Leading
With
Knowledge

Richard C. Huseman, Ph.D.
Jon P. Goodman, Ph.D.

with assistance from Daniel Rabinovitch

Leading
With
Knowledge

The Nature of Competition in the 21st Century

SAGE Publications
International Educational and Professional Publisher
Thousand Oaks   London   New Delhi

For information:

SAGE Publications, Inc.
2455 Teller Road
Thousand Oaks, California 91320
E-mail: order@sagepub.com

SAGE Publications Ltd.
6 Bonhill Street
London EC2A 4PU
United Kingdom

SAGE Publications India Pvt. Ltd.
M-32 Market
Greater Kailash I
New Delhi 110 048 India

HD
58.82
.H87
1999

Printed in the United States of America
Library of Congress Cataloging-in-Publication Data

Huseman, Richard C.
    Leading with knowledge: The nature of competition in the
21st century/by Richard C. Huseman and Jon P. Goodman.
        p. cm.
    Includes bibliographical references and index.
    ISBN 0-7619-1774-8 (cloth: acid-free paper)
    ISBN 0-7619-1775-6 (pbk.: acid-free paper)
    1. Knowledge management. 2. Organizational learning. 3.
Organizational change. 4. Employees—Training of. I. Goodman, Jon P. II. Title.
    HD58.82 .H87 1998
    658.4'06—ddc21   98-25433

99   00   01   02   03   04   10   9   8   7   6   5   4   3   2   1

Acquiring Editor:	Marquita Flemming
Editorial Assistant:	MaryAnn Vail
Production Editor:	Diana E. Axelsen
Editorial Assistant:	Stephanie Allen
Copy Editor:	Linda Gray
Typesetter/Designer:	Marion Warren
Indexer:	Trish Wittenstein

CONTENTS

Introduction   ix

Changes in Corporate Education and the Emergence
of Knowledge Organizations   x

The Early Roots of Knowledge Organizations   xi

Overall Approach of This Book   xiii

The Realm of the Red Queen   xiv

National Survey of Corporate Education and
Knowledge Practices   xv

Acknowledgments   xvii

PART I

THE PAST AS PROLOGUE

Chapter 1. The Classic Corporation   3

The American Mass Market: Implications for
Production and Distribution   5

Mass Production and Scientific Management   5

The Organization Man   13

The Success of the Classic Corporation   16

Chapter 2. The Impact of Change on Corporate America   19

International Competition   20

The Rise and Impact of Domestic Competition   29
The Impact of Information and Communication
    Technology   32
The Classic Corporation Attempts to Change   38

Chapter 3. Major Strategies for Coping with Change   **41**

Realignment   42
Restructuring   43
Downsizing   44
Downsizing: A Report Card   52
The End of a Workplace Contract   54
The Cumulative Impact of Competition, Technology,
    and Downsizing   57

PART II

THE PRESENT AS TRANSITION

Chapter 4. The Evolution of Corporate Learning   **61**

The Roots of Corporate Education   62
The 1980s and 1990s: Management/Executive
    Education Comes of Age   66
The Emergence of Corporate Universities   67
The New Learning Paradigm   69
Communities of Practice   75

**Chapter 5. The 1998 Strategic Report on
             Workforce Education**   **79**

Percentage of Employees Receiving Training   80
Types of Employees Receiving Training   81
Geographic Coverage   82
Current Delivery Methods   83
Future Delivery Methods: A Shift Away from the
    Classroom   84
Corporate Universities and Learning Centers   85
Partnering Practices with Outside Developers   86
Corporate America's Reaction to MBA/Executive
    MBA Programs   92

The Future of Training   99

**Chapter 6. The Emergence and Growth
              of the Knowledge Economy**   **103**

What Is Knowledge?   103
The Progression Toward Knowledge   105
The Five Elements of Knowledge   108
Knowledge: The Latest Store of Economic Value   115
Knowledge as a Corporate Asset   116
Knowledge as a Competitive Advantage   125
Knowledge as a Manager of Change   128

PART III

THE FUTURE AS EPILOGUE

**Chapter 7. Charting the Knowledge Path:
              A Survey of America's Largest Companies**   **135**

Knowledge Organization: What Does It Mean?   136
Knowledge Organizations and Continual Learning   141
Knowledge Organizations Manage Their Intellectual
   Capital   145
Degrees of Knowledge Organizations   150
Tier 1: Four Distinct Exemplars   153
Conclusion   155

Chapter 8. Intellectual Capital Accounting   **157**

Mill Valley: Knowledge Accounting Gains Momentum   158
The Vision-Guided Intellectual Capital Report   160
Intellectual Capital Accounting   164
How Skandia Developed Its Intellectual Capital
   Report   173

Chapter 9. Conceptualizing and Leveraging Knowledge   **177**

Phase 1: Identifying and Capturing Knowledge   178
Phase 2: Valuing and Prioritizing Knowledge   180
Phase 3: Sharing and Leveraging Knowledge   182

Phase 4: Knowledge Creation and Connection   194

10. Leading With Knowledge   211

Leadership in Knowledge Organizations   211
The Role of Vision   212
Phase 1: Identifying and Capturing Knowledge   214
Phase 2: Valuing and Prioritizing Knowledge   215
Phase 3: Sharing and Leveraging Knowledge   215
Phase 4: Creation and Connection of New Knowledge   216
Risk Taking and the Knowledge Organization   217

Notes   219
Introduction   219
Chapter 1   220
Chapter 2   222
Chapter 3   225
Chapter 4   227
Chapter 5   229
Chapter 6   229
Chapter 7   231
Chapter 8   231
Chapter 9   233

Index   237

About the Authors   253

INTRODUCTION

*To know that we know what we know, and that we do
not know what we do not know, that is true knowledge.*

—Confucius

The hierarchical structure that once characterized corporate
America has become much flatter. The giant corporations that
first appeared on the scene at the end of the 19th century and
dominated the economy for most of this century, although not gone, no
longer define the economic landscape. This may appear to oversimplify
what has and is taking place in corporate America, until one considers
the following:

- In 1979, 43% of the workforce was employed in corporations of 500 or larger.
- In 1998, 19% of the workforce was employed in corporations of 500 or larger.
- In 1979, 6% of the total workforce was employed in companies with 20 to 250 employees.
- In 1998, 47% of the total workforce was employed in companies with 20 to 250 employees.[1]

In 1954, *Fortune* magazine published its list of the 500 largest
companies in the United States for the first time. By 1997, 66% of the
companies that were on the initial list were out of business, merged with
other companies, or were no longer large enough to be included.

Not only are companies becoming flatter and smaller, but giant companies are also seeking out niche strategies to survive. Consider that not too long ago corporate "giants such as Proctor & Gamble might have ignored market segments of less than $200 million. Today, they [and other large corporations] covet niches a quarter of that size."[2]

CHANGES IN CORPORATE EDUCATION AND THE EMERGENCE OF KNOWLEDGE ORGANIZATIONS

Less obvious than the changes in corporate structure and size are changes in the role of corporate education and the emergence of knowledge organizations. Yet these changes will have far greater impact on the future of corporate America than the more easily observable changes in corporate size and structure, and companies are beginning to balance the short-term fixes of restructuring with the long-term opportunities of relearning.

In today's corporate America, we live in an age of rapid change—mergers, reengineering, downsizing. Countless popular books, consultants, and seminars offer prescriptions on how to survive in flatter, high-speed, customer-oriented organizations. But despite the flood of available literature and advice, many in corporate America, from entry-level employees to CEOs feel they are drowning in the flood of change. Concurrently, there is also an emerging theme that an emphasis on corporate training and education or perhaps even becoming a "learning organization" or "knowledge organization" will enable both individuals and organizations to survive and perhaps even prosper in these turbulent times. Always, there is the hope of finding the "silver bullet"—the appropriate management tool or approach. Micklethwait and Woolridge, in their 1996 book, *The Witch Doctors,* take the position that the business world is overrun by management fads. The authors maintain that the management gurus—high-powered consulting firms, business school professors, and motivational speakers—are latter-day "witch doctors," each in his or her own way promising a cure for the ills of corporate America. The authors state that 72% of managers believe the "right" management tools can ensure business success, even though 70% also state that most of the tools promise far more than they deliver.[3] Frequently, the results include thousands of people losing their jobs or having their work lives dramatically changed forever.

THE EARLY ROOTS OF KNOWLEDGE ORGANIZATIONS

Ours is a time of great change, and the flood of management advice may seem to muddy the waters, making it unclear which remedy is fact and which is fad. One may gain some comfort from knowing that even the most current batch of management buzzwords—*knowledge management, intellectual capital, learning organizations*—all stem from theories set forth long ago. Sixty years ago, in 1938, long before management theorists began to underscore the importance of sharing knowledge, Chester Barnard emphasized in his classic work *The Functions of the Executive* the importance of employee expertise and the role of communication in the organization.[4] According to Barnard, an essential role for executives to perform was to "provide the system of communication . . . promote the securing of essential efforts . . . formulate and define purpose."[5]

Nearly 40 years ago, in 1960, Douglas McGregor published the first edition of *The Human Side of Enterprise*.[6] McGregor's Theory Y celebrated the mind of the worker and warned managers that authority in an organization is a two-way street.

> The Church as an organization rests on dependence which is essentially one way. The ultimate source of all authority and all power is God, and all members of the organization are, therefore, dependent upward. In the military . . . individuals are required to sacrifice their personal goals and needs to the necessities of the national crisis and to accept dependence upward.[7]

In industry, on the other hand, dependence is mutual. The manager may not escape dependence on the worker to get the job done, says McGregor, a situation he describes as interdependence. McGregor made a prescient insight into the nature of human resource management. According to the dominant mode of management—what he calls Theory X—direction and control are the bases of organizational management. This paradigm, vividly apparent in scientific management, stands in stark comparison to McGregor's Theory Y. According to Theory Y, managers must create

conditions in which members of an organization may best achieve their
personal goals by working toward the goals of the enterprise.[8] Theories
X and Y really are diametrically opposed when one considers the
implications for managerial roles. Warren Bennis illustrated the difference through General Motors' example, in the foreword to the 25th
anniversary edition of McGregor's work.

> It used to be that the old fashioned GM philosophy of management could
> be summed up by this phrase: "DON'T THINK, DUMMY—DO WHAT
> YOU'RE TOLD!" Now, in GM's Buick City plant as well as a number
> of others, there is a new and very different credo which goes, "THINK!
> I'M NOT GOING TO TELL YOU WHAT TO DO!"[9]

Participatory management lies at the heart of Theory Y, and it is startling
to note how similar McGregor's (1985) definition of the term sounds to
today's discussion of knowledge management.

> The effective use of participation is a consequence of a managerial point
> of view which includes confidence in the potentialities of subordinates,
> awareness of dependence downwards, and a desire to avoid some of the
> consequences of emphasis on personal authority.[10]

In hindsight, it may appear that McGregor predicted the coming of
today's knowledge worker, someone whose worth to the organization is
based on intellect and expertise. What makes *The Human Side of
Enterprise* remarkable is its resonance today, in the midst of economic
realities that were barely on the horizon in the 1960s.

Similarly, *The Social Psychology of Organizing*,[11] by Karl Weick,
seems to have foreseen today's interest in learning and knowledge
organizations. Published in 1969, Weick's book stressed the importance
of being responsive to one's environment. This advice came at the exact
time that many U.S. corporations were discovering just how out of touch
they were with their customers, competitors, and suppliers. Organizing,
Weick said, consists primarily of adapting to an environment that is the
result of "interdependent human actors." In today's discussion of knowledge organizations, we hear echoes of Weick's assertion, "Organizations
continue to exist only to the degree that they are able to maintain a
balance between flexibility and stability."[12] There must be a dichotomy
in the organization, said Weick, for without flexibility the organization

may not adapt to unforeseen circumstance. And without stability, the organization may not amass any history and organizational knowledge.[13]

Has the world nothing left to learn or say about management after McGregor's and Weick's books? Would that it were so. Circumstances and technologies that could never have been foreseen 30 years ago are now embedded in the corporate landscape. We cite classic theorists to point out that management advice must have a memory. In place of fads, the aim of this work is to provide facts about continuous corporate development that may lead to greater understanding. But how can we achieve understanding and offer useful direction for the future?

One of the first great futurists of modern times was H. G. Wells. Wells was trained as a historian, and his study of history led him to believe it was possible to understand and predict the future. Wells argued that if the long course of events is determined by our reaction to economic and technological events, then we could, in fact, make meaningful projections of what the future is likely to bring.

OVERALL APPROACH OF THIS BOOK

Our basic approach is that, following in the tradition of H. G. Wells, one can best gain perspective on the current chaotic corporate scene by considering both a historical and futuristic view of the corporation. In this book, we will do the following:

1. Examine the evolution of the corporation, from the early classic to the more recent adaptive model.
2. Illustrate the forces of change on corporate structure and the techniques used to restructure the corporation.
3. Analyze the impact of change on corporate education and the emergence of knowledge organizations.
4. Present a strategic model for conceptualizing and leveraging knowledge.

Represented by Figure I.1, our strategic model for conceptualizing and leveraging knowledge synthesizes much of what has been written to date on the topic of knowledge, current practices in corporate America, and the results of our national survey on the current state and future of corporate knowledge.

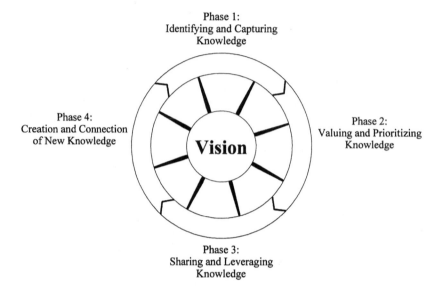

Phase 1:
Identifying and Capturing
Knowledge

Phase 4:
Creation and Connection
of New Knowledge

Vision

Phase 2:
Valuing and Prioritizing
Knowledge

Phase 3:
Sharing and Leveraging
Knowledge

Figure I.1. A Strategic Model for Conceptualizing and Leveraging Knowledge
SOURCE: Copyright © 1999 by Richard C. Huseman, Ph.D., and Jon P. Goodman, Ph.D.

This book seeks to examine changes in corporations in a way that enables one to put the current turbulence in perspective and position strategically for the following:

- ▶ A future in which the only constant will be change
- ▶ A future in which the corporation's primary advantage will be the ability to create, capture, leverage, and measure intellectual capital
- ▶ A future in which the sum of the company's intellectual capital will determine its competitive position
- ▶ A future in which corporations will strive to improve as quickly as they can, in some cases, just to maintain their current market position—a competitive environment that can be characterized as the realm of the Red Queen

THE REALM OF THE RED QUEEN

First proposed in 1973 by Dr. Leigh Van Valen, "the Red Queen hypothesis" suggests that in a highly threatening environment, organisms have to evolve as quickly as possible just to survive. The theory, which took its name from Lewis Carroll's book *Through the Looking Glass*,[14] holds telling implications for the modern corporation. Carroll's fictional character, Alice, remarked that no matter how fast she ran in the Red Queen's world, she made little progress.

> "Well, in our country," said Alice, still panting a little, "you'd generally get to somewhere else—if you ran very fast for a long time, as we've been doing."
> "A slow sort of country!" said the Queen. "Now, here, you see, it takes all the running you can do, to keep in the same place. If you want to get somewhere else, you must run at least twice as fast as that!"[15]

Today and for the foreseeable future, the modern corporation competes in the "realm of the Red Queen." Although some companies may appear to master change today, perpetual technological innovation and rapidly increasing global competition frequently negate any advantages that seem to be secure. We think it will become increasingly clear that becoming a knowledge organization will greatly enhance one's chances of surviving and even prospering in the realm of the Red Queen.

Attempting to build a knowledge organization, however, is neither a short-term effort nor a one-off project. The process of becoming a knowledge organization can be visualized as traveling along "the knowledge organization path." Some organizations are not even on the path, others are just starting on the path, and still others are further along. The underlying assumption is that those companies on the knowledge organization path envision and behave differently from the more traditional 20th-century companies. Those with a knowledge orientation focus on ideas, creativity, and knowledge. They speak of "intellectual capital" as opposed to traditional assets. Most important, the leaders of knowledge organizations fully realize that their most important assets walk out the door every night. Whether those assets show up the next day is of vital importance to the future of the knowledge organization.

NATIONAL SURVEY OF CORPORATE EDUCATION AND KNOWLEDGE PRACTICES[16]

In an attempt to identify some of the many steps along the knowledge organization path, we surveyed 202 of the 1,500 largest companies in

America. We asked respondents at those companies a series of questions regarding the ways they capture, store, and leverage knowledge. The results of our study were finalized during the first quarter of 1998. We share the results of our national survey with you later in this book and believe they provide some helpful illumination along the knowledge path.

But before you turn to those results, spend some time making your way through the rest of the book. If you want to create a knowledge organization, understand the backdrop and the context from which knowledge organizations are evolving. Knowledge is not another passing fad. In an age when reengineering and downsizing are commonplace for most organizations, the resulting consequences of losing valuable knowledge with the shedding of employees will haunt many organizations for years to come. Those employees who have survived and continue working in their organizations fully understand that the "employment for life contract" is no more. Many of these employees are beginning to understand the value of the knowledge they possess for their company—or perhaps for a competing company. Whereas the 1980s and 1990s will be remembered by many as a time when organizations abandoned employees, we are now at the beginning of a time when good employees increasingly will abandon their organizations—taking their knowledge with them. The leaders of knowledge organizations understand that we are in a dramatically different world when it comes to recruiting, rewarding, and retaining knowledge workers.

As we approach the new millennium, the key to running faster and faster in the realm of the Red Queen will be knowledge. Indeed, capturing knowledge, leveraging knowledge, and creating knowledge will provide the ongoing, sustainable advantage for a rapidly increasing number of successful organizations.

ACKNOWLEDGMENTS

Every book contains the weight of the authors' intellectual antecedents; this book, possibly more than most. We've been fortunate to have had generous mentors, stimulating colleagues, challenging business experiences (as well as hair-raising ones), and smart students.

During our careers, we've seen more than a few management theories become the latest hot practice. Somehow, we've avoided being charmed by most of them. But over the past 5 years, we have become intrigued with the impact of information systems and technology, and we are convinced that the most important element of them is people.

We've been in literally hundreds of corporations and agencies. Nowhere is the issue so clear as on the front line. Downsizing's little regard for knowledge management has gutted the competitive core of many companies because the people didn't just walk out the door at night . . . many left forever and took their invaluable knowledge with them.

This book is the result of many long talks with each other and our colleagues, but we alone are responsible for any ideas we've mangled or facts we've skewed. We would like to think the good people at EC², the Annenberg Incubator Project at the University of Southern California—most particularly James Klein and Cindy Mitchell. John Faier of the Omnitech Consulting Group provided valuable assistance and support for our national survey of 202 knowledge organizations that we report on later in this book. Zulema Seguel has been invaluable, as have been our friends at Sage Publications.

We hope the ideas and information we've presented will make you think, and puzzle, and act. It has been that way for us. We believe these ideas can speed the knowledge journey.

PART

1

THE PAST AS PROLOGUE

THE CLASSIC CORPORATION

*Knowledge is the only instrument of production that is
not subject to diminishing returns.*

—J. M. Clark

The modern American corporation was born in a train wreck.
During the early expansion years of the American railroad
system, stretches of track were usually no more than 50 to 100
miles long and trains traveled in only one direction. Individual superin-
tendents and their assistants managed them. As the railroads expanded,
switching technology enabled trains to travel in both directions and share
the same piece of track. However, the more extensive a railroad became,
the more difficult it became to manage. Head-on collisions, scheduling
problems, and the need for effective cargo management finally brought
about a new system of organizational structure and management. These
problems prompted the earliest forms of managerial organization, which
became the roots of the classic corporation.

The classic corporation, exemplified by large, manufacturing industry, began evolving in the 1850s and matured in the 1970s and 1980s.

The classic corporation is primarily defined by two salient characteristics: First, it is the sum of a number of distinct operating units, each one with its own managers, administrative support, and its own books, which can be audited as distinct from the larger organization. Each unit can, in theory, operate as a distinct business enterprise. The corporation acts as an umbrella for a diverse range of business activities. The second characteristic is that the classic corporation is structured in a hierarchical fashion. Middle and upper managers oversee and direct the activities of the business units. These two characteristics developed beginning in the middle of the 19th century. Prior to 1840, there were no middle managers in America. Businesses were largely single-unit operations run out of a single office. For example, a group of owners operated a bank, a dry goods store, a factory. It was not until the rise of a national railroad system that a more segmented corporation and its emphasis on hierarchy started to evolve.[1] In an 1856 report, Daniel C. McCallum, superintendent of the New York and Erie Railroad Company, began forming the guidelines for a managerial hierarchy when he stated,

> A Superintendent of a road fifty miles in length can give its business his personal attention. . . . [For] a road five hundred miles in length a very different state of things exists. Any system which might be applicable to the business and extent of a short road, would be found entirely inadequate to the wants of a long one.[2]

McCallum went on to describe the basic requirements of an operable railroad system. McCallum's guidelines, however, described more than the requirements of running a railroad. His guidelines were the beginnings of a structure that could manage multiple divisions and far-flung operations in a wide variety of organizations. Rapid growth in the number of employees and the miles of track a railroad company oversaw gave rise to three core traits of the classic corporation: (a) Management was distinct from operation, (b) a managerial hierarchy developed with defined channels of communication, and (c) decisions were made with a major emphasis on cost analysis.[2]

With these basic tenets of a corporate hierarchy emerging, the American corporation was poised to be influenced by two great transformations—mass marketing and mass production.

THE AMERICAN MASS MARKET: IMPLICATIONS
FOR PRODUCTION AND DISTRIBUTION

Prior to the rise of the railroads and telegraph, businesses were single-unit enterprises that usually lacked any sort of internal structure. Typically, owners ran a shop that sold an array of goods or performed a single function. National brands did not exist because there was no system by which to transport goods efficiently. Businesses served local markets but exercised very little control over them. However, the completion of a national railroad network and the invention of the telegraph set the stage for mass marketing and mass production. The era of the national mass market was one in which a small number of firms realized economies of scale to an unprecedented degree by expanding their distribution from coast to coast and border to border.[3]

Of these mass market seekers, Henry Ford, Asa G. Candler, and Richard W. Sears shared three characteristics: They and their companies each sought to unify a cluttered market, they each saw opportunity in serving the unserved, and they all sought profit through high volumes of mass production and mass distribution. In the America of the late 1880s, there were only 38 states. Their total population was 58 million, and about 65% of these people lived in rural areas. This was the opportunity that Ford, Candler, Sears, and others attempted to leverage. The legacy of their accomplishment continues to influence the modern corporation to this day because it was not merely the feat of mass marketing that formed the modern corporation; it was the means and methods by which these companies made their visions come true.

MASS PRODUCTION AND SCIENTIFIC MANAGEMENT

Henry Ford sought to create and build an automobile so inexpensive that any working man could afford one. To build such a car, he eventually decided to use an assembly line approach to mass produce it. Prior to the introduction of the assembly line, workers at Ford's Highland Park plant built the Model T in "gangs." Long rows of car chassis sat on wooden horses, waiting for a gang of workers to assemble them. Laborers delivered the necessary parts to each chassis just before the next gang arrived. Each member of the gang was specially trained to perform one task: install the transmission, drop in the engine, or assemble the flywheel magneto. This method depended heavily on timing and could be easily disrupted by late delivery of parts or assemblers who worked too quickly or too slowly.

But back in the early 1900s, Ford decided the solution was to bring the work to the assemblers. Ford Motor's assembly line was the synthesis of several existing production techniques. William Klann, head of the engine department, began talking about the line after he toured Swift's Chicago slaughterhouse. He observed that if cows and pigs could be slaughtered using line production techniques, "we can build cars that way and build motors that way." Klann also drew on his experience as a machinist repairing mechanical conveyors in breweries for the Huette-man & Cramer Machine Company in Detroit. The Ford assembly line was in fact the next stage of evolution of the assembly line technology, not the beginning. On April 1, 1913, workers in Ford's flywheel magneto assembly department stood before the company's first assembly line, a waist-high, smooth-sliding surface built on pipe frame. Where the work-ers were once expected to perform all the steps of assembly, they were now required to perform one simple task on the magneto and then push it down the line.

The initial results from what was essentially an experiment at Ford appeared to have potential. With the workbench method, 29 workers would put together 35 to 40 magnetos per day. With the assembly line, the same 29 men put together 1,188 in a day. To solve the recurring problem of various work paces among the laborers, the line was fitted with a lateral chain that moved the magnetos along at a pace that would speed up the slower workers and slow down the quicker ones. The news of this experiment spread through Highland Park quickly, and soon other assembly departments began to implement their own lines. The transmis-sion line went into effect in June 1913, the chassis line in October 1913, and the engine line in November 1913.

These assembly lines at Ford were refined over time through contin-ual testing. For example, on October 7, 1913, 140 chassis assemblers worked on a 150-foot line. Man-hour figures were three hours per chassis with that configuration. In December, the line was 300 feet long and had 177 men working on it. Chassis assembly with the 300-foot line took two hours and 38 minutes per chassis. Before the end of the year, the chassis were pulled along the line by a long chain. After several months of experimentation, the line yielded more returns. By the end of

April 1914, three 300-foot lines were in use, producing 1,212 chassis assemblies in an eight-hour day or 93 man-minutes per chassis. The jump in productivity showed up dramatically in the price of Ford's cars. The Model T touring car cost $805 when introduced in 1908. In 1916, the same automobile cost $360. In 1905-1906, Ford sold 1,599 cars. In 1920-1921, the company sold 933,720. Before the start of World War I, Ford had captured nearly half of the U.S. car market.[4]

Henry Ford expected a high level of efficiency from his employees, and although Ford publicly denied that his processes borrowed from the scientific management theories of Frederick Winslow Taylor, the two men's philosophies did share some common points. Taylorism, like Fordism, held that a company could accurately predict output from a set of variables such as machine productivity, work processes, and time motion analysis of individual workers. Taylor was an engineer who made a name for himself with research he conducted at Bethlehem Steel Company. Taylor conducted time-motion analyses of pig iron handlers at Bethlehem to determine the most efficient ways to work. According to Taylor,

> The most prominent single element in modern scientific management is the task idea. The work of every workman is fully planned out by the management at least one day in advance, and each man receives in most cases complete written instructions, describing in detail the task which is to be solved, as well as the means to be used in doing the work.

Scientific management reserved all decision making (and arguably creative thought) to middle and upper management. The worker was essentially viewed as a unit of production. Taylor's experiments yielded the following results: The number of pig iron handlers was reduced by 76% to handle the same amount of work; the average number of pounds of pig iron handled per day increased 207%; and the average cost to Bethlehem Steel to handle one ton of pig iron decreased by 54%.[5]

Similarly, at Ford Motor Company, Henry Ford had specific expectations for the functioning of each and every laborer, machine, and tool. As far as he was concerned, the worker was subordinate to the system of production and management. According to Ford,

> We expect the men to do what they are told. The organization is so highly specialized and one part is so dependent upon another that we could not for a moment consider allowing the men to have their own way. Without

the most rigid discipline we would have the utmost confusion. . . . The men are there to get the greatest possible amount of work done.[6]

Scientific management, or the systematic management practiced at the Ford Motor plant, became a widespread practice because it was well crafted to the worker demographics in contemporary corporations. In the late 19th century, the United States began the largest wave of immigration that the world had ever seen, with 14 million immigrants arriving between 1865 and 1900.[7] At Ford Motor in 1914, 71% of the company's workers were foreign-born, representing 22 nationalities. Many of these people were from a rural background, and few spoke English.[8] Thus, Taylor provided a management style and Ford provided a manufacturing process well suited to the composition of the unskilled workforce and to the production process.

The crux of scientific management was to replace "rule-of-thumb" techniques used on the shop floor with a scientifically formulated and tested process. The origin of such a model is best illustrated by the managerial experience of F. W. Taylor himself. In 1880, at the age of 24, Taylor left the ranks of his fellow workers and took the position of foreman at Philadelphia's Midvale Steel corporation. After serving as an apprentice for six years, he brought with him a reputation for being, as biographer Robert Kanigel reports, "bullheaded," "tactless," and, above all, exacting in the level of productivity he felt Midvale workers could attain.[9] As a manager,

> Taylor lacked the personal skills, the seductive blarney charm, to worm cooperation from the men, to get more out of them and have them love him for it. So at Midvale, he bludgeoned the men, cajoled them, threatened them, and drove them in the only way his temperament permitted.[10]

The seed of Taylor's discontent was that he felt he was not getting a full day's work out of his men. Ultimately, however, there was a natural limit to the amount of work he could demand from the workers. That limit existed at the boundaries of Taylor's experience. After his six years on the shop floor, Taylor was an apt machinist but ranked as a beginner when compared with the older hands he was expected to manage. When Taylor tried to push the men harder, their answer was invariably, "You simply can't get any more out of this machine." Of course, Taylor did not know whether this was true or not, and in point of fact, even the seasoned workers did not know for sure how productive they could be. "Much of their wisdom was shop lore, guesswork, built up over the years into serviceable rules of thumb, based on what they'd heard from others, or on what worked well enough day by day, or on chance remembered incidents." As it came to pass, through time analysis and experimentation, Taylor exercised his control over his subordinates by depriving them of the one piece of knowledge held exclusively in their domain: the knowledge of how to get the job done.[11]

Taylor's most enduring contribution to industry was to move "knowhow" off the shop floor and into the manager's office. His critics called this effort "de-skilling the workforce."

> Scientific management gathered knowledge and fed it back to the worker in the form of instruction cards, books of standard operating procedures, standing orders, standardized jigs and fixtures, fixed machine settings, printed forms, posted work rules, and so on. The worker need only check off the right blank, or press the right block on the computer touch screen, or otherwise follow simple rules.[12]

The term *de-skilling* may mislead the reader into thinking that practitioners of scientific management sought to create cadres of unskilled automatons to man their stations on the shop floor. Certainly, it must have seemed that way to labor representatives in the early 1900s who violently opposed Taylor's techniques. From the perspective of corporate leaders, however, scientific management represented a distinct move from chaos to order. In the case of the Scovill Manufacturing Company, a brass company in Waterbury, Connecticut, scientific management represented a competitive advantage.

In the 1870s, the 50-year-old Scovill Manufacturing Company began to see its profit margins drop owing to competition and industry overproduction. Rather than join one of several groupings of brass companies as their competitors were doing, Scovill aggressively adopted scientific management practices to cut costs. Led by executives Chauncey Porter Goss and M. L. Sperry, the "artisans" and foremen who had long controlled the productivity of the corporation were systematically removed. At the Scovill plant, casters—the men who shaped brass into buttons, wire, and fixtures—dictated the speed at which production would ensue. They were artisans whose craft was mysterious and their knowledge closely held. Scientific management techniques would be difficult to implement in such a diversified work environment, but Goss and Sperry spent 20 years, between 1900 and 1920, taking control of the production process from those who controlled it.

Management had to be able to trace materials throughout production, and the various components of the industrial process had to be coupled, linking casting and fabrication divisions that formerly operated as separate fiefdoms. Early on, Goss introduced self-contained furnaces, allowing him to replace the skilled casters with unskilled laborers. Goss also wrested control from the foremen who often hired family, friends, and members of their own ethnic group into Scovill. In the 1918 employee manual, Goss made it clear that foremen could recommend workers for hire, but the ultimate decision for hiring, transfer, and termination rested in the hands of the newly formed employment office. Goss further systematized management by issuing time-keeping cards to all employees. Back-office timekeepers, not foremen, administered the cards. (Prior to this, workers were able to leave their posts at any time and go without fear of official reprimand.)

Eventually, every employee at Scovill was issued an identifying number by which the "cost office" tracked attendance, payroll, and employment records. This system allowed for rapid creation of employee census and statistical summaries. Goss and Sperry did not limit the use of scientific management techniques to the shop floor. Secretaries who sought promotions were required to take a test in the employment office to rank their ability. In retrospect, Scovill's strategy worked. Although it caused much pain and outcry from worker representatives, Scovill became one of the 200 largest industrial corporations in the United States by 1917.[13]

Throughout the early 1900s, Henry Ford and Frederick Winslow Taylor did not keep secret their techniques for dramatically increasing productivity. Detailed descriptions of Ford's techniques appeared in *The American Machinist* in 1913 and *Engineering Magazine* in 1914 and 1915. Taylor unveiled his steel-cutting technology at the Paris International Exposition in 1900, and his *Principles of Scientific Management* reached international audiences soon after its 1911 publication.[14] Other industries also began using scientific management strategies. The story of the American chain grocery store tells of vertical integration, the rise of national brands, and a formula approach to retailing. In designing the grocery chain A&P, knowledge was again grounded in middle and upper management. In this case, scientific management dictated store layout and design, buying based on corporate information, and enhanced communication with the customer through research.[15]

Examples of scientific management in diverse industries abound:

▶ When pharmacist John Styth Pemberton invented the formula for Coca-Cola on May 8, 1886, he added one more soda to a national spectrum of flavors. "Jobbers" or fountain operators in drugstores throughout the country offered their own soda concoctions. Coca-Cola may have joined a crowded field, but through the efforts of company president Asa G. Candler, Coke became the first brand to dominate the national market. Candler's marketing strategy hinged on uniformity. Salesmen had the job of stocking the drink with jobbers at drugstores and soda fountains throughout the country. Charles Howard Candler, the president's son, described the training for a new salesman:

> If he was not already sold on Coca-Cola, he was thoroughly acquainted with its merit, and was afforded the opportunity of watching its manu-facture, particular attention being called to the quality of ingredients used; the profit to be derived by a retailer in dispensing Coca-Cola was demonstrated to him; the various pieces of advertising material were displayed to him and he was taught how best to use them. He was also informed respecting a selling plan to both wholesalers and retailers, known as the rebate contract plan, and impressed with our preference that, as far as possible, all sales be made through jobbers. His attention was called to any customers on his proposed route who were not in good credit standing, and specific instructions were given him as to how these customers might be best approached and handled.[16]

Coca-Cola unified the cluttered soda market and created the first domi-nant national consumer brand with just one product. From the time Candler bought the company in 1889, the company did not introduce any other version of the soda until 1955. Until that time, the company marketed only the syrup and the soda in the familiar 6.5-ounce bottle.[17]

▶ Scientific management spread into health care when researchers at the University of Iowa designed a work space for dentists that clustered equipment and tools traditionally located throughout a room into one tight space. It was determined at the time that the design saved 29% of the dentist's time. The same model was implemented in the surgical operating room, affecting the layout of implements and techniques for suturing.

▶ Banks were redesigned to run as a factory assembly line. Low-paid tellers handled routine tasks such as accepting deposits, cashing checks, and recording bill payments. Complex problems were handled by college-educated "service representatives." The design, it was found, reduced the amount of time a customer spent in the bank.

▶ Even academia felt the pressure of the stopwatch. The Carnegie Foundation for the Advancement of Teaching reported in 1910 that "one is struck with the absence of any gauge of efficiency which even remotely resembles, for instance, profits in an industrial undertaking." The foundation called for measurement of faculty productivity based on the amount of time spent with a student, class inspections, and other objective measures.[18]

The spread of scientific management has had a lasting impact on the structure of the classic corporation. It gave rise to a "back office" throughout industries of an unprecedented size. Economic theorists credited the size of the classic corporation for much of this success. In 1958, John Kenneth Galbraith, in *The Affluent Society,* described the success of General Motors: "There is no clear upper limit to the desirable size. It could be that bigger is better."[19] Returning to the Scovill case, it is remarkable to note the lopsided growth of this company. Between 1911 and 1920, the number of main office workers—clerks, managers, executives, accountants, timekeepers, and secretaries—quadrupled, whereas the people really doing the company's work—casters and manufacturing workers—barely doubled. Put another way, in 1911, there were 3 support staff members for every 10 Scovill employees working on "the line." By 1920, that ratio had become 6 support staffers for every 10 line workers.[20]

Companies throughout the country were investing heavily in scientific management and, in the process, swelling the ranks of middle management. Ultimately, the legacy of scientific management is best captured by Taylor's prediction that "in the past the man has been first. In the future the System must be first."[21]

The almost religious devotion to scientific management among corporations was earned. In the United States, where many companies took note of these messages, manufacturing output per worker increased 150% between 1890 and 1930. Companies in Europe were not as quick to adopt American techniques. Citroen (French) did not install a moving assembly line until 1919. Renault (French) followed in 1922 and Opel (German) in 1924. Skoda (Czech) built a factory with a moving line called "America" in 1925. And Morris, Britain's largest manufacturer, waited until 1934 to install a moving assembly line in its plant. While Europe was slow to adopt moving assembly lines, factories in the United States increased production until it was producing 80% of the world's cars and trucks just prior the outbreak of World War I. America had entered an era of world automotive dominance that would continue until the early 1970s.[22] Just as the success of scientific management has earned the devotion of corporations, economic stability earned the trust of middle management, giving rise to a new class of employee: the Organization Man.

THE ORGANIZATION MAN

First used by William Whyte in 1956, the term *Organization Man,* coined at a time when it was usually men who filled management positions, described a worker who was totally dedicated to the company in which he worked. The Organization Man's work ethic—his devotion to the company and its goals—was noted by Whyte as a departure from the Protestant ethic. The key assumption of the Protestant ethic was that a man's success had little to do with luck or environment but was a function of the employee's qualities and hard work. As corporations continued to grow in size, the Protestant ethic became less relevant and nearly the opposite became true. "Be loyal to the company and the company will be loyal to you," went the new credo. Following this maxim to its logical conclusion, Organization Men understood that, as Thomas Watson, Sr., founder of IBM, put it, "The good of each of us as individuals is the greater good of the company."[23]

Viewed from a historical perspective, the Organization Man's allegiance put him in an interesting position that Whyte described by metaphor:

A middle-management executive is in a spot of trouble. He finds that the small branch he's helping to run is very likely to blow up. There is a way to save it: if he presses a certain button, the explosion will be averted. Unfortunately, however, just as he's about to press a button his boss heaves into view. The boss is a scoundrel and a fool, and at this moment he's so scared he is almost incoherent. Don't press the button, he says.

The middle-management man is no rebel and he knows that the boss, stupid as he is, represents the Organization. Still, he would like to save everyone's life. Thus his dilemma: if he presses the button he will not be acting like a good organization man and the plant will be saved. If he doesn't press it they will all be blown to smithereens.[24]

So why didn't the organization men push the proverbial button? It was a matter of conditioning and training. In the classic corporation of the 1950s (when Whyte did the research for his book) there was a discouragement of extraordinary talent. Industry did not ignore brilliance, but it favored "normal" personalities. In other words, those who did as they were told, without question, were praised. The indoctrination of this mind-set began in the recruitment phase. Whyte draws on the example of a recruiting film from the multinational Monsanto Chemical Company. The film was made to inspire college graduates for a career in chemistry. In it, one sees young boys watching trains go by and dreaming of faraway lands and adventure. Later, the film shows the young men at Monsanto in white coats. The voice-over in the film announces, "No geniuses here; just a bunch of average Americans working together."[25] The implication of the commentary was that the organization is better served by "ordinary" minds than extraordinary ones.

Fluidity—the ability to do whatever asked and go wherever asked— became a sign of success among Organization Men. This dynamic had obvious effects on the career drive of the Organization Man. If genius was shunned and normalcy was celebrated, then why shouldn't the Organization Man seek a middle ground in the organization? In fact, this is what most did.

When Whyte interviewed 200 corporation-bound college graduates in 1956, he found that only 12% said they wanted to get involved in production work. Most wanted to be middle managers, lending support and guidance to the front line. The most sought-after positions in the company were in the personnel department. The original Organization

Men came out of the military after World War I to assume leadership of the personnel function. To them, handling people was a natural fit after their years in the military. For the newer Organization Men—those graduating from college in the 1950s—Whyte said the impulse to manage people was driven more by an urge to escape competition. Even in the positions where a competitive attitude was called for, the Organization Man found a way out. Consider the approach the Organization Man took to sales:

> What they mean by sales is the kind of work in which they will be technical specialists helping the customer, or, better yet, master-minding the work of those who do the helping. They want to be sales engineers, distribution specialists, merchandising experts—the men who back up the men in the field.[26]

The ethic of the Organization Man was born of a search for stability. Some had lived through the Great Depression and then gone into the regimented organization and stability of the military. The large corporation provided men returning from the war with a hierarchical organization that they knew well. Like the military, the corporation was built in units. People with titles and rigid job descriptions operated it. And there were clearly articulated avenues of communication between one unit and another. Like the military, large corporations codified every process and procedure that an employee might undertake. At the Department of Defense (DOD), 4,000 laws and 30,000 pages of regulations guide the actions of its 134,000 employees. The DOD rules for acquisitions are embodied in 1.2 million typed lines. (The rules for purchasing fruit cake are 20 pages long.) Before it split into the Baby Bells, AT&T provided rules for every contingency as well. Its *Bell Systems Instructions* manual took up 24 feet of shelf space. The section on "How to Properly Take an Order" was 1,200 pages long.[27] This level of detail fit well into an ex-military man's experience with a hierarchical, highly routinized organization.

For other Organization Men—those born in the 1920s and 1930s—large corporations were attractive because they provided an environment largely sheltered from economic turbulence. From the 1950s through the mid-1970s, American corporations dominated their markets. The gross national product grew at an average annual rate of 3.7% between 1946 and 1969. Total national wealth was $334 billion in 1922. It grew to $700 billion by 1946. And by 1958, it had grown to $1.7 trillion. Family income rose in constant dollars from $4,531 in 1946 to $8,473 in 1969.[28] Corporations considered foreign competition minimal, and domestic competition was predictable and orderly. This level of stability manifested itself inside the corporation. Organization Men heard the message: If they did as they were told and went where they were ordered, they would enjoy a long career with the same company. Productivity was not necessarily part of the job requirement.

THE SUCCESS OF THE CLASSIC CORPORATION

The structure of the classic corporation was not built according to arbitrary theories and practices of a group of business leaders. The classic corporation evolved over a period of years, adopting practices that served it well and abandoning those that did not. The reader should put the stories told in this chapter in their proper perspective. To assume that the assembly line was the most logical production method is to fall into the same trap that much of corporate America did prior to the mid-1970s. The basic tenets of the classic corporation—(a) hierarchy, (b) mass production, (c) mass marketing, and (d) scientific management—endured over the years because they worked, taking the United States to a position of economic dominance.

Retrospective data show that U.S. corporations from the late 19th century through the early 1970s served a market of enormous proportions. By 1970, American families had the highest material standard of living in the world.[29]

In the process of serving this market, American corporations thrived. By the mid-1960s, the United States manufactured more goods than the next 9 largest industrial nations combined. All but 2 of the world's 20 largest corporations were American. General Motors earned as much in profits as the 10 biggest companies in France, Great Britain, and West Germany—30 companies in all. *Fortune* magazine's 500 largest companies in 1954 took in $137 billion, or 37%, of the gross national product (GNP). In that year, the same 500 companies employed 8 million people—50% of the U.S. manufacturing force. By 1969, Fortune 500 firms dominated the economy, employing 15 million people (three quarters of the workforce) and earned $445 billion or 46% of the GNP.[30]

Against the backdrop of scientific management, mass marketing, and mass production, the classic corporation was led to believe that nothing could go wrong. As we will see in Chapter 2, it was precisely this level of success and confidence, this form of economic hubris, that became a liability as major drivers of change caught the classic corporation unaware and unprepared.

2

THE IMPACT OF CHANGE ON CORPORATE AMERICA

A little knowledge is a dangerous thing, but a little want of knowledge is also a dangerous thing.

—Samuel Butler

hange can build quietly, remaining unnoticed until it explodes onto the scene, challenging the very paradigms on which your company has built its most successful systems. Never has change affected American corporations to the degree that it has during this past decade. Igor Ansoff refers to this change as *discontinuous* when a corporation "makes a departure from the market which it knows how to serve, from the technology on which the firm's products are based, or from the geographical, economic, cultural, social, or political settings in which it knows how to do business."[1] At the core of today's discontinuous change is a fundamental shift in the way corporations are structured, how they function, and how they compete. Two major drivers of change have had an effect on corporate America: competition (both international and domestic) and information technology.

INTERNATIONAL COMPETITION

In Chapter 1, we saw how Henry Ford's use of scientific management techniques in the production of the Model T exemplified the founding principles of the classic corporation. We now look again to the U.S. automobile industry as a vivid example of international competition as a driver of change. For years, Detroit was the control center for the world's automobile market. It was one of many U.S. industries that enjoyed such a high level of market dominance that the threat of major foreign competition seemed a very remote possibility. However, the story of the Big Three auto manufacturers—Ford, General Motors, and Chrysler—provides a particularly instructive example of the impact that international competition has had on corporate America.

In post-World War II America, car manufacturers produced increasingly large, elaborately styled cars. General Motors' Chevrolet division led the charge to sell cars as a sign of youth and vigor. In 1953, the Chevy Eight measured 198 inches in length and had a wheel base of 155 inches. The Eight weighed 3,385 pounds and cost $1,659. Just six years later, in 1959, America was introduced to the Chevrolet Bel Air—a heavier, longer, and pricier car than the standard market had yet to see. More important, the Bel Air sported a pair of oddly shaped tail fins—which would come to be "the look" for cars of that era. Not to be outdone, John Delorean presented a new Pontiac that same year. Compared with the previous year's model, the new car was longer by a foot, was heavier by 400 pounds, and had a lot of added chrome and some really splashy colors. These new heavyweight contenders in the automobile market were a big hit with consumers. Sales for the Pontiac alone hit 380,000 in 1959 (up 41% from the previous year), and in 1962, Pontiac sales hit and passed the half-million mark. These Chevrolet and Pontiac design specs were to become beacons for the rest of the industry. In 1959, total American car sales reached 5.9 million. Chevrolets accounted for 1.4 million of that—one of four cars purchased that year was a Chevy. In America, bigger, faster, and more expensive had become king.[2]

The Small Car From Germany

> To the average American of the early 1950's, the adjective *small* con-
> noted inexpensive and inferior. . . . Price was directly correlated to size,
> and size was related to status. One should not be ashamed of driving a
> small car, but a small car certainly was not thought of with pride—by
> most Americans, that is. The idea was to move from small to large as
> rapidly as possible, large being a symbol of success.[3]

When the Germans began to market a squat, rounded car called the
Beetle in the early 1950s, Detroit did not take great notice. This was not
the first time the Europeans had tried to penetrate the U.S. market. The
English had made a brief foray into the U.S. market with the Mynx, one
that was doomed by weak service and parts availability. So Detroit was
unconcerned by the Beetle. They "knew" the American consumer adored
size, power, and speed in large quantities. The little intruder from
Germany did not meet any of these requirements.

Volkswagen sold only 20,000 Beetles in 1955, but by 1959, 120,000
were on U.S. roads. Beetle clubs began appearing across the country.
Magazines sharing Beetle service tips were in distribution, and on college
campuses, the Beetle became a symbol of the new youth culture. Still,
the sales of the Beetle were minuscule compared with sales for the Big
Three. In 1961, VW sold 177,000 cars, the French Renault sold 44,000,
and the German Mercedes sold 13,000 of its high-status cars in the
United States. Compare this with Chevrolet's 1.6 million or Ford's 1.3
million car sales for that year. It is easy to understand why Detroit was
unconcerned by the sale of 177,000 Beetles compared with the 142,000
high-end, high-profit Cadillacs it sold that year. Detroit's only response
to this foreign competition was to promote used American cars as
having the power and comfort of the domestic car but at the competitor's
price.[4]

However, throughout the early 1960s, Volkswagen continued to lead
the pack of a growing number of foreign imports, selling two of three
imports in the United States in 1965. Detroit began to view Volkswagen
with some concern but never doubted that it could crush the German
company whenever it chose. The fact that the Beetle continued to
perform well through the mid-1960s was viewed by many as an aberration. According to one automobile executive, "There will always be 5
percent of the car market that will be made up of individualists and

nonconformists who cannot permit themselves to choose a car built by one of the Big Three."[5]

The Japanese Enter the U.S. Market

In 1965, two new names appeared on the list of top 10 imports: Datsun, which sold 13,000 cars, and Toyota, which sold 6,400. The arrival of Japanese cars seemed to come out of nowhere, since at the time, few were aware that the country even had much of a manufacturing base—let alone a car industry. Between World War I and World War II, Europe and the United States had turned their manufacturing focus to automobiles and their public works to laying down miles of roads. At the same time, Japan, being largely agrarian, lacked the capital and the impetus to do the same. In 1924, for example, American manufacturers sold 3.1 million cars, and total registrations reached 17.6 million. In that same year, Japanese car registrations were at 17,939, only a fraction of the number of registered rickshaws (105,000). Not only was Japan seen as having little incentive to join the automobile manufacturing ranks, but World War II had decimated Japan's ability to produce. One quarter of the national wealth had been destroyed, one of every four buildings had been leveled, and one of three machines was rendered useless.[6]

Most people outside of Japan were unaware that in 1960, the Japanese government embarked on a 10-year plan to grow its economy. As Table 2.1 illustrates, results greatly surpassed expectations. Automobiles led the rise in Japanese exports, which rose at an average annual rate of 17.5% versus 7.7% in the United States.

As was the case with VW, Japanese success with imports initially went largely unheeded by the Big Three because they occupied such a small slice of the overall U.S. market. In 1961, 378,542 foreign cars were sold in the United States. Volkswagen sold roughly one half of that amount. Nissan and Toyota together sold 1,733 cars, one tenth the number of Fiats sold (11,839).[7] The Japanese at the time were far behind the Germans, French, Belgians, and Swedes, lending support to what *Business Week* ironically predicted on August 2, 1958:

> Japan is plunging into the foreign car market here with two entries, Nissan's four-door Datsun and Toyota's somewhat larger Toyopet Crown. With over 50 foreign carmakers already on sale here, the

TABLE 2.1 Prediction and Performance for the Japanese Economy in the 1960s (in billions of dollars)[8]

	Prediction in 1960	*Performance in 1970*
Gross national	72.2	173.4
Exports	9.3	19.3
Imports	9.9	18.9
Machinery and transport exports	3.5	11.3

> Japanese auto industry isn't likely to carve out a big slice of the U.S. market for itself. The Japanese companies, Nissan Automobile Co. and Toyota Motor Sales Co., feel that they have no other choice than making a stab at the small, second-car market here. Unlike Western European automakers, which in some cases can't keep up with local demand, the Japanese face an almost stagnant car market at home.[9]

However, it proved to be of little significance that the Japanese car market was stagnant at home. What mattered more was the fact that a tremendous market for cars existed in the United States and that, little by little, the Japanese manufacturers started to gain market share. The number of passenger cars that the Japanese produced in 1958—50,039—was only 6.4% greater than the year before. But the growth from 1956 to 1957 was an impressive 47%, from 31,968 to 47,045. Viewed in terms of growth, Japan was coming on strong, even if its volume did not compare with imports from Germany.

By 1972, Japan was the second-largest car manufacturer in the world, the same year it became the number-one exporter to the United States. In 1973, Henry Ford II, son of the father of the American automobile industry said, "What the hell do I want to go around the block to dinner in a Lincoln for? The big car as we know it is on its way out. That's gone forever. I'm a small-car man. I'm a promoter of small cars."[10]

The American Response

From 1972 onward, Japan continued to capture market share in the United States and assumed top position among world automobile manufacturers. Table 2.2 illustrates this rise. Japan's invasion of the U.S. car market finally prompted strong response from U.S. automakers.

TABLE 2.2 Production of Passenger Cars, by Country, 1961 to 1981
(in millions)[11]

	1961	1965	1969	1977	1981
United States	5.5	9.3	8.2	10.4	7.0
West Germany	1.9	2.7	3.3	3.8	3.6
Japan	.25	.69	2.6	5.4	7.0

In the first half of 1971—the year the United States ran a trade deficit for the first time in the 20th century—the Big Three lobbied for protection against imports. In 1950, the United States had the lowest tariff on automobile imports in the world (7%). This was less by almost one half the tariff in Europe. At the time, U.S. manufacturers felt that the tastes of the American consumer would be enough to repel the competition's smaller cars. However, Detroit did attempt a response to a growing market for small cars. The 1960 model year marked the introduction of the compact American car. For various reasons, each of the Big Three's entries in this market did not fare well.

Ford produced the Falcon. Three feet shorter and 1,400 pounds lighter than the Edsel, the Falcon's price tag ($2,300) was dangerously close to that of the Edsel ($3,000). The result for Ford was that its compact Falcon cannibalized sales on its more expensive line. In and of itself, the Falcon sold well—500,000 units in 1960. But overall, Ford's sales dropped that year by 917,000 to 14 million. More to the point of why the Falcon never made it is that its profit margins weren't as good as a big car. Before the Falcon's banner introductory year in 1960, Ford's engineers had already begun developing ways to make the Falcon a bigger car. Chrysler's Valiant also stole sales from the larger models, driving overall sales down 140,000 units. GM's Corvair was the only model to come from the Big Three that did not cannibalize the company. The low-riding, sporty car was loaded with design innovations. Its rear-mounted engine was reminiscent of the Beetle. To hold down production costs, Chevrolet excluded a stabilizing bar that was normally used in cars with rear-mounted engines. It also used 13-inch rather than 15-inch wheels. This move into the small car market revealed just how set Detroit was on manufacturing the big car. For all the corners Chevrolet cut to build the Corvair, it saved a mere $30 per car.[12]

The Big Three's response to foreign competition did work, stealing sales from every major foreign manufacturer except Volkswagen. The Corvair sold briskly for several years, but ultimately, design faults doomed it to failure. In 1965, consumer advocate Ralph Nader launched a campaign to expose the Corvair's faults. Nader revealed the car's steering difficulties in his book *Unsafe at Any Speed*[13] and touched off close to 100 lawsuits against General Motors. From 1965 on, the Corvair's sales dwindled until it was phased out in 1969. Nader's attack, although not focused exclusively on American autos (he called the Beetle the most unsafe car in the world), did tarnish Detroit's image as a center for blue-chip quality and design.[14] Unfortunately, many of the criticisms were warranted. In its effort to meet competition, Detroit had slipped. In 1976, Chrysler Corporation introduced the Volare/Aspen, a replacement for the Reliant/Dart. Problems with the carburetor and brakes and improper galvanizing led to massive recalls. Further reports of hoods flying off at high speeds cost Chrysler $200 million and untold sums in terms of lost trust among consumers.[15]

Japanese automobile manufacturers successfully rose to challenge Detroit. In the process, it came to light how advanced Asian manufacturing processes were. The comments of Harvard professors William Abernathy and Kim Clark, after an extensive tour of Japanese automobile manufacturers in 1981, capture the sentiment:

> We had been half-prepared to find them [the Japanese automobile makers] using process technology far more advanced than anything available to their American counterparts. What we saw about us at every turn, however, was not newer technology but better management of the technology in place—not the exotic gimmickry of wide-eyed public expectation but a sober master of manufacturing.[16]

Table 2.3 compares costs of small cars for General Motors and Nissan in 1981. Table 2.4 compares costs of manufacturing and stamping operations for Japanese and American plants in 1981.

The Challenge to the American Economy

American businesses were firmly on track throughout the 1960s, enjoying what appeared to be uncontested world dominance. Every now and then a foreign competitor would sprout up—the English Minx, the

TABLE 2.3 Comparative Costs for Small Cars, General Motors and
          Nissan, 1981[17]

Productivity/Cost, Category	General Motors	Nissan
Labor productivity, employee hours		
per small car	83	51
Costs per small car		
Labor	$1,826	$593
Purchased components	3,405	2,858
Other manufacturing costs	730	350
Nonmanufacturing costs	325	1,200
Total	$6,286	$5,001

TABLE 2.4 Comparison of Manufacturing/Stamping Operations in
          Japanese and American Automotive Plants, 1981[18]

Manufacturing/Stamping Operation	Japan	United States
Parts stamped per hour	550	325
Manpower per press line	1	7-13
Time needed to change dies	5 minutes	5 hours
Time needed to build a small car	31 hours	60 hours
Total workforce average at an automobile plant	2,360	4,250

German Beetle, the Japanese Toyopet—only to snare an inconsequential
market share. The Big Three made token efforts to meet the challenge
but ultimately imposed on the consumer what they knew how to build:
the large automobile. In the end, bigger did not sell as well. In a matter
of years, the balance of the industry took a dramatic turn, ending an era
of uncontested dominance for American car manufacturers. Of course,
the automotive industry was not the only industry to experience such
dramatic change. As a whole, American corporations lost their hold on
world markets.

▶ Even though imports of steel rose by 50% between 1970 and
1981, the industry as a whole failed to realize that domestic demand was
falling because Detroit was producing smaller, lighter cars.

TABLE 2.5 Distribution of the 100 Largest Industrial Corporations[19]

	United States	Europe	Japan
1970	64	26	8
1988	42	33	15
1995	24	37	36

▶ The Radio Corporation of America (RCA), once the largest consumer electronics manufacturer in the United States, prematurely assessed the new magnetic tape that would eventually be used in video-cassettes as too expensive to produce. Instead, it favored videodisk technology, an error borne of its inability to adapt to the better technology, the same technology that gave Japanese corporations a toehold on the U.S. consumer electronics industry. Even after losing $100 million in 1981 and 1982, RCA would not reorient its strategy and ultimately lost $580 million for its stubbornness.[20]

These stories do not simply tell the stories of American corporations in the face of international competition. More specifically, they illustrate the lethargy that characterized the classic corporation's reaction to changing economic circumstances and the implied arrogance that drove strategy.

The New World Economy

As you can see from Table 2.5, U.S. corporations once dominated world markets. However, rivals in Europe and Asia quietly grew until in 1995, the margin of U.S. companies in the world's top 100 companies actually fell below both Europe and Japan.[21]

Europe and Asia have eclipsed the United States in terms of worker productivity as well. From 1980 to 1990, American productivity grew at a rate of 1.2%. Meanwhile, productivity during that same period (1980-1990) grew in Japan at a rate of 3.1%, 1.9% in France, 1.4% in West Germany, and 2.9% in the United Kingdom. In terms of performance, the United States also lost stature during the 1980s. The United States was once home to the most educated workforce and finest industrial managers in the world. In 1990, the World Economic Forum ranked 23 industrial countries according to their competitiveness. For product quality, Japan ranked first, Germany third, and the United States 12th.

For on-time delivery, Japan was again number 1, Germany number 2, and the United States number 10. The Japanese were ranked number 1 for quality and quantity of on-the-job training. Germany was second best and the United States ranked 11th.[22]

The European and Japanese competitive advantages have been systemic in nature. In Germany, for example, job training begins at the grade school level. Students enroll in *Arbeitlehre,* a program in which young people learn about various industries. Students not continuing on to college can begin apprenticeships in one of 480 trades. Almost half of all German midsized firms and all major ones offer apprenticeships that last two to three years. The training curriculum is set by a consortium of industry, training experts, and government.[23]

The Japanese advantage was not solely one of management. It was equally a matter of economic systems. Japanese industries exist in a state of interdependence. Sometimes referred to as *keiritsu,* or industry groupings, this relationship encompasses all levels of the economy. In the Japanese automobile industry, for example, the large manufacturer and small supplier do not exist in an adversarial relationship. Quality, as practiced by the Japanese, is as much the responsibility of the supplier as it is the manufacturer. In the United States, as a counterexample, if a supplier ships faulty components, the manufacturer will monitor performance until there is an improvement in quality. If none occurs then the relationship will be terminated. The same situation in Japan would prompt a surprise inspection of the supplier's factory. Managers and workers would be interviewed, and perhaps suggestions for improvement would be offered. And if improvements were not forthcoming, *then* the contract would be canceled. This symbiotic relationship among small and large corporations is not solely a matter of collaboration. In many cases, large Japanese manufacturers take an equity stake in their suppliers. Toyota, for example, owns 9.8% of Hino Motor, 21.8% of Aichi Steel, 40.8% of Kanto Auto Works, 36.3% of Kyowas Leather Cloth, and 7.9% of Toyo Radiator.[24] In the United States, the tendency was for the manufacturers to buy the suppliers outright.

Throughout the rise and reign of the classic corporation in the United States, small businesses existed as a complement to large ones. With the rise of international competition, however, this dynamic has changed. The corporation now seeks ways to work with the small business, and increasingly to compete effectively against them.

THE RISE AND IMPACT OF
DOMESTIC COMPETITION

The *Washington Post* commented in 1989, "Once . . . such giants as Proctor & Gamble might have ignored market segments of less than $200 million. Today, they covet niches a quarter of that size."[25] Now, as we approach the 21st century, the classic corporation, a system engineered to service large, fixed markets, has found that such markets no longer exist. Large companies must now compete fiercely with small businesses that are agile and well suited to economic turbulence.

When John Kenneth Galbraith wrote his celebrated *Affluent Society* in 1958, he said the dynamic sector of the economy included large manufacturing, utilities, communication, and transportation firms. Smaller businesses were not included. "His independence," Galbraith said of the small business owner, "is often the caution, conformity, obeisance, even servility, of a man whose livelihood is at the mercy of his customers. His is often the freedom of a man who is pecked to death by ducks."[26] Galbraith's caricature of the small and medium-sized business stood in stark comparison with popular views just 30 years earlier. Early in the 20th century, small business was regarded as the core of the American economic system and representative of the American system of values. In 1917, Justice Brandeis was elevated to the Supreme Court. As the champion of small business, Brandeis connected the protection of that form of economic activity with the survival of the democratic system. He believed that bigness was a "curse," leading to inefficiency, concentration of power, and economic menace to competitors, consumers, suppliers, and the democratic ideals of our system.[27] However, since the early 1970s, the most dynamic sector of the U.S. economy has been the one driven by entrepreneurs.

Galbraith's portrait of the small business as a noncreative complement to the big business has come full circle. According to the Small Business Administration (SBA), small businesses are responsible for the majority of the economy's innovations. In 1993, the SBA studied technology, engineering, and trade journals and identified 8,074 innovations in 362 industries. Small firms, it was estimated, were at the root of 55% of these innovations. The study also found that there are 2.38 times as many innovations per employee in a small business as there are in a large one. Small businesses produce 1.91 times as many first-of-type innovations, 1.92 as many significant improvements, and 2.46 as many modest improvements per employee as do large businesses.[28]

Just as foreign companies came to challenge large U.S. corporations for traditional markets, so too have small and midsized businesses increasingly challenged larger ones for domestic markets. The U.S. economy, once dominated by large corporations, is now made up more of small and medium-sized businesses.

> In 1979, corporations of 500 employees or larger employed 43% of the workforce. In 1996, just 19% of the workforce worked at companies with 500 or more employees. Companies with 20 to 249 employees have experienced major growth in the past 18 years, growing from just 6% of total employees in 1979 to 46% in 1996.[29]

> Between 1976 and 1986, manufacturers with less than 500 employees added 1.4 million new jobs, at the same time that larger companies abolished 140,000 jobs.

> Between 1979 and 1989 the American economy added nearly 19 million new jobs. In this time period, Fortune 500 companies lost nearly 3.7 million.[30]

One interesting example is provided by the stock brokerage industry. Traditionally, the domain of large institutional trading houses, industry dynamics have changed since the arrival of the small-order execution system (SOES). The system was created by the National Association of Securities Dealers (NASD) in 1984, to ensure fair access to NASDAQ (National Association of Security/Securities Dealers Automated Quotations) among small investors. Block Trading is a Houston-based SOES trading house that runs its offices out of a strip mall. The founders, Chris Block and Jeff Burke, lease time on their computers to private traders (which are wired to NASDAQ) and take a small commission for each stock trade.

In 1995, when the company had only its Houston office, revenues were $1 million. In 1996, revenues hit $18 million, and the company is now spread across 13 offices in five states. Block Trading represents a quiet revolution (if it is a revolution at all). At the very least, the company represents a departure from the status quo, in the same way that Wal-Mart departed from the status quo with its retailing techniques, Nucor Steel departed from traditional manufacturing systems, and Southwest Airlines departed from standard airline operations.[31]

Whereas the classic corporation maximized size, the newer adaptive corporations are built for speed. Direct computer seller Dell is an example of the trend. If the established giants of the personal computer (PC) industry once thought direct sales were just a blip on the market's radar, they're now taking a second look. Direct sales account for almost one third of PC sales, up from 15% percent only six years ago.

Dell, based in Austin, Texas, is currently rewriting the book on high-tech retailing, and it is beating the leaders at a new game. Michael Dell, the company's founder and CEO, figures that the parts in his computers are, on average, 60 days newer than those in an IBM or Compaq computer sold at the same time. That's because the company holds onto only 13 days of sales in inventory versus 25 days at Compaq. In addition, Dell's computers are 10% to 15% cheaper than those sold by rival companies.

The company, founded in a college dorm in 1984, has achieved these advantages by striving for quicker operations and lower overhead. No Dell PC is assembled until it is ordered. When it is, the company ignites its supplier network no matter how large the order. Dell can turn the average sale to cash within 24 hours. Competitor Compaq Computer, which distributes computers by dealers, takes 35 days. The bulk of a Dell computer's components are warehoused within 15 minutes of its factories in Austin, Texas; Limerick, Ireland; and Penang, Malaysia. The company has worked for the past several years to speed the delivery of parts for computers. It used to take 22 days to receive circuit boards shipped by boat from India. Now Dell can truck the parts from Mexico in 15 hours. Dell has also trimmed its number of supplies from 204 in 1992 to 47 in 1997.

Dell is currently experimenting with new ways to bolster its speed to market. Working in partnership with network equipment maker 3Com, Dell is trying to reduce the typical 60 to 90 days required to test computer and networking configurations to 14 days. Dell's efficiency yielded a 71% jump in sales from 1995 to 1996, whereas the rest of the industry grew 13.6%.

Dell has received the most accolades for its performance on the Internet. As of November 1996, Dell had not invested a great deal of effort in selling PCs on the World Wide Web. Six months later, Dell was the number-one computer retailer in cyberspace, with sales growing 20% each month. CEO Michael Dell looks at this part of his business as a growth center. (As of their 1998 annual report, Dell's net profits continue to increase at four times the industry average.) Dell will put 75 of its corporate customers on a closed system whereby an employee at one of these companies will be able to order directly from Dell and receive the corporate discount.[32]

Innovations such as these introduce a new dynamic for the classic corporation. Information technology in general has introduced change at the most fundamental levels of the corporation and represents the second major driver of change.

THE IMPACT OF INFORMATION AND COMMUNICATION TECHNOLOGY

Technology has long been a major driver of change. Manual tools, interchangeable parts, electricity, and the automobile have each changed the corporation by redefining the very basic rules of production and distribution. Each of these advances also changed the very fabric of society, touching off fundamental demographic shifts. There are times, however, when new technologies may introduce even greater change. Certain technologies are so powerful, and are introduced at such a rapid rate, that they bring with them a level of change that is unexpected, dramatic, and seemingly uncontrollable.

The atomic bomb is one vivid example of the point. On August 6, 1945, the Enola Gay dropped "Little Boy" on Hiroshima. In one flash, the bomb's impact was equal to 12,500 tons of TNT. That same instant changed the entire world forever. World War II ended abruptly, and for more than four decades afterward, the world was locked in a global "cold war." Today, many corporations are experiencing change to a comparable degree. This time, information and communication technology are the main drivers.

"Moore's Law" and Technological Change

In 1965, Dr. Gordon Moore, cofounder of Intel, made a prediction that the number of transistors packed into a computer chip (and the proportional capacity of the chip) would double every year for the next 10 years. This may have seemed a fanciful statement considering that at the time, Moore's company was producing chips loaded with 200 circuits. Moore's prophecy came true, however, in the next 10 years. In 1975, he amended the prediction to a doubling of capacity every 2 years. This turned out to be an understatement. In fact, capacity has doubled every 18 months. Looking ahead, the only limit for growth on the surface of the silicon wafer Moore acknowledges is the atomic structure of matter.[33]

The electronics industry seems to be moving steadily toward that limit. IBM announced in 1997 that it would soon produce chips with copper transistors instead of the traditional aluminum ones. This innovation will allow IBM to produce circuits 0.2 microns wide, or 500 times thinner than a human hair.[34] This surpasses Intel's thinnest circuit by 0.05 microns, but the true significance of the invention is the implications of such a chip's performance, which will improve by 40%, and its production costs, which will be reduced 30%. Still other inventions threaten to challenge Moore's law for the better. Scientists in Japan announced at the end of 1997 that they had developed a process that could shrink chip sizes by 300%. By 2001, said the hotly contested research, chip performance would increase 64 times.[35]

In the past, however, although technology had the ability to change an organization, it typically took a considerable amount of time for the change to make its full impact on the corporation. Consider the case of electricity. Thomas Edison first harnessed the energy in the carbon filament incandescent light in 1879. The full impact of that invention was not to be felt in business for one generation's time. When it was felt, however, it altered the very structure of the typical manufacturing plant.

Factories at the end of the 19th century were housed primarily in four-story brick buildings. Large steam engines drove machinery by a complex system of vertical and horizontal shafts. These factories were quite literally vertical in orientation because the higher level of friction in horizontal shafts was more costly in terms of energy efficiency.

What factories saved in energy, however, they lost in productivity because, frequently, people and materials depended on elevators. When the central generating station was introduced in 1881, manufacturers simply stopped using the steam engine and converted to electricity. The new technology did slash coal bills by 20% to 60%, but the factory was still run through its lattice of shafts and belts. Over time, electric engines on each floor of the factory started to replace the large basement engine, but the cost of complete implementation was prohibitive. In the last year of the 19th century, electricity accounted for less than 5% of power used in American manufacturing.[36] Then, in the early 1920s a critical evolution took place. Factories made sweeping changes from the "group power drive" to "unit drive" so that individual machines each had their own power source. Only then did change come quickly. Factories literally flattened to one story, allowing for easier flow of materials. Real gains in productivity quickly followed. Labor productivity grew 1% every year from 1880 to 1900. Throughout the 1920s, that figure rose to 5% per year.[37]

An entire infrastructure had to be replaced for electricity to achieve its full potential in the workplace. In the digital age, an entire mind-set will have to be replaced. When the PC arrived in the American office, it was used in the same fashion as the old technology, the typewriter. Because the technology was new and the typewriter was kept as the standard tool, doubled costs for the same output smothered productivity. In addition, because companies introduced the technology piecemeal rather than across the board, work processes bottlenecked when they bumped up against the old techniques. But over time, managers found that computers allowed them to do different things, not merely the same thing differently.

Information technology is like electricity in its ability to transform the organization. Unlike electricity, however, the latest technological boom has spread widely across industries and penetrated deeply into corporations in a relatively short period of time. The rise of the Internet provides a dramatic example. In 1993, the traffic on the Internet was expanding at an annual growth rate of 643%.[38]

The PC has been an important driver of change largely because of its rapid infiltration into the everyday activities of the workforce and society at large. Between 1975 and 1980, the PC segment posted a 7,000% increase in the number of units shipped. The ubiquity of the PC is due to its plummeting cost. Consider Table 2.6. In 1975, it cost $1 million for the leading computer to process 1 million instructions. In 1994, a PC could process 1 million instructions for $45. The power to process information has had tremendous influence in many industries, including commercial banking.[39]

TABLE 2.6 Price and Speed of Computers, Selected Years, 1975 to 1995[40]

Year	Leading Device	Million Instructions per Second	Price	Price per Million Instructions per Second
1975	IBM Mainframe	10	$10,000,000	$1,000,000
1976	Cray 1	160	20,000,000	125,000
1979	DEC VAX	1	200,000	200,000
1981	IBM PC	0.25	2,000	12,000
1984	Sun 2	1	10,000	10,000
1994	Intel Pentium	66	3,000	45
1998	Intel Pentium II	500	1,000	2 [41]

The Impact of Information Technology

The commercial banking industry has been transformed since the early 1970s by electronic fund transfer (EFT) technologies. The automated teller machine (ATM) in particular has redefined the industry. In 1971, the first ATM came on line in Valdosta, Georgia, as a cash dispenser for a local bank. By 1995, restrictions on interstate transactions had lessened and ATMs did more than give consumers access to their money. Today, one can access detailed account statements, complete loan applications, transfer funds, purchase traveler's checks, and buy stamps from an ATM. In 1995, 9.7 billion transactions were processed on 123,000 ATM terminals. ATM technology has given rise to a similar application: point-of-sale (POS) transactions at retail stores. Since 1986, POS transactions have outpaced the growth of ATMs by roughly three to one.[42] Commercial banks have adopted a third technology that has driven change: computer-automated telephone transactions. One in three American households conduct their banking over the telephone at least once a month. The technology allows the consumer to transfer funds between accounts, order checks, stop payments, inquire about balances, and pay bills.

The rapid implementation of these technologies has been driven by attractive savings and overall gains in performance. In 1996, a transaction completed by a human teller cost a bank $1.07. The same transaction, run by an ATM, cost 27 cents. Using an automated telephone system, the transaction costs 35 cents versus $1.82 for a human telephone operator.[43] In terms of productivity, commercial banks have had the highest long-term growth in productivity among finance and service industries for the period of 1973 to 1993.[44]

The rising number of automated banking technologies, accompanied by their significant cost savings, correlates with the falling number of people employed in the commercial banking industry. The number of bank tellers fell by 41,000 between 1985 and 1995, a decade when the number of ATMs rose from just under 3 million to 9.8 million country-wide. Looking ahead, the U.S. Bureau of Labor Statistics projects a 27% decline in the number of bank tellers between 1994 and 2005.[45]

ATM and POS technology have not only changed the way banks move money and consumers access it, but also have changed the way banks are staffed. Information technology is currently redefining various business functions across every industry.

Billing

DuPont has streamlined its operations substantially by eliminating the requisition and billing process for 5% of its vendors. With a new electronic inventory system, suppliers don't have to wait for a requisition; they are automatically notified when supplies are low.[46]

Sales

Phoenix Designs, a Zeeland, Michigan, furniture reseller uses technology to dramatically speed up the amount of time it takes to fill orders. In the not-so-distant past, independent dealers would visit the site of a client and collect specifications for their office furniture. The rep would then feed these data to a designer who would put together some configurations. Six weeks later, after much back and forth, the customer would have a proposal to look at. All that changed when the company picked up a custom sales software application called Z-Axis. Now, the sales rep can design office systems and Phoenix can generate a proposal in five days. After a $1 million initial investment in technology, Phoenix has been rewarded with a 27% jump in after-tax income.[47]

Workflow

Aetna Life & Casualty used to generate policies through the combined effort of 3,000 employees spread throughout 22 business centers.

Sixty different employees had to handle a single application that took 15 days to process. In 1993, the company installed a computer system whereby a single employee could perform all the necessary steps. Aetna has pared down to 700 employees in four centers. Policies now go out in the next day's mail.[48]

Customer Service

Society National Bank in Cleveland installed a voice mail system that could handle 70% of customer service-oriented calls. This, combined with a fleet of laptop computers, has allowed loan officers to hit the streets to drum up business. Says Executive Vice President Allan Gula, Jr., "If you call us and say you want to refinance, we'll meet you in your parking lot at lunch."[49]

Inventory

The story of Wal-Mart Stores' rise to success is a classic case of technology fueling competitiveness. Satellite networks link POS terminals with distribution centers and the national headquarters in Bentonville, Arkansas. This allows for minute-by-minute tracking of inventory and continual analysis of consumer activity—and one of the most efficient inventory systems in America.[50]

Human Resource Management

At 7:15 in the morning, a group of Home Depot employees is gathered around a television screen in their Sunnyvale, California, store. The morning's lesson on the nutritional needs of plants, taught by the head of the nursery, will turn the 26 salespeople into experts ready for their customer's needs. The hardware megastore uses a proprietary satellite television network to distribute a stream of corporate learning.[51]

Technology as a driver of change is not new. Tools reoriented early civilization, as did the railroad in turn-of-the-century America. The impact of change in each of these cases has caused fundamental shifts in the way the economic system operates and in the social interaction of individuals.

> It can be said that in forty years computing has experienced a combined improvement in five dimensions—mass storage, reliability, cost, power

consumption, and processing speed—of thirty orders of magnitude. Such a level of change is almost beyond human compass. It is equal to the jump from the diameter of a single atom to that of the Milky Way galaxy. . . . it took a change of just two orders of magnitude to spark the Industrial Revolution and one of only four orders of magnitude in explosive power to end a world war and redirect human history.[52]

Ironically, it is the promise of information and communication technology that can aid the modern corporation as it strives to deal with massive change. The latter part of this work will elaborate further on the application of information technology: specifically, how the new adaptive corporations use information to capture and leverage knowledge throughout their organization.

THE CLASSIC CORPORATION ATTEMPTS TO CHANGE

The drivers of change—competition and technology—have had crippling effects on the classic corporation, an organization inherently designed to maintain the status quo. At the core of the classic corporation's inability to change is what Dr. Judith Bardwick, author of *Danger in the Comfort Zone*,[53] calls the "mentality of entitlement." Bardwick describes this dynamic as a function of economic dominance and corporate size:

> When this rich nation stopped requiring performance as a condition for keeping a job or getting a raise, it created a widespread attitude of Entitlement. Entitlement destroys motivation. It lowers productivity. In the long run it crushes self-esteem. And despite the layoffs of recent years, it is an epidemic in this country. It's our legacy of the boom times that followed World War II.[54]

Ironically, the "golden years" of the American corporation (the mid-1940s to the mid-1970s, depending on the industry) ultimately did it the most harm. In those years, unprecedented growth, prosperity, and stability diminished the employee's incentive to perform. This situation was a function of economics, demographics, and psychology. In the postwar boom years, corporations grew rapidly. At AT&T, for example, middle management grew by 500%. Profitability soared as well. Concurrently, there was a limited pool of people to fill these positions. Those people available to take these jobs were usually born in the 1920s and

1930s when the U.S. birthrate was at an all-time low. Taken together, these factors produced the entitlement mentality.[55]

"I've worked here a long time and have done what you expected. I've earned my security." This statement encapsulates the entitlement mentality. It became the legacy of the Organization Man to think of the company as "family" and that it "owes" him unconditional job protection. According to Bardwick, the entitlement mentality is a function of too much security in the workplace. She describes institutional forms of security as including the following:

> ▶ Informal "tenure" for everyone
> ▶ An appraisal system that has little impact
> ▶ A promotion system that doesn't reflect individual merit
> ▶ An emphasis on precedent
> ▶ A lot of rules
> ▶ A compensation system that doesn't reflect people's achievement
> ▶ Committees with no real authority
> ▶ Rewards for fine-tuners and punishment for innovators
> ▶ A formal hierarchy in which difference in power dictates permissible behavior
> ▶ Layers of people whose jobs are making sure no mistakes are being made[56]

As the classic corporation developed, it evolved with increasingly complex layers, divisions, and departments. One of the consequences of the hierarchical work organization was a workforce that paid more attention to the rules of the organization and less to the goals of the company. That emphasis on conformity to rules and regulation as a surrogate for goals, notes Bardwick, had four major effects: pseudowork, passivity, resentment and ambivalence, and greed.

First among the effects on the workforce is a tendency toward doing pseudowork. In this case, doing what looks good is more important than doing what is good. People are rewarded for "putting in time." Examples of pseudowork include meetings without follow-up and internal memos and status reports that don't get read.

Another effect of the top-down organization on the workers is passivity. Passive employees follow the boss's lead. They wait for orders and only then execute. Workers like these don't make any mistakes because they don't take any chances.

The third effect of the hierarchy on the organization is resentment and ambivalence. Taylor's scientific management prescribed that managers give subordinate employees concrete directions for what they were supposed to do and how they should do it. However, employees resent being stripped of any decision-making power. Concurrently, the rules of the organization make these same employees ambivalent about their work. So employees end up wallowing in the security of a regimented work organization.

The final effect of the hierarchical organization is greed. Although the company may be falling down around them, losing profit margins, and shedding units, entitled employees will complain about losing a percentage of their pay. The prevailing attitude becomes, "What will be done for me?"[57]

Whyte's metaphor of a factory on the verge of explosion, with a middle manager holding his finger on the panic button is an apt one to describe the classic corporation. No single middle manager can be blamed for the decline of an organization, just as no single manager can take credit for its renewal. The image of the Organization Man caught between what's right and what's expected poignantly captures this sense of paralysis. The very real result of entitlement was a declining level of productivity in the United States in the 1960s and 1970s culminating in the 1980s when the annual productivity per hour rate for nonfarm industry grew at a paltry 1.2%.[58]

What had become clear was that the classic corporation was unable to quickly recognize and react to the rapidly changing nature of world markets. What was not so clear was what these corporations could do to survive—much less prosper. In Chapter 3, the major strategies used by organizations to cope with change are laid out, as well as the consequences those strategies have had on the dynamics of corporate America today.

MAJOR STRATEGIES FOR COPING WITH CHANGE

Knowledge is the antidote to fear.

—Ralph Waldo Emerson

By the mid-1960s, the classic corporation was feeling the dual pressures of competition and technological change. Managers were desperate to meet the new challenge of competition, but the old hierarchy and management styles of the classic corporation were ill suited for a quick turnaround. The classic corporation was designed to maintain the status quo.

In this climate, a wave of management trends surfaced and affected the classic corporation and its employees. What is currently called *reengineering* has known many other names in the past, but one central theme remains: To compete, corporations have had to dramatically change the way they do business. As change became discontinuous, it challenged the basic systems on which a company's advantages rested. Because change came so quickly and hit corporations so hard, many needed to undertake dramatic strategies. The reactions of choice were to realign, restructure, and reduce.

REALIGNMENT

Mergers and acquisitions were not novel concepts to the classic corporation. As early as the 1970s, large corporations were formed of groups of smaller companies. This practice of rolling small companies into public shells became a frequent strategy for creating efficiency and pooling capital. This integration technique varied from the "M&A" (merger and acquisition) activity that became prevalent in the United States during the same period and that has lasted until the present day. Companies began to acquire others to be more competitive with increasingly aggressive foreign competition.

Frequently, other companies were growing by acquiring companies whose business was different. Between 1963 and 1972, three fourths of the assets acquired in M&A were for product diversification. One half of these were in unrelated product lines. In the years 1973 to 1977, one half of the assets obtained through M&A were unrelated to the buyer's core business.[1]

As companies grow by merger and acquisition, decision making for the entire conglomerate becomes a more complex matter. Prior to World War II, the corporate office of a large, undiversified corporation managed no more than 10 divisions. The largest corporations may have had 25 divisions. By 1969, many companies were operating 50 to 70 divisions. Between 1979 and 1985, there were more than 17,000 mergers and acquisitions totaling more than $500 billion. In the two consecutive years—1986 and 1987—6,920 takeovers worth more than $315 billion took place.[2] The record books continue to be rewritten as M&A activity increases every year. Although the number of deals has grown, the value of each deal has continued to increase exponentially. In 1996, there were 4,790 M&A transactions worth $369.3 billion.[3]

The implications of mergers and acquisitions are not limited to effects on boardrooms and back offices. The human consequences are considerable. Consider the 100 largest mergers of 1984. Over 4.5 million people, or 4.3% of the entire workforce, worked for the companies involved. If just 10% of that group were affected by the mergers, then 450,000 people had their professional lives altered.[4] This is not an unlikely scenario because M&A activity has implications beyond the transaction. As corporations fuse, the effects include having cultures clash, objectives become muddled, and the corporate focus becomes unclear. This in turn leads to a second major change strategy: restructuring.

RESTRUCTURING

In 1993, Michael Hammer and James Champy published *Reengineering the Corporation: A Manifesto for Business Revolution.*[5] In their book, the authors determined that to reinvent their companies, managers need to abandon the "classic corporation" organizational and operational principles and procedures they were using and create entirely new ones. The old operating rules are not only outdated, they are damaging to a company, claimed Hammer and Champy. The authors (and many other contemporary consultants before and after the book was published) advised companies that the best way to meet international competition was with massive changes. The reengineering movement is embodied in four key words:

> The first key word is "fundamental." In doing reengineering, business people must ask the most basic questions about their companies and how they operate.
> Next comes "radical," which means getting to the root of things: not making superficial changes or fiddling with what is already in place, but throwing away the old and inventing completely new ways of accomplishing work. Reengineering is about business reinvention— not business improvement, business enhancement, or business modification.
> After radical the key word is "dramatic." Reengineering isn't about making marginal or incremental improvements but about achieving quantum leaps in performance.
> The final key word is "processes," which, though the most important in our definition, is the one that gives most corporate managers the greatest difficulty. Most business people are not process oriented; they are focused on tasks, on jobs, on people, on structures, but not on processes. A business process is a collection of activities that takes one or more kinds of input and creates an output that is of value to the customer.[6]

The dramatic thrust of reengineering—rapid enterprise-wide changes— has had a lasting impact on the organization. The idea that major change was central to reengineering infiltrated boardrooms across the country. For example, Emmanuel A. Kampouris, chief executive of American Standard stated, "Re-engineering is not something you pussyfoot around and do a little here and a little there. Re-engineering is a radical redesign that makes 70% of the people mad at you. Some people won't even talk to you after a while. But that's the penalty you pay until you succeed."[7]

The following story regarding Seymour Cray, the founder of the supercomputer company, Cray Research, Inc., illustrates by metaphor the reengineering attitude:

> Seymour lived on a lake in Wisconsin, and he would pass the long winters there by building sailboats. Some of them were pretty big. In fact, the last one he built was 36 feet. He would build a boat in the basement and when the weather grew warm, he would drag the boat out on to the lake and sail around all summer. But at the end of the summer he wanted to dispose of the boat because he had so many ideas about the next boat he wanted to build. And so every fall, he would have a big party—a cookout on the beach with a big bonfire. He'd encourage people to dance around the fire, and at a certain point they would burn the boat. Just burn her right up![8]

Reengineering, as practiced by Hammer and Champy, began as a technique focused on internal process design and automation. It certainly was not the first management technique to address improvement concerns, but reengineering has had a lasting impact on the corporation that neither of the authors may have foreseen. According to the 1995 study by human resources consultanty Watson Wyatt, *Best Practices in Corporate Restructuring,* downsizing has been the single most prominent result of restructuring. Of companies that engage in restructuring actions, 74% downsize. The study found that one in four companies that engaged in downsizing reduced their workforce by more than 20%, cumulatively, in the early part of the 1990s, making downsizing a considerable pressure on the workforce.

DOWNSIZING

> *It's a sin to lose money, a mortal sin. [Statement made after the elimination of 10,500 jobs, one third of Scott Paper's workforce.]*
>
> —Albert J. Dunlap, ex-CEO, Scott Paper, Sunbeam[9]

> *We are exporting jobs to markets where workers get paid 35 cents an hour. Since American CEOs make 3.2 times*

> *the amount of British CEOs, shouldn't we be importing*
> *British CEOs?*
>
> —Joke on late-night talk show[10]

Downsizing: Impact on the Workforce

A June 27, 1986, headline in the *Washington Post* read, "IBM Rethinking Cherished Policy of No Layoffs."[11] With more than 405,000 employees worldwide—242,000 of them in the United States—"Big Blue" had become one of the largest corporations in the world. Still, it held onto the belief that it could offer its employees lifetime employment. For years, the company had attracted employees with its policy against layoffs. In 1984, the company was adding an average of 50 new employees a day. And IBM was not alone: Eastman Kodak and Xerox Corporation were among numerous companies that thought their size and market position would shelter them from instability.[12] Time and circumstances proved otherwise. Between the mid-1980s and mid-1990s, IBM and Kodak together laid off more than 200,000 employees. At Kodak, change came with five separate corporate restructurings that have saved the company $2.1 billion.[13] Once known as the "Great Yellow Father" among residents of Kodak's hometown of Rochester, New York, the film and imaging giant announced in November 1997, that it would lay off an additional 10,000 employees.[14]

It is little wonder that downsizing has followed closely on the heels of reengineering. Michael Hammer had promised that his style of corporate restructuring would result in the loss of more than 40% of the jobs in a company and could go up to a 75% reduction of the corporate workforce. Statistics bear out the prophecy. The largest of American companies have been hit hardest by the downsizing trend. According to one study, *Fortune* 500 companies slashed 4 million jobs in the 1980s. In 1991, cutbacks amounted to 2,600 a day.[15] And in 1993, the worst year for downsizing, IBM laid off 60,000; Sears, Roebuck & Co., 50,000; and Kodak, 10,000.[16]

At times, the numbers associated with layoffs have drawn attention from the trend of a shifting workforce. Headlines such as "40,000 to Be Laid Off at AT&T" do not represent the corporate restructuring story in its totality. Despite mass layoffs from the mid-1980s through the present day, unemployment levels have been falling in recent years. In 1993,

7.1% of the population was jobless. By mid-1996, the unemployment rate stood at 5.1%. In 1998, unemployment stood at 4.9%. Between 1993 and 1996 the economy produced 8.5 million net new jobs.[17] Despite this shift in the workforce, the impact of downsizing on the individual and the company at large remains.

Downsizing: The Guilty Parties

Shedding employees is certainly not a new phenomenon for many corporations. In the past, however, downsizing had been tied to business cycles. This was especially true in the auto industry. Starting in the early 1990s, downsizing became a matter of corporate strategy. The American Management Association (AMA) has polled its membership every year since 1990 on the effects of downsizing. In 1990-1991, 73.1% of companies engaged in layoffs because of business downturns. By 1992-1993, that number was 65.7%. In 1995-1996, only 36.6% of companies that downsized did so in response to business downturns. Other factors now influence the corporation's rationale for layoffs. For example, in 1990-1991, automation and new technology were cited as the reason by 8.1% of companies that downsized, versus nearly 20% in 1995-1996.[18] Downsizing has given rise to a growing level of public outcry in terms of its impact on individuals. The media began to focus critical attention on the fallout in corporate America in 1996, the year that headlines such as "Corporate Killers," "Does America Still Work?" and "The Downsizing of America" ran in some of the nation's most respected journals. Journalists reflected a sense of betrayal among their readers, many of whom had personal experience with downsizing. In fact, the *New York Times* found that nearly three quarters of all households have had a close encounter with layoffs. One in three households have a family member who has lost a job to downsizing. One in 10 adults say getting laid off precipitated a major crisis in their lives.[19] These statistics make for some grim comparisons. Almost 50% more people are affected by layoffs each year, 3 million more than those who are victims of violent crime.[20] An examination of downsizing's recent history and publicity indicates three responsible parties (in the eyes of many journalists): the CEO, Wall Street, and the shareholder.

At the CEO level, one figure has emerged as the archetype of corporate downsizing: Albert Dunlap. A graduate of West Point Military Academy, Dunlap has turned downsizing into an art form and has increased scrutiny of the relationship between a CEO's restructuring responsibilities and his or her compensation. Dunlap's techniques have included massive downsizing, management restructuring, and shedding of "noncore" products and services. At Scott Paper, for example, Dunlap earned his nickname "Rambo in Pinstripes." Scott was the world's largest tissue maker in 1994. Founded in the 19th century, the company began to seriously falter in the 1980s. Former CEO Phil Lippincott began a three-year downsizing of 8,300 workers. However, in 1993, the company still lost $227 million. Dunlap arrived in April 1994 with the statement, "If you don't like dramatic change, I'm the wrong person." He then dismissed 10 of the 11 top executives at the company.[21] In that same year, Dunlap eliminated 11,200 jobs: an estimated one third of the workforce, or 70% of its headquarters staff, 50% of its managers, and 20% of the rank and file. Dunlap also unloaded over $3 billion in assets and transported the corporate headquarters from Philadelphia to Boca Raton, Florida. In what some considered a bizarre irony, Dunlap sold the company to its chief competitor, Lilly Tulip, for $7 billion in stock. Rambo in Pinstripes walked away from the deal $100 million richer.[22]

Late in 1996, word came that Dunlap was sharpening his ax for an assignment at consumer goods manufacturer Sunbeam Corporation. His first actions there included (a) closing all six corporate headquarters and regrouping them into 50,000 square feet in Delray Beach, Florida; (b) reducing the number of factories from 26 to 8 and the number of warehouses from 61 to 24; and (c) focusing the product mix—shedding furniture, bedding, thermometer, and scale businesses. Dunlap fired 3,000 of Sunbeam's 12,000 employees, leaving 9,000 workers, one third of whom worked for business divisions that were sold off.[23]

After many road shows and analysts' meetings, in which Dunlap waxed eloquent on the successes under his leadership and the company's strong return to financial health (even though the company lost money in the last two quarters during which Dunlap was CEO), Dunlap and his chief lieutenant were summarily (and very publicly) terminated by the Board of Directors in June 1998. This was followed by a very public network news program on the missteps of Dunlap's management and

BOX 3.1

**From the *Glenn Falls Post-Star*
March 11, 1994**

IBM Corp., as part of its goal to cut over 30,000 jobs in this year, laid off 800 New York workers Thursday from its Large Scale Computing Division. . . .

IBM announced last July that it would trim its work force from 256,000 to 225,000 by 1994. The plan has resulted in the first IBM layoffs since the company was founded in 1914. . . .

"It's something we must do to stay competitive," spokesman Stephen Cole said.

BOX 3.2

**From the *New York Times*
March 11, 1994**

The chairman and chief executive of the IBM Corporation, Louis V. Gerstner, Jr., has earned $7.71 million in salary, bonuses and other cash compensation since he joined IBM in March.

Mr. Gerstner, 52, also received stock options that could be worth up to $38.2 million, IBM said in its annual proxy statement filed today with the SEC. . . .

He is to receive a total of $8.5 million for his last 12 months of service, a spokesman for IBM said.

strategy. As of this writing, there are charges of accounting irregularities, and the board has decreed that there will be no severance.

Some management writers have noted strong relationships between corporate downsizing, corporate performance, and compensation for the CEOs who are actively engaged in reengineering. Alan Downs, for example, illustrated such a correlation in his 1995 book *Corporate Executions*,[24] when he juxtaposed the articles shown in Boxes 3.1 and 3.2, both of which appeared on March 11, 1994.

TABLE 3.1 The Layoff-Stock Surge Correlation[26]

Company	Number of Employees Laid Off	Date Layoff Was Announced	Rise in Stock Price by December 27, 1993
Boeing	21,000	February 18, 1993	31%
IBM	60,000	July 27, 1993	30%
United Technologies	10,500	January 26, 1993	30%

Downs is not the only one to point out the correlation between CEO pay and the toll of layoffs. *Newsweek* singled out AT&T CEO Robert Allen in its February 26, 1996, story "The Hit Men." Allen was rewarded for his decision to downsize 40,000 employees with $5 million when the value of his stock options soared after announcing the action. Is Allen a ruthless hit man? (One joke that circulated in the wake of his 1996 announcement was that AT&T will soon stand for Allen and Two Temps.) He admits to feeling both regretful that he had to take the action and glad that he was able to save the company.[25] In either case, Wall Street adores downsizing.

Wall Street—and the rewards it indirectly heaps on CEOs who slash jobs—has increasingly been viewed as a major enabler to the downsizing trend. Consider the data shown in Table 3.1.

Heightened scrutiny of CEOs and their practices may be warranted, especially in light of their rising status. Since 1974, the average CEO's after-tax salary has risen by more than 300%, whereas the average worker's pay fell by 13%, both adjusted for inflation. Viewed on a global perspective, American CEOs are disproportionately rewarded for their work. In Japan, for example, the ratio of a typical worker's pay to a CEO's is 1 to 16. That same ratio is 1 to 21 in Germany, and 1 to 33 in the United Kingdom. In the United States, the ratio is 1 to 120.[27]

Shareholders, once individuals, now increasingly institutions, are also implicated in downsizing. In 1955, close to 95% of corporate stock was held directly by households. At that time, pension funds and mutual funds owned less than 5% of the stock. By 1975, roughly 70% of corporate stock was in the hands of individuals and 30% was with institutional investors. In 1994, the two almost came even with 55% of corporate stock owned by individuals and 45% owned by institutions. Some observers charge that this evolution has driven a disturbing trend in corporate America. Many of the decisions made by corporations, including those that implicate people's jobs, are based solely on shareholder return. One often-cited example is the 1996 merger of First Interstate Bank Corporation with rival Wells Fargo.

On October 18, 1995, San Francisco-based Wells Fargo & Company announced a hostile takeover of Southern California's First Interstate Bancorp. The two companies were studies in opposites. Wells Fargo was the beloved of Wall Street for its aggressive replacement of human tellers with automatic teller machines. First Interstate, which had been failing for years, had prided itself on its "old-fashioned" banking, relying heavily on tellers. First Interstate's chairman William Siart backed away from Wells Fargo's $10.1 billion offer and began looking for a "nicer" company as a merger partner. That search brought Minneapolis-based First Bank System, Inc., into the fray with a bid of $9.9 billion worth of stock for First Interstate.

Wells Fargo's plan for First Interstate would seek short-term gain and large shareholder return. Due to a redundancy of offices, 10,000 people would be laid off (mostly Californians from First Interstate), and 350 branches would be closed, for a savings of $700 million. The alternate, "nicer" plan from First Bank took a longer view. To save $500 million, the bank would fire 6,000 people, but it would close few branches because there was little overlap in the operating areas of the two companies. In this way, employee cuts could be thinly spread across the combined 1,500 branches. With the two deals on the table, the CEOs from the three banks began lobbying shareholders for support. The value of Wells Fargo's deal was readily apparent: quick and substantial shareholder return. The First Bank offer, on the other hand, offered long-term growth potential and less impact on First Interstate's employees. This last point would eventually sink the deal for First Bank. When Los Angeles Mayor Richard Riordon called Wells Fargo's plan a "job killer" and a "disaster for lower income communities" where branches would close, First Interstate shareholders responded angrily. The quick and predominant reaction among stockholders was that they had no obligation to preserve jobs in Southern California.

Four fifths of First Interstate's stock was held by 50 large institutional investors: mutual funds, pensions, and investment partnerships. Each of these groups in turn was under pressure to maximize shareholder return.

Some investors favored the Wells Fargo deal because it proposed layoffs and branch closings, a route to quick profits. This point did not escape Wall Street. As if to signal which proposal was favored, Wells Fargo stock began to be traded up. This action increased the value of the Fargo offer dramatically. By January 15, 1996, the active offer had increased by $1.5 billion. On January 25, 1996, First Interstate announced its acceptance of Wells Fargo's bid. One year later, in the 1996 annual report, Wells Fargo announced that 8,900 jobs had been eliminated and 350 redundant California branches had been closed. However, on the executive level, 39 executives received golden parachutes worth $29 million. The top five were to receive $2 million each. First Interstate's CEO got $4.57 million.[28]

Downsizing: The Heart of the Matter

Aggressive downsizing advocates like Al Dunlap do not assume any responsibility for individual employees or the communities affected by a corporate restructuring. He says, "The responsibility of the CEO is to deliver shareholder value. Period. It's the shareholders who own the corporation. They take all the risk."[29] Dunlap has become a standard bearer for corporate pragmatism, wielding his cost-saving chainsaw at 11 companies. His most recent slash and burn exploits at Sunbeam have done nothing to support his philosophy of management or executive skill.

Robert Reich, former U.S. secretary of labor, has stood in direct opposition to Dunlap, once debating the topic of downsizing on national television. Reich's views represent the other side of the responsibility question. In his estimation, a corporation has a connection to its employees and a duty to weigh that bond in its decision making. In a roundtable discussion with Dunlap, Reich illustrated the point:

> AT&T—a highly profitable company—announced on the first business day of 1996 that it would be laying off 40,000 people. Now, quite apart from the question of whether that was wise or good for AT&T's own business strategy, let us at least acknowledge two things. Number one, there are social costs in doing that. There are communities in New Jersey that are now different than they were before. Property values may be lower, people are less secure. But number two, there are consequences

extending beyond AT&T. Every time a large company announces a major layoff, a chill is sent through the living rooms and kitchens of millions of American homes. People feel less secure. To the extent that we're concerned about social tranquillity, that sense of insecurity is a real cost.[30]

And so, we have two sides of the same coin. Downsizing, says the reengineer, is a necessary evil, but it speaks to the company's responsibility to its shareholders and its ability to survive in the long run. The other side acknowledges the necessity of change but encourages companies to take responsibility for the lives of employees and neighbors. Somewhere in between these two points, people like Edward Luttwak, a fellow at the Center for Strategic and International Studies in Washington, D.C., indict the system.

> The corporation is not a moral entity and should not be treated as one. But it is an entity that's guided by rules. And as a society we ought to fix those rules so that corporations only interested in making money nevertheless do the right thing.[31]

As a hypothetical solution to CEO's using downsizing for short-term personal gain, Luttwak proposed a 105% tax on one-year stock options.[32]

The question of downsizing is, after all, multifaceted, implicating the CEO, the employee, the company, and its community. This debate, although important, does not get to the heart of the matter, however. The more important question about downsizing is, How has it affected the workplace?

DOWNSIZING: A REPORT CARD

> The past decade has seen downsizing evolve from an act of desperation into a calculated choice. . . . The transformation of downsizing is the result of two tends in management training. One is the realization that size in itself is no longer a source of competitive advantage. The past decade has seen the humbling of a series of giants: Du Pont, Salomon Brothers and Westinghouse, as well as General Motors, IBM and Sears. Rather than celebrating their size, big companies have taken to hiding it; they try to imitate the agility of their smaller rivals by shrinking their

headquarters, slashing away layers of management and breaking themselves into smaller units. Some have gone the whole hog and broken themselves up into separate companies. In 1995, ITT, America's quintessential conglomerate, showed AT&T the way to do that.

The other new management fashion is to focus on your "core competencies": the things that you—and you alone—can do better than anyone else.[33]

Just two years after the publication of their book, *Reengineering the Corporation,* authors Hammer and Champy admitted that three of four times, companies would fail in their transformation. Similarly, downsizing has had its share of shortcomings. The AMA found that only 40% of companies that downsize report a long-term decrease in operating expenses. And only 35% see an increase in the quality of their products and service.[34] The promise of reengineering has fallen short of expectations as well. Although 90% of companies that restructured did so to reduce expenses, less than 50% actually did. Of 75% that had hoped for productivity improvements, only 22% achieved them. And over 50% expected to reduce bureaucracy or speed decision making; only 15% actually did.[35]

On the individual level, restructuring has had an adverse impact at many companies. Watson Wyatt surveyed 531 large companies and found that restructuring weakened employee commitment to the company among 53% of the respondents, with 31% of respondents having difficulty retaining high performing employees and only 13% noting an increase in productivity. Interestingly, 63% found that employees were more willing to take risks.[36]

It is not within the scope of this discussion to examine best practices in corporate restructuring. As with any business process, there are some who do it well and many who do not. The issue at hand is, What has downsizing wrought and where do we go from here? To answer the first question, the legacy of downsizing is the end of what was known as a workplace contract. Many companies in the past "provided" for their employees, and in return, employees gave the company their allegiance. That type of contract is no more. The loyalty implicit in such a contract is also gone. Corporate America has shed much of its middle-management talent. It now finds itself reliant as never before on the knowledge of the remaining employees and their ability to learn.

THE END OF A WORKPLACE CONTRACT

The corporation as the provider of security and belonging was a corner-stone of the Organization Man's worldview. For the Organization Man, corporate downsizing does not simply mark the end of a job. It signals the breach of a social contract and can bring severe emotional trauma.

> I was hurt. After 34 years with the company, I was surprised that it came down to an economic relationship between the two of us. I thought I was in a family kind of thing.
>
> —Married man, 57, retired early from
> a large pharmaceutical company

> It was pretty traumatic. My self-worth was nil. It was the worst period of my life. Today you can't count on working for a company for 20 to 30 years.
>
> —Married man, 43, victim of cutbacks
> at a large mineral company[37]

Classic corporations across the country have been forced to respond to heightened competition. The transition from an organization built to withstand change to one surrounded by it can have dramatic implications for employees.

Similar to the merger of Wells Fargo and First Interstate, the union of Chase Manhattan Bank and Chemical Bank was spurred by sharehold-ers' demands. In April 1996, investor Michael F. Price became Chase Manhattan's largest shareholder. He immediately demanded better per-formance from a company that had been shedding employees since the mid-1980s. Four months later, the bank was purchased by Chemical for $10 billion. The planned merger called for the closing of 100 of the two banks' 480 branches and the elimination of nearly 12,000 jobs, all within 3 years. The merger spawned jokes at the acquired bank such as, "What do you call a Chase worker who is downsized? Chemical waste."[38]

Employees had once called their company Mother Chase, describing an employer with a reputation for jobs as secure as civil posts. After the merger, that sense of entitlement quickly became replaced with fear. Said one "surviving" loan officer,

> Chase has always been my identity. Chase is part of my name. But I'm not going to roll over and die because I don't work for the new Chase.

Yet if this keeps up, who's going to go to work anymore? Why bother? Why get out of bed?[39]

Implicit in this worker's comments is the end of an entitlement mind-set and the social contract that guaranteed a job despite performance.

Beyond the end of a worker-employee contract, downsizing introduces an air of fear and uncertainty among employees. In the Chase-Chemical merger, for example, the whole three-year process is orchestrated by a computer system called the Merger Overview Model. Ironically nicknamed MOM, the system keeps track of every detail that must be handled to reach the new bank's goals, including an emphasis on downsizing. Employees receive regular updates on the reengineering process in the form of a newsletter called the *Merger Update.* Sometimes there are town meetings, or company-wide voice mail messages announcing merger news. Meanwhile, employees know MOM continues to tick, counting down the days to the completed merger. Many are gripped with fear, unsure of their job security—a situation reflected in unauthorized mock *Merger Updates* published by employees. One excerpt reads as follows:

Frequently Asked Questions

Why am I facing layoffs, why is my career in ruins, why can't I sleep at night?

Your largely insignificant life is being sacrificed to bring into existence the best banking and financial services company in the world, bar none, without par, post no bills, void where prohibited.

When will I know if I'm being laid off?

You, you, you, is that all you care about, you? Please understand that we need to think about "us," which probably doesn't include you. It's about time you started to think about the greater whole, buddy. . . . It should be an honor to be laid off.[40]

The sardonic humor speaks volumes about the effects on a workforce in the throes of downsizing.

Psychiatrist Judith Bardwick notes several distinct reactions among workers in an uncertain environment. The primary three coping techniques are good behavior, self-protection, and tendencies to seek safety. When security is gone, says Bardwick, the ratio of "yes" people to the entire workforce goes up. Employees spend more time trying to impress their superiors. The second reaction is for people to stake out what they consider their "turf" and surround it with barbed wire. In other instances, workers will seek safety through anonymity. They will seek ways to minimize risk.[41] Others may react more aggressively. In one company, news of downsizing prompted one secretary to start bringing in issues of *Guns and Ammo* magazine. She would ask her supervisor what he thought of certain guns; whether it would be a good gun to get.[42]

Although low employee morale is an immediate by-product of downsizing, the productivity payoff may be late in coming for many companies and may never arrive for some. An examination of AMA's latest survey of its membership found that a surge in productivity may never accompany layoffs. In fact, more than one year after a downsizing, 41% of the AMA's respondents reported saw no change in worker productivity or it had decreased. Forty eight percent said the quality of the products or services had not improved. And almost 50% said the quality of customer relations had remained the same or deteriorated.[43]

The current state of the corporate workplace has come full circle from the age of entitlement. According to Bardwick, the level of anxiety or urgency in a workplace has a direct bearing on productivity. When anxiety is low, she says, as was the case at the height of the classic corporation, workers feel entitled and productivity is low. When anxiety is extremely high, workers are hampered by paralysis and productivity suffers again. The right mix, says the psychologist, is somewhere in between entitlement and paralysis.[44]

The Shedding of Talent

The most lasting legacy of downsizing and reengineering has been a widespread shedding of talent and knowledge from within the corporation. The largest target for streamlining continues to be middle management—the legions of supervisors who in the classic corporation made decisions and added creative input to the company's value chain. In 1990-1991, 17.1% of middle managers were let go from member corporations in the AMA. Throughout the early 1990s, that figure held steady, reaching 19.9% of middle-management ranks in 1995-1996. These numbers have greater impact when one considers that middle management composes only 5% to 8% of the American workforce, but their jobs represent 15% to 20% of corporate downsizing. The AMA found that between July 1995 and June 1996, downsized corporations cut three management jobs for every one created. Supervisory and professional positions did not fare well either. In 1995-1996, they accounted for 15.9% and 15.5% of laid-off employees, respectively.[45] Frequently, the decision to eliminate a job was not based on any evaluation of an individual's performance. Many workers have been eliminated because they were at the wrong company at the wrong time. It must also be acknowledged that as corporations shift the responsibility and authority down to the worker, middle management becomes a surplus item—not worth the cost of carrying.

THE CUMULATIVE IMPACT OF COMPETITION, TECHNOLOGY, AND DOWNSIZING

It may be argued that corporate structure is a function of environment. For the better part of this decade, the prevailing blueprint for corporations was based on a predictable and stable business environment. In *From the Ground Up,* John Case characterizes this blueprint:

- ▶ The bigger you were, the more resources you could bring to bear on the task. Suppliers could be dominated or bought up, and labor commandeered with the promise of high wages.
- ▶ Big, technologically sophisticated plants could pour out products by the truckload, and heaving marketing budgets could (usually) persuade consumers to snap them up.
- ▶ Competitors, most of them American, faced similar costs and business conditions. Since no big company was likely to be driven out of business, "competition" meant jostling for a point or two of market share.[46]

Companies continued along these lines as long as everything remained stable. One change in the nature of competition, technology, costs, or consumer behavior and the whole system would break down. In the last quarter-century, not only one characteristic changed, but nearly all of them did, wreaking havoc in corporations and forever changing the nature of the world economy. Many companies still have not completely recovered from the change.

Before the drivers of change hit corporations, bigger staffs, stronger machines, and more capital were sustainable competitive advantages.

That is no longer true. In a business environment marked by international and smaller-firm competition and the meteoric development of information technology, a new corporate model is needed. Today, companies need to be fast—faster than ever before in new product development, speed to market, and change management. They have to be intimately tied to their customers, and most of all, they must cultivate their only source of sustainable competitive advantage: knowledge. As we shall see in Part II, "The Present as Transition," there is only one way for a company to stay on top. It must tap the potential of the knowledge it comes into contact with every day: knowledge inherent in its processes, its structure, and the minds of its employees.

PART

II

THE PRESENT AS TRANSITION

4

THE EVOLUTION OF CORPORATE LEARNING

Any piece of knowledge I acquire today has a value at this moment exactly proportional to my skill to deal with it. Tomorrow, when I know more, I recall that piece of knowledge and use it better.

—Mark Van Doren

For the better part of this decade, terms such as *knowledge management, learning organizations,* and *intellectual capital* have gained increasingly in popularity and interest. But the question is, Haven't businesses always valued knowledge? The answer is, of course they have. Henry Ford certainly placed a great premium on the cadres of young engineers who designed his manufacturing systems. And knowledge management never rang more true than when scientific management was implemented in organizations. The changing nature of knowledge throughout history does not pertain to its importance: It has always been and will always be a key to business success. So the question becomes, Why is knowledge going to be even more important in the future? The answer is that knowledge is the only renewable resource a company can capture, leverage, and create to maximize its advantage.

Who owns knowledge? Where does it come from and where does it go? How can companies encourage knowledge generation? These are questions that come under the heading of *knowledge management*. The term assumes that corporations can readily distinguish between information and knowledge and that they can manipulate this knowledge to attain strategic advantage. The truth is, it is little easier today to generate, measure, and apply knowledge than it was in Ford's time. With the rise of purely information-based businesses, however, the absolute need to do so has never been more necessary. From the earliest executive education programs to today's sophisticated multimedia-based training, corporations have tried to capture those elusive kernels of knowledge that will win them a competitive advantage. Is knowledge different today? No. The way it flows through the company, however, has changed.

THE ROOTS OF CORPORATE EDUCATION

Since its inception, corporate education has been a reactive foil to the dominant trends in the organization. In the late 19th and early 20th centuries, the role of corporate education was to codify and explain the factors of success in large corporations—scientific management, mass production, mass marketing, and hierarchical structures. At that time, the management of business was becoming recognized as an important consideration in business organizations and a demanding function for its practicing managers. The concept of management as a distinct kind of work and field of learning was emerging, and with it, a new managerial class within organizations. As a consequence, some university educators and business leaders saw the need for special kinds of education that were not being provided by the liberal arts and natural sciences programs at universities.

In 1881, the University of Pennsylvania established the Wharton School of Commerce and Finance. The universities of Chicago and California followed with curricula in business just before 1900. In addition to credit programs in business, some universities started noncredit courses and seminars. In 1911 and 1912, Dartmouth sponsored a series of seminars for businessmen based on Frederick Taylor's work in scientific management. Along with the YMCA seminars, described next, this series appears to have been among the first widely known seminars to be held solely for practicing business executives.

Another interesting, but frequently overlooked, organization that influenced management/executive education in its early years was the YMCA and its summer conferences. The YMCA was started in England and officially organized in 1845. The 1851 World's Fair in London attracted people from around the world and also exposed them to the new "Y" movement. A visiting New York University student, George Van Derlip, was so impressed that he later wrote a series of articles published in the *Boston Newspaper*, which then prompted one reader, Thomas Sullivan, to set up the first American YMCA in Boston.

As the Y movement caught on, the number of YMCAs grew, and so did the need for people to manage these facilities. Early on, the YMCA started to provide training through summer conferences held at various camps the Y had acquired. Although there were a number of such camps, four are important in terms of training and continuing education. The camp at Lake Geneva in Wisconsin was the first, created in 1886. It was soon joined by Silver Bay on Lake George, New York, in 1902; the Blue Ridge Assembly in Black Mountain, North Carolina, in 1912; and Camp Estes in Colorado, in July 1908.

The first summer conference at Lake Geneva was sponsored by a group of leaders from the Chicago YMCA. It was titled, "Addresses of the Industrial Railroad Conference on New Ideals in Industrial Betterment." Attending this conference were 7 company presidents and approximately 70 other company officials and managers, including representatives from Westinghouse Air Brake, John Deere, and Western Electric.[1]

The success of the conferences held at Lake Geneva inspired the first weekend industrial conference in 1918, at Silver Bay. H. H. Westinghouse of Westinghouse Air Brake chaired this first conference. It was titled "Human Relations and Betterment in Industry and Transportation During the War." The invitation for the conference stated that President William Taft would be present. Whether that actually occurred is unclear. However, a number of prominent industrial leaders, including W. H. Woodin, president of American Car and Foundry; C. S. Cheng, vice president of U.S. Rubber; G. E. Emmons, vice president of General Electric; Seth Chandler of Tidewater Oil Company; and several different representatives from American Telephone and Telegraph, attended, along with 100 other people.

The summer conference at Silver Bay grew rapidly in stature and size. The title was changed in 1920 to "Human Relations and Industry," a title that continues to this day. Ten years later, in 1928, 600 participants attended the Silver Bay Conference. By 1948, more than 15,000 participants had attended the annual Silver Bay Conferences.[2]

As the United States emerged from World War I and business thrived, the number of undergraduate business schools grew and more graduate schools appeared. Yet for years, there was no sustained thrust toward executive education programs for midcareer businesspeople. However, in the early stages of the business discipline, a number of theories and experiments in industrial psychology evolved. These theories were soon put to use in the business classroom and further developed in business practice.

In 1928, the Harvard Business School started conducting summer sessions for experienced businessmen. In 1931, the yearlong Sloan Fellowship Program was started at MIT, and a similar program was begun that same year at Stanford. In 1935, Harvard initiated a series of executive discussion groups, called the Philip Cabot Weekends. In 1941, an executive education program was established at the University of Iowa. In 1943, the federal government asked both Harvard and Stanford to retrain business executives in the intricacies of the war production effort. At Harvard, the program gradually evolved into a general course of study, and in 1945, it was renamed the Advanced Management Program, which continues today.

The Postwar Years

The Great Depression, followed by World War II, created pent-up demand for high-quality business talent at all managerial levels. New technologies and new markets were rapidly changing the way business was conducted. General management programs were started at Dartmouth, Western Ontario, Pittsburgh, Toronto, Indiana, and Stanford universities. Using techniques borrowed from law schools, Harvard and Western Ontario developed the use of small-group studies and business cases. The Aspen Institute for Humanistic Studies focused its programs on the problems of power and responsibility, topics later treated in many other executive programs. Large companies started their own internal programs, usually to supplement those offered by business schools.

A study by the U.S. Naval Institute in 1948 reported that executive education was an active component in the executive development efforts of more than 100 medium- to large-sized companies. By 1958, there were 40 residential university programs two weeks or more in length. Between 1949 and 1958, there had been roughly 10,000 attendees from over 2,700 companies enrolled in these programs.[3]

The Formalizing Period: 1950-1979

Almost from the beginning, management/executive education in America has derived much of its intellectual content from established faculties of colleges and universities. Teaching faculties, not only in business schools but also in more traditional disciplines, found this new market both professionally stimulating and financially rewarding.

By 1958, there were seven schools devoted exclusively to the graduate study of business: Chicago, Columbia, Cornell, Dartmouth, Harvard, Pittsburgh, and Stanford. In addition, more than 100 universities offered some graduate courses in business. There were hundreds of shorter courses, seminars, workshops, and specialized functional programs. For example, Michigan State carried 130 offerings, along with 8 nonresidential broad-coverage programs taking a year or longer. Annual attendance at the longer general management programs rose from about 3,900 in 1969 to 5,800 in 1979.

A National Industrial Conference Board report in 1969 analyzed 45 business education programs of 2 to 16 weeks in length. It noted that 66% of those programs were 2 to 4 weeks long. Most were continuous, but some were split-session offerings. Of the university brochures, 90% listed two common objectives: (a) to make generalists out of specialists and (b) to increase the attendees' effectiveness through their exposure to decision making, communications, and behavioral science findings. Seventy-one percent said that they tried to acquaint their participants with forces in the external environment of business. Thirty-three percent included methods of research and statistical analysis in their courses. Other program objectives listed were to broaden and deepen business understanding, provide opportunities to discuss ideas with people from other organizations, and allow participants to reflect on their career development.[4]

Education has had an inestimable effect on the performance of the most influential American corporations. The classic corporation thrived by capitalizing on brawn—bigger machines manned by more efficient laborers—rather than brains—that is, the "thinking" employee. Taylorism and Fordism yielded fantastic results when combined with new technologies such as the moving assembly line, and, soon, scientific management principles spread even to the grade school.

William T. Harris, a leading architect of the American public schooling system commented, "The student must have his lessons ready at the appointed time, must rise to the tap of the bell, move to the line, return; in short, go through all the evolutions with equal precision."[5] Inside the corporation, education has also served to codify and enhance the structures and methods of the classic corporation. Since much of the training was done by case study, the lessons learned from successful practices of mass production, mass distribution, scientific management, and the hierarchical approach to communication became the primary focus of corporate education.

THE 1980s AND 1990s: MANAGEMENT/ EXECUTIVE EDUCATION COMES OF AGE

The new orientation for corporate education in the 1980s was characterized by a closer affiliation with business strategy, specific learning objectives, uniquely tailored content, and more systemic determination of objectives and results. Program development had to be more flexible to provide the results an ever-changing business environment demanded. During the 1980s, corporate America continued to look to university business schools to provide much of what it consumed in the way of management/executive education. Indeed, for decades, the university was the source of much of corporate America's intellectual capital in the form of freshly minted MBAs and timely executive education courses.

Although business schools were still offering a lot of executive education, dissatisfaction from the corporate community was growing. At the beginning of the 1990s, the popular media began to run stories critical of corporate education.

▶ Consider this one on the cover of *Business Week:* "Where the Schools Aren't Doing Their Homework: Critics Say They Churn out MBAs Lacking Leadership Skills and Operations Know-How."[6]

▶ Or this one in the American Management Association's (AMA's) *Management Review:* "Business Schools: Striving to Meet Customer Demand," which opens with, "Business schools have long been criticized for not addressing the needs of today's global competitive business environment."[7]

▶ Or a 1991 story in *Fortune:* "The Trouble with MBAs," in which journalist Alan Deutschman quips, "Who needs managers who have just spent two years with such an out-of-date crowd?"[8]

Even some of the "pillars" of corporate education began to show signs of wear and tear. Starting in 1957, executives from this country's most successful corporations convened in a rustic Vail, Colorado, retreat for three weeks of study in philosophy, economics, and business classics. The University of Chicago hosted the event, and for many of those years, it turned people away because of too many applicants. In 1996, Chicago shuttered the windows of this retreat, citing declining profitability. In its last year, the program earned just $30,000. Explaining the reason for the fall in popularity, the university's Center for Continuing Studies said, "Many executives can't afford to be away for long periods."[9]

THE EMERGENCE OF CORPORATE UNIVERSITIES

Heightened competition and the ubiquitous presence of information technology in business have forced a new role for knowledge creation in the corporation. Business schools have not kept pace with the dramatic change that has taken place in corporate America, say management writers Davis and Botkin, authors of *The Monster under the Bed.*[10]

> Students still come to classes to learn, the classes are still sixty, seventy-five or ninety minutes long, and courses are still offered in semesters, trimesters, or quarters. Instructors still stand in front of the room and students sit in rows that, at most, have been bent from straight lines into a horseshoe shape for case discussions. Typical classroom technology is still hardly beyond what it was three and four decades ago. Computers are used extensively, but so are pencils. Indeed, the process and products of business school education have changed as little as the process and products of any kind of school education, whereas business itself has gone through revolutions.[11]

As a reaction to the criticism of business schools and a growing recognition of corporate education, many corporations have internalized education, in some cases developing "corporate universities" of their own. By some estimates, there are currently over 1,200 corporate universities in the United States.[12]

Motorola University exemplifies internalized education in a corporate university setting. In 1979, CEO Bob Galvin set up the Motorola Executive Institute, a curriculum that would give top staffers an MBA built around Motorola's philosophy. But lower-level managers didn't see any reason to change the status quo, and it did not succeed.

In 1980, Galvin set up the Motorola Training and Education Center (MTEC) with the goal of improving quality tenfold in five years. The curriculum included statistical process control, basic industrial problem solving, how to present conceptual material (intended for employees to aid them in recommending new processes to their managers), how to conduct and participate in productive meetings, and how to set goals and measure progress. Managers came to the courses and learned the material, then continued to manage as they always had. Frontline workers saw this and decided the courses must be useless.

The next round of courses was adjusted to include one that analyzed what competition would do to Motorola if the company did not make serious quality gains. Galvin himself attended the seminar along with 11 of his top people. Each of them sent out "invitations" to join the program. This time, the initiative took. Following this success, the company decided to stress learning at its new cellular phone plant in Schaumburg, Illinois. Frontline workers would be responsible for quality control, flexible manufacturing, and the mentorship of several thousand new hires. What the company discovered was that half its frontline workers could not calculate 10% of 100.

The company quickly arranged basic skill courses, and this time around, Galvin took measures to ensure participation. Motorola began a new policy—employees who did not enroll in the courses would be fired. Providers of training and education were given clear descriptions of what kind of knowledge was needed for the first time.

Eleven years after its first initiatives, Motorola's budget on training and education had mushroomed from $7 million to $120 million. In 1981, Motorola University was founded. Three years later, in 1984, a new policy was instituted that required managers to invest at least 1.5%

of the department's payroll in training. Frontline workers are required to have at least ninth-grade math and science skills.[13] Today, Motorola University has its own press, consulting services, and close to 100 courses in areas such as these:

- Customer service
- Engineering support
- Manufacturing management and supervision
- Quality
- Sales, marketing, and distribution

Historically, corporate education has closely followed on the heels of change, providing businesses with the knowledge they needed to survive and excel. In today's age of increasingly rapid change where businesses seek to maximize new ideas and processes quickly, education has become more than a reaction to change. Corporate education, once a course, then a place, has become an integral part of the company's everyday functioning. This paradigm shift has demanded a new look at the ways corporations build and disseminate knowledge.

THE NEW LEARNING PARADIGM

Executives at multinational corporations such as Hewlett-Packard and the Canadian Imperial Bank of Commerce (CIBC) were abolishing traditional classroom style education. What was happening? Was it possible that education had become unfashionable at the same time that terms such as *learning organizations* were beginning to gain popularity? In fact, learning has never been as vital to the success of the corporation as it is today. It is the typical training method that has become unpopular.[14]

> Everything that's wrong with training can be stated in four words: It's just like school . . . School isn't really about learning; it's about short-term memorization of meaningless information that never comes up later in life. The school model was never intended to help people acquire practical skills. It is intended to satisfy observers that knowledge is being acquired (for short periods of time). (Roger Schank, Director, Northwestern University's Institute for the Learning Sciences)[15]

Other complaints from the business world underscore the ineffec-
tiveness of some corporate training programs.

▶ Hubert Saint-Onge, formerly of CIBC, states, "Most companies can't tell
you how much they spend on training. It took us six months to decipher—
$30 million a year! And one penny out of a hundred hits the mark."[16]

▶ "Most training programs are pitched too high or too low, are delivered in
classrooms to an audience that needed the information last month or
won't need it for two years, and cost the earth," says Thomas Stewart of
Fortune magazine.[17]

▶ John Sealy Brown, Director of Xerox's Palo Alto Research Center, says,
"The false correlation of learning with training or education is one of the
most common and costly errors in corporate management today."[18]

The model for traditional training—to impart static knowledge
(formulas, history, technique) from an expert to a student—is quickly
being replaced by a new paradigm, now known popularly as the learning
organization. The two key characteristics of the learning organization
are that

1. it seeks to be adaptive to its environment, and
2. the transfer of knowledge within the organization is accomplished in
   social environments and sometimes through informal means.

Whereas the classic corporation existed largely as an island among
its competitors, customers, and suppliers (as illustrated by the history of
the Big Three auto manufacturers in the United States), the learning
organization thrives on the connections it has with its business environment. Peter Senge, management professor at the Massachusetts Institute
of Technology, broadened the definition of learning in his landmark
book, *The Fifth Discipline: The Art and Practice of the Learning Organization.*[19]

Through learning we re-create ourselves. Through learning we reper-
ceive the world and our relationship to it. Through learning we extend
our capacity to create, to be part of the generative process of life.
This, then, is the basic meaning of a "learning organization"—an
organization that is continually expanding its capacity to create its
future.[20]

The implications of learning for the modern organization are part conceptual and part structural. In many cases, the classic corporation was built to shelter itself from its environment. The results of this kind of sheltering were illustrated earlier with the reaction of the Big Three automakers in the face of international competition. The learning organization, on the other hand, embraces involvement with its environment. Leaders in learning organizations promote thinking in terms of systems in which few decisions or processes are viewed as unrelated. Actions and events are all part of a large, interrelated web.

Systems thinking is Senge's fifth and most important discipline for learning organizations. The other disciplines—personal mastery, mental models, shared vision, and team learning—must develop in tandem with the growth of the organization. Without systems thinking, however, the vision may not be rooted or operable in real working situations.[21]

Senge illustrates systems thinking when he describes the act of filling a glass of water from a faucet. The act intuitively seems linear in nature, not involving anything but the hand and the faucet. One holds the glass under the faucet, turns on the water, turns off the water, and removes the glass from underneath the faucet. However, viewed systemically, filling the glass is actually a highly complex water regulation system. The glass is placed under the faucet. The water is turned on. From then on, thousands of messages are sent from the eyes that monitor the water level to the brain that keeps the end goal to the hand that controls the flow of water. When the water reaches the desired height, the eyes report to the brain that fires the order to the hand to end the process. A complex system, indeed.[22]

Systems thinking has the power to work negatively or positively. Senge cites the U.S./U.S.S.R. arms race as a negative effect generated by systems thinking. Fear of one side caused the other to bolster its defense capabilities by stockpiling more and more deadly weapons. This, in turn, led to fear on the other side of the conflict who reacted in exactly that same manner.[23]

On the other hand, systems thinking took a positive role in the form of "word-of-mouth" marketing. In the late 1960s, the Volkswagen Beetle gained a reputation as a dependable, comfortable, and well-styled car. As this reputation spread and was reinforced by more word of mouth, the popularity of the Beetle soared.

Mental Models

Learning is not simply about acquiring new information; it is about expanding the ability to achieve goals and to check our visions against reality. One major roadblock to organizational learning is mental models. These are our deeply held images of how the world works. Ian Mitroff suggests that there were powerful mental models at work at General Motors when the Japanese and Europeans began to take shares of the American auto market, including the following:

- GM is in the business of making money, not cars.
- Cars are primarily status symbols. Styling is therefore more important than quality.
- The American car market is isolated from the rest of the world.
- Workers do not have an important impact on productivity or product quality.
- Everyone connected with the system has no need for more than a fragmented, compartmentalized understanding of the business.[24]

Other mental models have been at work in the classic corporation for decades, including these:

- Bigger is better.
- There is one best way for a worker to get the job done.
- Knowledge is the domain of management.

Companies that are able to identify and understand their mental models—for strategy, operations, marketing, and so on—may become better suited to adapt to new business realities. Arie De Geus, former group planning manager for Royal Dutch/Shell Group, studied the defining characteristics of corporations in North America, Europe, and Japan that had existed since the fourth quarter of the nineteenth century and were still thriving. The most dramatic case study in the lot, a European paper and chemical company called Stora, had survived since the Middle Ages. Starting out as a copper foundry, it weathered the Reformation, the wars of the 1600s, and two world wars in the 20th century. Finally, it emerged as a chemical manufacturer. Along the way, it depended on runners, horses, and ships to distribute products and information. Ultimately, the company embraced electronic networks and overnight mail. Stora's success, De Geus hypothesized, came from an inherent ability to adapt to its changing business environment.

> There are times when a company's know-how, product range, and labor relations are in harmony with the world around it. The business situations are familiar, the company is well organized, and employees are trained and prepared. During those times, managers do not need to develop and implement new ideas.
>
> But just when the company has organized itself, outside circumstances may change. New technologies come on the scene, markets shift, interest rates fluctuate, consumers' tastes change, and the company must enter a new phase of life. In order to stay in sync with the outside world, it must be able to alter its marketing strategy, its product range, its organizational form, and where and how it does its manufacturing. And once a company has adapted to a new environment, it is no longer the organization it used to be; it has evolved. That is the essence of learning.[25]

Being sensitive to the world around the business, De Geus stresses, is among the key characteristics of learning organizations. At Royal Dutch Shell, the practical application of this sensitivity does not rely solely on training. It focuses on planning.

Shell had grown from a union of Royal Dutch Petroleum and London-based Shell Transport and Trading Company in 1907 to a multinational conglomerate with over 100 operating companies in the early 1970s. The new corporation had at its core a tradition of decision making by consensus. As the organization grew to include managers from varied nationalities, consensus became increasingly important but difficult to achieve. What emerged was an understanding that consensus was based on shared mental models. If decision makers from each of the key operating companies were to act in unison, their pictures of reality would have to be influenced in a uniform manner.[26] This realization came on the verge of massive industry-wide change touched off by the Organization of Petroleum Exporting Countries (OPEC). On October 20, 1973, OPEC banned oil shipments to the United States. By 1974, the price of oil shot up 80%, and the price of gasoline increased by 50%. Throughout the 1970s, OPEC controlled the price of crude oil. During that time, the price of one gallon went from $3 per barrel to $30.[27]

Interestingly, one year prior to OPEC's action, Shell had begun to note changes on the way for the petroleum industry.

Oil-exporting nations such as Iran, Iraq, Libya, and Venezuela were becoming increasingly concerned with falling reserves. Others, such as Saudi Arabia, were reaching the limits of their availability to productively invest oil revenues. These trends meant that the historical, smooth growth in oil demand would eventually give way to chronic supply shortfalls, excess demand, and a "seller's market" controlled by the oil-exporting nations.[28]

Shell does not claim to have predicted the Saudi action. However, the company had taken note that some dramatic change was at hand. At first, their efforts to influence decision makers in holding companies failed to prompt significant change. At the time, Group Planning had begun to disseminate a new technique called "scenario planning." Potential future trends, with problems built into them, were disseminated to managers at holding companies. At first, the managers dismissed the scenarios because their premises—market fluctuations, high prices, shifting roles—ran contrary to the steady growth they were accustomed to. Shell's Group Planning unit saw that by handing the managers new visions of the future, they had failed to address the most basic assumptions on which the managers made their decisions.

Starting on a new tack, Group Planning asked managers to identify the basic assumptions they had about the current state of the oil industry and global geopolitics. With these in hand, they went about deconstructing the assumptions, pointing out real trends that would refute the managers' basic mental models.

For example, exploration for oil would have to slow down because of higher prices and consequently slower demand growth. Also, with greater instability, nations would respond differently. Some, with free-market traditions, would try to keep it low. Thus, control of Shell's locally based operating companies would have to increase to enable them to adapt to local conditions.[29]

The scenario-planning technique did not result in Shell managers' completely reevaluating their thinking. It did, however, shake them out of their set mental models and get them to begin questioning their assumptions and resulting worldviews. When the OPEC oil embargo hit in 1973, Shell responded differently from other oil companies. They saw the change as a new market reality rather than an aberration that would come and go. Management in the operating companies reacted accordingly, adapting their refineries to whatever crude oil was available. The net result: Royal Dutch Shell leapt from a weak position among the world's 7 largest oil companies in 1970 to one of the top companies in 1979.[30]

Companies such as Royal Dutch Shell have shown that learning is the process by which we perceive and manage our position in the world. Learning organizations are also defined, however, by a second trait: the ability to transfer knowledge socially and, in some cases, informally.

COMMUNITIES OF PRACTICE

In 1994, Xerox's Louisville, Texas, customer service center hosted an experiment that juxtaposed modern learning techniques against traditional corporate training. For years, customers calling into the Louisville center complained that they were shunted from one department to another, seeking the right person to answer their questions. Xerox's Integrated Customer Service (ICS) experiment combined three customer service departments, each with its own area of expertise, into one. Initially, Xerox consulted with its internal training division, based in Leesburg, Virginia. To make a customer service representative an expert in two new areas, Leesburg calculated, would take at least 52 weeks of training per employee.

The procedure for building an original course was sequential. First, the training department made a visit to ascertain baseline-training requirements. That information was passed on to a team of curriculum designers in Virginia who put the course together. Several months later, trainers arrived at the Xerox location to begin the course. Unfortunately, after all this preparation, workers generally found the training to be irrelevant to their jobs. It focused too much on tasks that were rarely performed, and by the time employees got out of the classroom, they forgot much of what they had been taught. Worst of all, the workers said, none of the trainers had ever set foot in a customer service situation.[31]

At this point, Xerox turned to the Institute for Research on Learning (IRL), a research and consulting firm in Menlo Park, California, that specialized in developing learning organizations. The IRL researchers suggested a dramatically reduced number of hours in the training room and a redesigned seating arrangement. From then on, ICS staff members were moved from their isolated cubicles to work in cross-functional teams of six or seven. So instead of being pulled out of work for weeks on end, the ICS reps began learning from one another. When asked how well the experiment worked, Rick Hawkins, who came to ICS from account administration said, "It was the best sort of team-building I'd ever seen. It forces us to rely on each other daily." Hawkins estimated that he spent just 8 hours off the job to learn skills from his co-workers, versus the 52 weeks initially proposed by Xerox's Virginia-based training department. Dede Miller, also in the ICS experiment, said,

> We shared information with each other all the time. Even when we weren't asking for help. We were learning because we could hear other people in our work group on the phone with customers, and we'd pick up tips about how they handled certain kinds of calls. None of us wanted to go back to our old jobs. For the first time ever we were able to solve all of a customer's problems without having to pass them off to someone else. That made us and the customer very happy.[32]

The most surprising finding to come out of the ICS experiment was that it was not the first time Xerox employees had engaged in this kind of learning. Learning by example is hardly a newly noted phenomenon in social systems. In fact, at this moment, in any given corporation, in any number of departments, employees are engaged in active, fruitful learning. There may not be a training session scheduled, but informal learning groups dubbed "communities of practice" function as a main artery for the transfer of knowledge within an organization. A "community of practice" is a group of individuals who share a common interest and trade information to reach a common goal.[33]

Any group, from secretaries exchanging filing tips around the water-cooler to a group of employees who take charge of throwing holiday parties, qualifies as a community of practice. These groups function as forums for the transfer of knowledge—that is, learning.

At Nynex, James Euchner, a vice president in research and development, wanted to find out why some departments were so quick to adopt new technologies and others were not. He hired an anthropologist to study two different groups of people. She found that in departments where people didn't communicate informally, there was a low level of

learning. Euchner reorganized these departments to have these employees working in the same room to increase their level of informal contact.
The result was that the time needed to adopt a new technology dropped
from 17 to 3 days.[34] Euchner found, as many in corporate America are
recognizing today, that groups are essential to learning.

Do communities of practice and the learning organization spell the
end of individual training? Yes and no. Individual knowledge is still an
important driving force for organizational learning. Otherwise, why
would a proven learning organization like Royal Dutch Shell spend
$2,400 per employee every year on training? Experiments by Allan
Wilson, a professor of biochemistry and biology at the University of
California, Berkeley, indicate that the role of individual learning is
integral to the generation of organizational learning.[35] Wilson hypothesized that groups may learn to adapt to their environment if three
conditions are met:

- First, the members of the group must have the freedom to move around
  rather than sit in isolated areas.
- Second, individuals within the group must have the ability to learn new
  skills.
- Third, the group must have some means for learning the skill from the
  individual through direct communication.

Wilson's test case was not a multinational corporation. It was a
species of birds. Wilson examined the well-documented history of two
species in Great Britain in the late 19th century. At that time, milkmen
would leave open bottles of milk on the doorsteps of people's houses.
The two species—robins and titmice—would raid the bottles for the rich
cream that had risen to the top. By the 1930s, it became common practice
to cap the bottles with aluminum seals to keep the birds out. Twenty years
later, the entire population of titmice had learned how to pierce the seals,
whereas the robins could not. Wilson deduced that the titmice were
better able to acquire the new skill because of their flocking tendencies.
Recall that one of Wilson's requirements for organizational learning is
that individuals within the group must have the ability to interact with
the larger group and not remain in isolated areas. Such is the case with
titmice, which tend to flock in large groups. Robins, on the other hand,
are territorial and do not interact with other birds not in their territory.[36]

In large corporations, there will always be a number of individuals curious enough to find a solution to a new problem. Management training programs may play a critical role as the source of such innovations. Research by the AMA seems to indicate that training played an invaluable role in corporate America's recovery from an era of radical downsizing.[37] The AMA has found that corporations that downsized and increased their training efforts were

> ▶ more than twice as likely to report quality improvements (59% vs. 27% of those that do not increase their training activities),
> ▶ 75% more likely to increase worker productivity (64% vs. 36%), and
> ▶ 60% more likely to increase their operating profits (68% vs. 43%).[38]

In an attempt to gain a broader perspective on the current state of education and training in corporate America, we undertook a national survey of education and training practices in America's largest companies. The results of our survey are the basis of the next chapter.

THE 1998 STRATEGIC REPORT ON WORKFORCE EDUCATION

*Learning is acquired by reading books; but the much more
necessary learning; the knowledge of the world, is only to
be acquired by reading men, and studying all the various
conditions of them.*

—Lord Chesterfield

n January 1998, the Annenberg Center for Communication at
the University of Southern California published its study, *Workforce Education: Corporate Training and Learning at America's
Companies.*[1] (The authors of this volume were the principal
investigators of the research.) This national survey was done in cooperation with Chicago-based market researcher OmniTech Consulting
Group.

Telephone interviews were conducted with 202 senior-most persons
responsible for corporate education and training. Respondents were
drawn from both publicly and privately held companies, all with 1996
annual revenues greater than $1 billion. A cross section of industries was
represented in the sample. The average number of people employed by

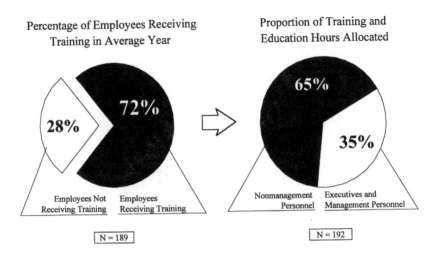

Percentage of Employees Receiving Training in Average Year

Proportion of Training and Education Hours Allocated

Figure 5.1. Percentage and Types of Employees Receiving Training
NOTE: Across respondent companies, nearly three of four employees receive training in an average year. The majority of training is delivered to nonmanagement personnel.

each company was 16,753. The majority of respondents (60%) had 10,000 or fewer employees in their companies. Of respondents, 6% indicated that their companies employ more than 50,000 people.

Respondents worked in companies representing a variety of industries: 33% manufacturing, 22% finance/insurance, 19% retail/wholesale, 8% utilities, 7% services, 6% technology/information systems (IS), 4% transportation, and 1% entertainment. Industry representation in this study was consistent with industry representation in the population of companies with revenues of $1 billion and more.

PERCENTAGE OF EMPLOYEES RECEIVING TRAINING

Our survey shows that in a typical year companies train anywhere from 15% to 100% of their workforce. The average percentage of employees receiving training is 72% in all companies (see Figure 5.1). Companies with larger workforces tend to train a greater percentage of personnel than do companies with fewer employees. Companies with smaller workforces provide training and education to 57% of their employees in

TABLE 5.1 Breakdown of Respondent Responsibilities Among
Respondent Pool

Task/Responsibility	Percentage of Respondents
Identifying training and learning needs	99
Recommending sources for training delivery and course development	99
Overseeing development of training courses and products	97
Managing training budgets	97
Approving partnerships with outside training entities	96

an average year. In comparison, companies with midsized to large workforces provide training and education to 78% of their employees. The breakdown of responsibilities for respondents can be seen in Table 5.1.

TYPES OF EMPLOYEES RECEIVING TRAINING

Of respondent companies, 67% spend the majority of all training and education hours (at least 60%) delivering to nonmanagement personnel. A much smaller percentage of companies (22%) spend the majority of training hours delivering to executives and management personnel. Only 11% of respondents indicate that nonmanagement and management personnel receive comparable proportions of training and education hours (41% to 59% of hours).

Looking across all respondents, the proportion of training and education hours delivered to nonmanagement personnel is almost double the proportion delivered to executive and management personnel. On average, nonmanagement personnel receive 65% of all training and education hours; executives and management personnel receive 35% (see Figure 5.1).

A similar allocation is expected in the year 2000. On average, respondents anticipate that they will still spend only 38% of training and education hours providing education to executives and management personnel. The majority of hours (62%) will remain focused on nonmanagement personnel. The type of employee receiving the bulk of available training hours does not vary by industry or respondent type.

GEOGRAPHIC COVERAGE

Of all respondents, 42% indicate that training is provided regionally. Twenty-seven percent provide training nationally, and 31% provide training internationally. Differences in the geographic scope of training provided are seen among the various industries. Furthermore, training on an international basis is found to be more prevalent in large companies, companies with large training budgets, and companies with a large workforce. Finally, there appears to be a relationship between training on an international basis and the presence of a corporate university.

Companies in different industries tend to conduct business on different geographic scales. This in turn affects the geographic coverage of training provided. Most utilities respondents (82%) indicate that training and education are provided regionally. In comparison, a smaller percentage of manufacturing (30%), retail/wholesale (37%), and finance/insurance (48%) respondents provide training regionally. More than half (53%) of manufacturing and approximately one quarter (24%) of retail/wholesale respondents provide training internationally.

It is not surprising to find that significantly more large companies provide training internationally, compared with smaller and midsized companies. Approximately half (49%) of large companies provide training on an international basis. In comparison, only 23% of smaller and midsized companies train internationally.

A significantly greater percentage of companies with large training budgets provide training internationally, compared with companies with smaller training budgets (47% vs. 16%).

There is also a relationship between the size of a company's workforce and the geographic scope of training it provides. Of respondents in companies with a large workforce, 47% indicate that training is provided on an international basis. Comparatively, only 24% of respondents in companies with a smaller to midsized workforce indicate that training is provided on an international basis.

Companies that have a corporate university or learning center are more likely to provide training internationally than are companies that do not have one. Training is provided internationally by twice as many companies with a corporate university as companies without a corporate university (44% vs. 22%).

The methods by which employees learn serve as a broad indicator of how well corporations have integrated learning into their operations and how widely accessible it has become.

All respondent companies are training and educating their employees, providing their workforce with the knowledge and skills needed to be successful. At the companies surveyed, an average of 72% of employees receive training, and the majority of training hours are delivered to nonmanagement personnel. How is training currently being provided to these employees? Is this expected to change in the future? Specifically, we addressed the following questions:

▶ How is training provided at America's largest corporations today? How will it be provided in the year 2000?

▶ How prevalent are corporate universities today? What will be their prevalence in 2000?

CURRENT DELIVERY METHODS

Across all respondents, classroom training currently accounts for the majority of total available training hours. On average, respondents spend 56% of all available training hours delivery in the classroom. Of training hours, 28% are available in other forms, including videotapes, manuals, and on-the-job training. The smallest percentage of hours, 16%, is available via computer (see Figure 5.2).

There is no relationship between a company's revenues and the proportion of training hours available via computer. From smaller companies to large companies, on average, 16% of training hours are available via computer.

However, there is a relationship between a company's revenues and the proportion of training hours available through the classroom and through other forms of delivery. On average, smaller companies deliver 51% of available training hours in the classroom. In smaller companies, 31% of training hours are available in other forms such as videotapes, manuals, and on-the-job training. In comparison, large companies deliver 62% of available training hours in the classroom, and 21% use other forms of training. Aside from training via computer, which companies of

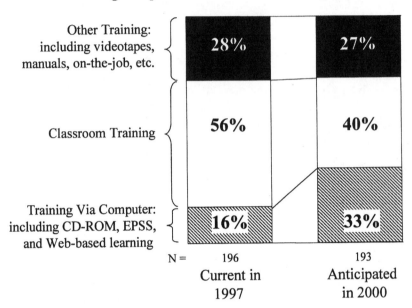

Average Proportion of Available Training Hours

Figure 5.2. Training Delivery Methods
NOTE: Although classroom training currently accounts for the majority of available training hours, in the year 2000 a more even distribution across the three delivery categories is expected. Specifically, a greater proportion of training hours is expected to be available via computer and a smaller proportion via classroom. (The acronym EPSS stands for electronic performance support systems.)

all sizes are using to a comparable degree, large companies tend to spend more time training in the classroom than do smaller companies.

FUTURE DELIVERY METHODS:
A SHIFT AWAY FROM THE CLASSROOM

Respondents anticipate a shift away from classroom-based training and toward computer-based training. In 2000, although classroom training is still expected to account for the greatest proportion of available training hours, respondents anticipate a more even distribution of available training hours among the three categories of delivery. Classroom training, expected to decrease by 16%, is predicted to account for only

40% of all hours. Training via computer, on the other hand, is expected to double, moving from 16% to 33% of available hours. Other forms of delivery are expected to remain consistent, accounting for 27% of total available training hours in 2000 (see Figure 5.2).

The relationship between a company's revenues and the proportion of training hours available through the classroom and through other forms of delivery is expected to disappear in the new millennium. Companies of different sizes foresee making available similar proportions of their training hours in the classroom and through other forms of delivery in 2000.

The turn of the century will apparently bring differences in the way training is delivered among companies with different 1997 corporate training budgets. Companies with midsized training budgets anticipate making an equal proportion of training hours available via computer and classroom. Each method will make up 37% of total available training hours. For companies with large training budgets, however, the proportions will not be equal. These companies, on average, expect that 30% of hours will be delivered via computer, with 48% of hours delivered in the classroom.

CORPORATE UNIVERSITIES AND LEARNING CENTERS

Across all respondents, the majority (58%) indicate that their companies currently do not have a corporate university or learning center. Certain types of respondents are more likely to have corporate universities than others. Corporate universities are found more frequently in large companies, companies with large training budgets, companies with large workforces, and companies that provide training internationally. Other findings regarding corporate universities include the following:

▶ Corporate universities are more likely to be found in large companies. Of large companies, 57% have a corporate university or learning center, compared with 30% of smaller companies.

▶ Corporate universities also exist in significantly more companies with large training budgets than in companies with smaller training budgets. Of companies with large training budgets, 63% have corporate universities, compared with 24% of companies with smaller training budgets.

▶ Companies with large workforces are more likely to have a corporate university than companies with smaller workforces. Corporate universities exist in 57% of companies with large workforces and in only 31% of companies with smaller workforces.

▶ Finally, corporate universities exist in considerably more companies that provide training on an international basis than in companies that provide training on a regional basis. Of companies that train internationally, 59% have corporate universities. Only 31% of companies that train regionally have corporate universities.

The Future of Corporate Universities: A Snapshot

Less than half of all respondents (42%) currently have a corporate university, but will this change? An additional 20% of respondent companies plan to have a corporate university by 2000. Assuming that all of the companies that currently have a corporate university will also have one in the future, 62% of all respondents will have a corporate university in 2000 (see Figure 5.3).

PARTNERING PRACTICES WITH OUTSIDE DEVELOPERS

Often, companies will partner with outside developers to provide corporate education and training. Companies can partner with a variety of outside developers, including consultants, private vendors, universities, or corporate training units in other companies. To what extent are America's largest corporations partnering with outside developers? When partnering, which type of outside developer do companies turn to?

As we move into the new millennium and technology becomes increasingly more advanced and accessible, we are likely to see more outside developers offering courses in a multimedia-based training (MBT) distance learning format. Will companies be more inclined and interested in working with outside developers if and when these courses are available?

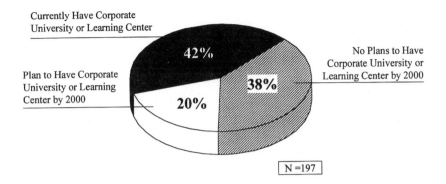

Figure 5.3. Corporate Universities

NOTE: The majority of companies currently do not have a corporate university or learning center. Of these companies, approximately one third plan to have a corporate university in the year 2000.

Budget Allocated to Outside Developers

Companies currently have a variety of options for outside development. Specifically, respondents were asked about outside consultants or private vendors, universities, or corporate training units in other companies. We found the following:

▶ The percentage of an organization's training budget allocated to these outside developers ranges greatly, from 0% to 90%. The mean percentage across all respondents is 38%.

▶ Compared with manufacturing and utilities respondents, who spend 45% and 51% of their budgets on outside developers, respectively, retail/wholesale respondents spend a significantly smaller percentage of their training budgets on outside sources (27%). This is not surprising, as findings also show that the majority of retail/wholesale training budgets (56%) are allocated to internal custom development.

▶ The amount of custom development done by a company also coincides with the amount of budget spent on outside developers. Companies that make us of custom development on a light to moderate basis spend 43% of their training budgets on outside sources. Companies that rely heavily on custom development spend only 26% of their training budget on outside sources.

Partnering Practices

Across all respondent types, the overwhelming majority (97%) indicate that they currently partner with outside consultants or private vendors. Sixty-eight percent currently partner with universities. A much smaller percentage (22%) partners with a corporate training unit in another company. Although not asked about it directly, respondents indicated other outside developers, such as associations or foundations, consortiums or conglomerates, specific individuals, and industry-related schools (see Figure 5.4).

Certain respondent types appear more likely than others to form university partnerships. Differences in university partnering practices are seen among respondents with different training budgets and different workforces. The industry in which a respondent works and the geographic coverage of training the company provides are also related to the likelihood of partnering with a university. Finally, the amount of custom development a company does influences its likelihood to partner with a university (see Table 5.2). Other observations in regard to corporate partnerships with universities include the following:

▶ Companies with large training budgets are more likely to partner with a university than are companies with smaller training budgets. Most companies (92%) with large training budgets currently partner with universities. In contrast, only 61% of companies with smaller to midsized training budgets do the same.

▶ More than three quarters (79%) of companies with large workforces currently partner with universities. Exactly half (50%) of companies with smaller workforces have partnerships with a university.

▶ Partnerships with universities are much more common in the manufacturing sector than they are in the retail/wholesale or finance/insurance sectors. Whereas 86% of manufacturing respondents indicate that they partner with a university, only 45% of retail/wholesale and 61% of finance/insurance respondents indicate the same.

▶ University partnerships are more common among companies who provide training on an international basis than among those who provide training on a national basis. Of international trainers, 76% partner with a university, compared with only 53% of national trainers.

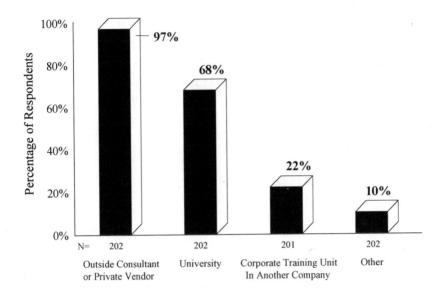

Figure 5.4. Current Partnerships
NOTE: Nearly all respondents currently partner with an outside consultant or private vendor. A much smaller percentage of respondents currently partner with a corporate training unit in another company.

▶ Companies that allocate a smaller proportion of their budgets to custom development are more likely to partner with a university than are companies that allocate a larger proportion of their budget to custom development. University partnerships are seen among 74% of light to moderate builders but among only 57% of heavy builders.

Partnering With Training Units in Other Companies

Using a corporate training unit in another company is an option adopted by significantly more companies providing training internationally than by companies providing training nationally. Of inter-

TABLE 5.2 Differences in University Partnerships Across Respondent
Type (in percentages)

More Likely to Partner With University		Less Likely to Partner With University	
Large training budgets	92	Small to midsized training budgets	61
Large workforces	79	Smaller workforce	50
Manufacturing	86	Retail/wholesale, financial institutions	45
Train internationally	76	Train nationally	53
Light to moderate builders	74	Heavy builders	57

NOTE: University partnerships are not formed equally among different industries and different types of respondents. Certain types of companies are more likely than others to partner with universities.

national trainers, 32% partner with a corporate training unit in another company, whereas only 11% of national trainers do the same.

Partnering with another company's corporate training unit is also more common for companies with a large number of employees than it is for companies with fewer employees. Of companies with large workforces, 34% partner with another company's corporate training unit, compared with 15% of companies with midsized workforces.

Partnering in the Future

Respondents were asked whether their use of outside consultants or private vendors, universities, corporate training units in other companies, and business schools would increase, decrease, or stay the same in 2000 (see Figure 5.5).

▶ Slightly more than half of all respondents (55%) expect to increase their use of outside consultants or private vendors in 2000. Approximately one third (34%) state their use will stay the same. Only 11% of respondents expect their use of outside consultants or private vendors to decline.

▶ Approximately half of all respondents (51%) expect their use of universities to increase in 2000, while an additional 45% indicate that their use will stay the same. Only 4% expect university partnerships to decline.

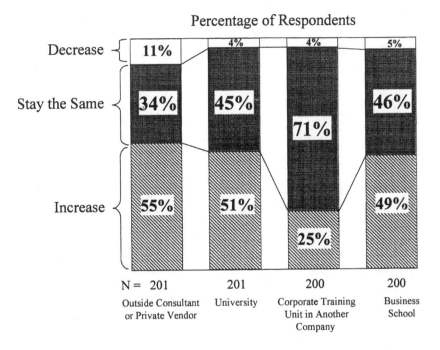

Figure 5.5. Partnering in 2000
NOTE: A similar percentage of respondents expect their use of outside consultants or private vendors, universities, and business schools to increase in the year 2000. A much smaller percentage of respondents expect their use of a corporate training unit in another company to increase in 2000.

▶ Most respondents expect to use corporate training units in other companies to the same degree in 2000 as they do today. Of all respondents, 71% state that their use of these units will be the same in the future, whereas one quarter (25%) anticipate increased usage. As is the case with using other outside developers, a very small percentage (4%) of respondents predict their use of other companies' training units will decrease.

▶ Respondents who currently allocate a large proportion of their training budget to custom development appear less likely to increase their usage of corporate training units in other companies, compared with respondents who allocate a smaller proportion of their budget to custom development. Twice as many light to moderate builders as heavy builders expect their use of another company's corporate training unit to increase (31% vs. 15%).

Respondents were also asked whether their use of business schools would increase, decrease, or stay the same in the future. Approximately half (49%) expect their use of business schools to increase, whereas slightly less than half (46%) expect use to stay the same. Only 5% expect business school use to decrease.

CORPORATE AMERICA'S REACTION TO
MBA/EXECUTIVE MBA PROGRAMS

The most significant use of business schools over the years has been sending employees for degree education, specifically the MBA or the executive MBA degree. Employees are receiving education and training from their respective companies. Regardless of whether training is received in a classroom, via computer, or in other forms, companies are making an effort to train employees in the skills they need to prosper. Is the responsibility for education solely that of the employer? Can employees learn all the skills and absorb all of the information they need through corporate education and training programs? Statistics suggest that they cannot. In 1996 alone, 94,000 people received MBAs and executive MBAs. Often, employers will help foot the bill for an MBA, which for certain programs can be a hefty investment. According to a recent *Business Week* survey, the average tuition among the 20 leading executive MBA programs is around $50,000. At the low end of the range is North Carolina's Kenan-Flagler school with a total tuition of $27,800. However, at the opposite end of the scale is the University of Pennsylvania's Wharton school with a total tuition of $82,500.[2]

In this section of our survey, the following questions were addressed:

▶ How valuable are MBAs in the eyes of corporate educators today? How valuable in the year 2000?
▶ What percentage of respondent companies reimburses employees for MBAs or executive MBAs?
▶ What factors are considered most important when selecting an MBA or executive MBA program?

Value of an MBA: Today and in 2000

Using a 5-point scale in which 1 is *not at all valuable* and 5 is *extremely valuable,* respondents were asked to rate the value of an MBA in today's business environment as well as its value in the year 2000.

▶ Approximately half of all respondents (49%) feel an MBA is valuable in today's business environment, providing ratings of 4 or 5. That an MBA is extremely valuable (rating of 5) is a belief held by only 15% of respondents. Of respondents, 15% do not think an MBA has much value, assigning ratings of 1 or 2. The mean value rating across all respondents is 3.4 (see Figure 5.6).

▶ Opinions are predicted to be the same in the year 2000, suggesting that MBAs will be just as valuable in the future as they are today. The same percentage of respondents (49%) believe an MBA will be valuable in 2000, providing ratings of 4 or 5. Eighteen percent of respondents believe an MBA will be extremely valuable in 2000, and 17% do not think an MBA will have much value in the future, giving ratings of 1 or 2. The mean value rating across all respondents is 3.4.

▶ MBAs are considered to be more valuable in certain types of companies than in others. Respondents in companies with fewer employees believe an MBA is more valuable in today's environment, compared with respondents in companies with a greater number of employees. The mean value rating across respondents in companies with smaller to midsized workforces is 3.6. The mean value rating across respondents in companies with large workforces is 3.1. These opinions are predicted to hold true in the future. As in today's business environment, companies with a fewer number of employees feel the MBA will be more valuable in 2000 than do companies with a greater number of employees. On average, respondents in companies with smaller to midsized workforces rate the MBA's value in 2000 at 3.6. The mean value rating across respondents in companies with large workforces is 3.1 for the future.

▶ Companies that spend a smaller percentage of their budgets on custom-developed training believe that MBAs have more value today and will have more value in 2000 than do companies that spend a greater percentage of their budgets on custom-developed training. For light builders, the mean value rating of an MBA in today's environment is 3.7.

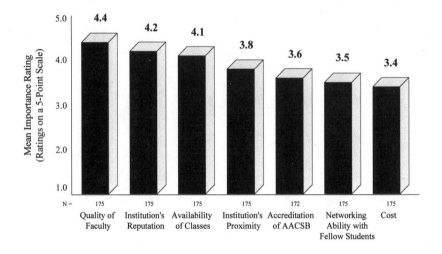

Figure 5.6. Factors in Selecting an MBA Program
NOTE: Relative to all other factors, respondents rate the quality of faculty as being the most important factor in selecting an MBA or executive MBA program. The least important factor is cost.

For moderate to heavy builders, the mean value rating is 3.3. For both groups of respondents, mean value ratings for 2000 are exactly the same as they are today (3.7 and 3.3, respectively).

▶ Light, moderate, and heavy users of computer-based training (CBT) currently perceive the value of an MBA to be the same. Looking toward the future, however, moderate to heavy CBT users believe the MBA will be more valuable in 2000 than light CBT users. When asked about the value of an MBA in 2000, the mean value rating across moderate to heavy CBT users is 3.6. The mean value rating for light CBT users is 3.2.

Reimbursing for MBAs and Executive MBA Degrees

Another indication of the value a company attributes to an MBA is whether the company reimburses employees for the degree. The large majority (90%) of companies currently reimburse for an MBA or executive MBA. Of the 21 respondents whose companies do not currently reimburse for an MBA, only three say their companies reimbursed in the past but no longer do so. Reimbursements for an MBA do not vary among different types of respondents.

Factors in Selecting an MBA Program

A company evaluates several factors when selecting an MBA or executive MBA program. Respondents were asked to rate factors that may influence program selection on a 5-point scale in which 1 is *not at all important* and 5 is *extremely important*. The following factors were considered: the institution's reputation; the institution's proximity, cost, and accreditation by the American Assembly of Collegiate Schools of Business (AACSB); availability of classes; quality of faculty; and networking ability with fellow students. Factors are discussed in order of their perceived importance (see Figure 5.6).

▶ Across all respondents, the most important factor in selecting an MBA or executive MBA program is the quality of faculty. Of respondents, 89% believe quality of faculty is important, providing ratings of 4 or 5. The mean score across all respondents is 4.4.

▶ The perceived importance of quality of faculty varies across industries. Retail/wholesale respondents believe more than manufacturing respondents that the quality of faculty is important. Of retail/wholesale respondents, 70% think the quality of faculty is extremely important (assigning ratings of 5). The mean importance rating across retail/wholesale respondents is 4.7. In contrast, only 42% of manufacturing respondents believe quality of faculty is extremely important (ratings of 5). The mean importance rating across manufacturing respondents is 4.2.

▶ The second most important factor in selecting an MBA or executive MBA program is the institution's reputation. Of all respondents, 85% give an institution's reputation an importance rating of 4 or 5. The mean importance rating is 4.2.

▶ Respondents who make different amounts of training available via computer have different opinions regarding the importance of an institution's reputation. Moderate to heavy CBT users believe an institution's reputation is more important than light CBT users. The mean

importance rating for moderate to heavy CBT users is 4.3, compared
with 4.0 for light CBT users.

▶ Availability of classes is the third most important factor in selecting a program. Class availability is considered important (ratings of 4 or
5) by 81% of respondents. The mean importance rating for this item is
4.1. Any one type of respondent does not view availability of classes as
more important.

▶ According to respondents, an institution's proximity is the next
most important factor. Of all respondents, 69% think proximity is
important, providing ratings of 4 or 5. The mean importance rating is
3.8.

The Importance of Accreditation

Accreditation by the AACSB is the fifth most important factor in
selecting an MBA program. Of respondents, 58% indicate that accreditation is important, assigning ratings of 4 or 5. The mean importance
rating is 3.6. Other findings include the following:

▶ Accreditation is more important to respondents in companies
with midsized workforces than it is to respondents in companies with
smaller workforces. Exactly half (50%) of respondents in companies with
smaller workforces feel that accreditation is important (ratings of 4 or
5), compared with 67% of respondents in companies with midsized
workforces. More than four times as many companies that train internationally view accreditation as unimportant, compared with companies
that train nationally. Of respondents in companies that provide training
internationally, 30% think accreditation is unimportant (ratings of 1 or
2), compared with only 7% of respondents in companies that provide
training nationally. Mean importance ratings are 3.2 and 4.0, respectively
(see Figure 5.7).

The Cost: The Least Important Factor

The least important factor in selecting an MBA or executive MBA
program is cost. Of respondents, 49% indicate that cost is important,
giving ratings of 4 or 5. The mean importance rating across all respondents is 3.4. The importance of cost does not vary across respondent

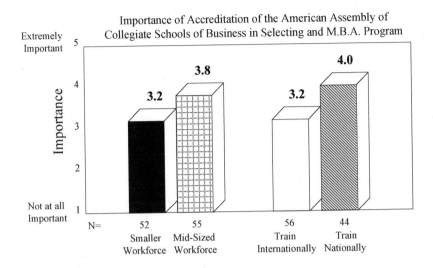

Figure 5.7. Differences in Importance of Accreditation by the American Assembly of Collegiate Schools of Business (AACSB)
NOTE: In selecting an MBA program, accreditation of AACSB is more important to companies with midsized workforces than to companies with smaller workforces. In addition, it is found to be more important to companies that train nationally than to those that train internationally.

type. That cost falls at the bottom of the importance list implies that if the institution has a good reputation and high-quality faculty and if students can enroll in the classes they want, companies are not as concerned with the cost of the program. Companies are willing to make an investment in an MBA or executive MBA program if it meets the other criteria they deem important.

Effect of an MBT Distance Learning Format on Partnerships

Some outside developers are beginning to offer courses in multimedia-based distance learning format (MBT distance format). MBT distance learning formats can be used to deliver single courses and even entire programs. For example, Duke University's Fuqua School of Business offers an on-line MBA through its Global Executive MBA program (GEMBA). GEMBA students spend as much as 30 hours a week on-line attending CD-ROM video lectures and downloading supplemental programs and interactive study aids.[3] Would respondents be more inclined to partner with an outside developer if the developer were to offer courses in an MBT distance learning format? Findings suggest that many would be more inclined. For several respondents, it would not make a difference. One thing is certain: It would not do any harm. Very few respondents say the introduction of MBT distance learning formats would cause their interest in partnering with an outside developer to decline (see Figure 5.8).

▶ Of all respondents, 61% state that if an outside consultant or private vendor were to offer courses in an MBT distance format, their interest in working with the developer would increase. An additional 38% say their interest would stay the same. Only 1% would have a decreased interest.

▶ If a university were to offer courses in an MBT distance format, 59% of respondents would have an increased interest in partnering with the university. Of respondents, 40% indicate that their partnering interest would stay the same, and 1% indicate that their interest would decline.

▶ The interest change in university partnerships varies by type of respondents. If a university were to offer courses in an MBT distance format, significantly more companies with a large workforce would have increased partnering interest than would companies with smaller to midsized workforces (72% vs. 55%).

▶ A greater percentage of respondents with midsized to large training budgets state that their interest in partnering with a university would increase, compared with respondents with smaller training budgets (67% vs. 46%).

▶ Nearly three quarters (73%) of moderate builders state that their interest in partnering with a university would increase if courses were offered in an MBT distance format. Comparatively, only 48% of heavy builders indicate that their interest would increase if this occurred.

▶ Of respondents, 55% indicate increased interest in partnering with business schools if courses were offered in an MBT distance format. Of respondents, 44% would have no change in partnering interest, and only 1% believes their interest would decrease.

Interest in partnering with business schools is found to be related to two factors: size of training budgets and the proportion of training hours

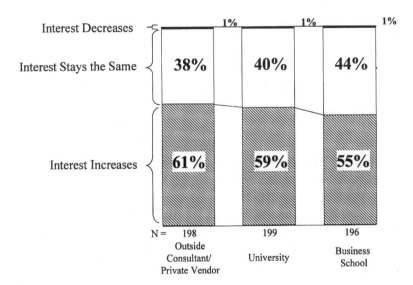

Figure 5.8 Availability of MBT in a Distance Learning Format: Effect on Partnering
NOTE: If outside consultants or private vendors, universities, or business schools were to offer courses in multimedia-based distance learning format, almost all respondents indicate that their interest would either increase or stay the same.

available via computer. Significantly more respondents in companies with midsized to large training budgets state that if business schools were to offer courses in an MBT distance format, their interest in partnering would increase, compared with respondents in companies with smaller training budgets (64% vs. 40%).

▶ Of moderate CBT users, 67% say their interest in partnering with a business school would increase if courses were offered in an MBT format. In comparison, 47% of light CBT users and 51% of heavy CBT users indicate that their interest would increase.

THE FUTURE OF TRAINING

Whether causal or coincidental, the advent of a knowledge-based economy has grown in tandem with a growing role of training at America's largest companies. Budgets and other trends tell the tale.

1997 Corporate Training Budgets

The estimated amount of money that organizations spent on corporate education and training in 1997 (excluding salaries and overhead but including outside expenditures with developers) varies greatly across respondent companies. Among respondents who were able to estimate the exact amount spent on corporate education and training, budgets for 1997 ranged from $13,000 to $120 million. The average corporate education and training budget across these respondents was $6.3 million. The median budget was $2 million.

A Look to the Future: Year 2000 Corporate Training Budgets

Looking toward the future, approximately three quarters (77%) of all respondent companies expect the amount of money spent on corporate education and training to increase in the year 2000. An additional 18% expect their budgets to stay the same, whereas only 5% foresee a decrease in the amount of money spent on corporate education and training (see Figure 5.9). There are no differences in expectations across different company types or industry sectors.

Companies expecting to see an increase in year 2000 corporate education and training budgets expect to see varying degrees of growth. When companies were asked the percentage increase expected, answers ranged from 1% to 600%. The average growth expectation across these respondents is 36% (see Figure 5.9).

A small group of companies expect their year 2000 budgets to decrease. Expectations for the magnitude of this change range from 3% to 60%, with an average anticipated decrease of 25%.

Multimedia-based training promises to grow along with corporate training in general, and corporate campuses continue to grow in size and scope across the country.

▶ Motorola University began with a $2 million budget and three staff members. Today, it administers a $120 million budget and operates out of the 133,000-square-foot Galvin Center for Continuing Education at Motorola's headquarters in Schaumburg, Illinois. Motorola University also runs satellite campuses in 14 cities in the United States, Europe, Asia, and Latin America.[4]

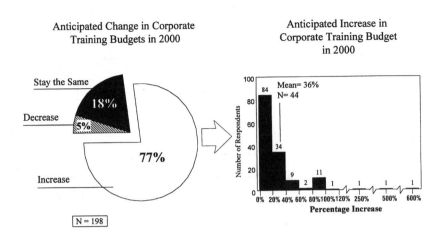

Figure 5.9. Future Corporate Education and Training Budgets
NOTE: The majority of respondents predict corporate education and training budgets will increase by the year 2000. The average growth rate expectation is 36%. However, there are a few that predict increases of more than 250%.

▶ McDonald's Hamburger University, begun in the basement of an outlet in 1961, now runs its management training courses from a 130,000-square-foot campus in Oak Brook, Illinois. The university has satellites in each of McDonald's 40 U.S. regions and training programs in 91 countries. Three thousand managers graduate from Hamburger University every year.[5]

▶ Arthur Andersen invests $300 million per year on corporate education, roughly 7% of the company's total revenues. In 1971, it purchased a college campus outside of Chicago to build the Andersen Center, a sprawling monument to corporate learning. Andersen has invested $150 million on the 645-acre campus. Staffed by 200 education specialists, the center can accommodate 1,700 overnight students. It has 130 classrooms, 6 auditoriums, 5 conference centers, 1,000 computer workstations, several restaurants, a 9-hole golf course, and a discotheque. Over 60,000 trainees visit the Andersen center every year, half of whom are employees of the company; the other half are clients or outside customers.[6]

Although the most celebrated corporate universities are housed in brick and mortar, many companies have contained their learning efforts in virtual universities, a combination of rented conference rooms, community college courses, and MBT.

▸ Federal Express, for example, spends 5% of payroll annually on education for its 40,000 couriers and customer service agents. Using interactive videodisks (IVDs), employees receive four hours of company-sponsored training and two hours of self-administered testing every 6 months. The course materials are based on 25 videodisks (the equivalent of 37,500 floppy disks), which are updated monthly. Trainees may view the disks on one of FedEx's 1,225 IVD units kept at 700 locations.[7]

Multimedia-based training has captured the attention of many corporate education departments for its speed, ease of use, and long-term savings. Before dismantling the training room and trading in the overhead projector, knowledge managers must learn to strike a balance between a "high-tech and high-touch" approach to learning.

Although training plays an integral role in the generation of knowledge, the critical element for organizational learning lies in dissemination. Does the company provide ample opportunities for individuals to share what they have learned? Few would question that a company filled with competent, intelligent individuals would generate new knowledge. The corporation skilled in transferring what it knows from one person to the rest of the group, however, holds the keys to the future.

CHAPTER

6

THE EMERGENCE AND GROWTH OF THE KNOWLEDGE ECONOMY

Where is the wisdom we have lost in knowledge?
Where is the knowledge we have lost in information?

—T. S. Eliot

WHAT IS KNOWLEDGE?

Scholars since Socrates have wrestled with this question. Even when the question is limited to the context of knowledge in the world of business, answering it comprehensively exceeds the scope of this book and, most likely, the patience of the reader. Still, it is worthwhile to spend some time constructing a working definition of knowledge for two reasons. First and foremost, managers must begin to grapple with the complexity of knowledge because deciding what it is (and what it is not!) is the first step to harnessing its power. Thomas Stewart of *Fortune* magazine has said that managing knowledge can be like fishing with your bare hands. It is indeed a slippery topic, but the only way to leverage the value of knowledge is to embrace it for all its complexity. It is in the difficult-to-grasp nature of knowledge that much of its power resides. As Davenport and Prusak say,

Although it is tempting to look for simple answers to complex problems and deal with uncertainties by pretending they don't exist, knowing more usually leads to better decisions than knowing less, even if the "less" seems clearer and more definite. Certainty and clarity often come at the price of ignoring essential factors.[1]

Second, defining knowledge is a necessary first step before proceeding with the rest of this book. We cannot go into a discussion of how to locate, measure, and manage knowledge without first understanding what it is.

Already a great deal of effort has been expended trying to define knowledge. Unfortunately, the tendency to avoid complexity has lead some to label everything people know and much of the intangible things a company owns as knowledge assets. As a starting point, such a broad definition of knowledge is problematic because it obscures what makes knowledge valuable and knowledge organizations extraordinary. Skandia is the Swedish insurance and financial concern that first issued an intellectual capital report to accompany its annual report to stockholders. The company measures intellectual capital according to 164 variables. Skandia's report will be explored in more detail later in this book because it is the first and most coherent effort to measure the knowledge assets of a sizable company. However, Skandia does define intellectual capital too broadly. In addition to skill, innovativeness, and knowledge, Leif Edvinsson, Skandia's corporate director for intellectual capital says intellectual capital consists of software, hardware, and "all that is left behind when staff is going home."[2] Although a knowledgeable worker may sit in front of a computer all day, that does not necessarily mean he or she invests knowledge in the object. By placing a value on all intangible assets—"the difference between the company's market value and its book value," according to Skandia CEO Lars-Eric Petersson[3]—Skandia assumes that if you can't hold it, it must have value. Unfortunately, this is just not so, as *Forbes* columnist John Rutledge alludes to in the following satire:

"You've got to be kidding" I told the voice on the phone. She had called me during dinner time to tell me she would cut off my credit line if I didn't make a payment the next day. "Do you know how *rich* I am? I may not have any money, but I am . . . an intellectual capital millionaire! I have a doctorate in economics and a Phi Beta Kappa key. My wife studied psychopharmacology, plays the flute, and speaks French. And on my family balance sheet my five children have already capitalized one Ph.D., two and a half bachelor degrees, three prep school degrees, and two fancy East Coast private-grade-school honor-roll certificates. We have books all over the house and our own Web site, sophist.com. We recycle everything. We value diversity. My children have studied Latin, for crissake. And with all this intellectual capital, you want to cut off my credit card?"

"With all that intellectual capital, maybe next time you can figure out how to pay your bills," she said, and hung up.[4]

Rutledge pokes fun at the concept of intellectual capital, but he points out a very important aspect of knowledge. Although a company may be brimming with data and information—most are today—it may never translate the assets into true value. The U.S. Internal Revenue Service, for example, is awash in data, but many would not quickly refer to it as an organization wealthy with intellectual capital. Only those companies skilled at transforming data into information and information into knowledge will harvest the sustainable competitive advantages that we speak of. We will return to the process of knowledge generation in a later chapter, but to appreciate the essence of knowledge, it is important for a manager to understand how it is derived from its raw building blocks—data and information.

THE PROGRESSION TOWARD KNOWLEDGE

Data

A masterful symphony incarnates knowledge. The skill of the performers, the experience of the conductor, the decor of the concert hall, the mood of the audience, and some elements that are impossible to express all combine in a presentation that says perfection. Broken down, however, even the most complex symphony or business operation begins with data.

Data are objective facts describing an event without any judgment, perspective, or context. In the symphony, musical notes are data. They have no meaning themselves, unless read (played) by someone with the knowledge to translate these marks into music. In this sentence, words are data. Unless words are grouped appropriately, they do not convey any meaning or understanding. Data are like the points in a "connect-the-dot" puzzle without the lines filled in or like individual pieces of a jigsaw puzzle. In our economy, we are primarily concerned with four forms of data: numbers, words, sounds, and images. Because data are highly portable and easy to generate, the principal activities surrounding data are its creation, collection, movement, and storage.[5] Some companies are more data intensive by virtue of their business. Banks, insurance companies, and utilities, for example, depend heavily on their ability to create, process, move, and store data. However, all companies, no matter their size, manage data in the form of marketing research, financial accounts, and sales reports. When a person analyzes even the most simple data points, he or she adds some meaning to the numbers, and a set of data becomes information.

Information

Peter Drucker describes information as *data endowed with relevance and purpose.*[6] Gregory Bateson calls information "the differences that make a difference."[7] Essentially, information is a message. It draws together data points, puts them in context, adds perspective, and is delivered to change people's minds or reinforce their beliefs. The notes a musical composer chooses and the order in which he or she places them create information. The composer takes raw data, endows it with meaning, and makes a presentation that affects the listeners. The word *inform* originally meant to give form. Information gives shape to data and to people's perceptions. It has the power to convince, describe, and provoke. Davenport and Prusak have observed five ways in which data change into information.

- ► *Contextualized:* We know for what purpose the data was gathered.
- ► *Categorized:* We know the units of analysis or key components of the data.
- ► *Calculated:* The data may have been analyzed mathematically or statistically.
- ► *Corrected:* Errors have been removed from the data.
- ► *Condensed:* The data may have been summarized in a more concise form.[8]

Information travels through a company by soft and hard networks. At staff meetings, for example, department heads provide information to bring the rest of the company up to speed on projects. In annual reports, a company boils down a year's worth of data, describing performance in a way that is understandable to the shareholders. Although information, in any form, may convey well-crafted meaning, perhaps even some insight, it cannot convey knowledge without several critical elements. The difference between information and knowledge is like the nutritional difference between bon-bons and broccoli.

Knowledge Defined

Knowledge is information laden with experience, truth, judgment, intuition, and values; a unique combination that allows individuals and organizations to assess new situations and manage change.[9]

Information is often mistaken for knowledge because they both move through an organization via networks. There are important distinctions, however—clues to be discussed in a later chapter that will help managers distinguish between the two. For now, let's say that knowledge exists in communities and is codified in rare documents. Cross-functional teams hold knowledge, as do procedure manuals that are the culmination of 20 years' experience. Job descriptions, culture, strategy, procedures, and, often, stories are vessels for knowledge. Howard Gardner, of Harvard's School of Education, has called stories "the single most powerful weapon in the leader's arsenal." He believes that stories can be the most efficient ways to contain and transfer knowledge. Says Edward O. Welles in *Inc.* magazine,

> In a perilous economy, a story can serve as a competitive tool that defines a company's sense of self and its place. It's not just a question of having a story that can open wallets on Wall Street or among other swanky investment types: you need a story to tell employees, suppliers, customers, and—most of all—yourself. By forcing its teller to reveal what is unique about a company's aims, a story helps a company's management, acting as a useful reminder that what matters is focus.[10]

Telling an effective story is not easy work, but for many companies, a story has meant a great deal. For example, SatCon Technology is a Massachusetts-based manufacturer of electromechanical products. Its customers range from aerospace industries to automakers. Although it is a market leader and can tell the story of what is does through a hundred equations, SatCon has the experience and understanding to grasp the essence of what it does: "We bring a higher level of intelligence to machines."[11]

Davenport and Prusak describe the processes for generating knowledge from information:

> ▶ *Comparison:* How does information about this situation compare with information from other situations we have known?
> ▶ *Consequences:* What implications does the information have for decisions and actions?
> ▶ *Connections:* How does this bit of knowledge relate to others?
> ▶ *Conversation:* What do other people think about this information?[12]

As must be clear by now, knowledge is not as neat as data and requires much more work than information. Managers must be careful not to simplify knowledge. It does not create itself, as purveyors of computerized "knowledge management" products might have us believe. Just as data *endowed with relevance and purpose* make information, so information endowed with the five elements makes knowledge.

THE FIVE ELEMENTS OF KNOWLEDGE

Experience

The value of experience lies in its historical perspective. Having "been there" before translates into tremendous value when entering a time of change. Experience is the essential bridge between what happened in the past and what is happening in the present. General Electric crystallized the value of experience when it launched its Answer Center in 1982. At GE, telephone operators respond to over 14,000 calls a day. Experience is embedded in every response to a customer's question or complaint. GE launched the Answer Center in Louisville, Kentucky, to leverage this experience. Within the Answer Center's database sit the descriptions for 1.5 million customer problems and their solutions. Operators may retrieve the answer to a question by simply describing the situation, and through artificial intelligence programming, the Answer Center will find the appropriate solution. If none exists, 12 on-site specialists, each with at least four years of repair experience, will devise one. Computer programmers are also on site to rapidly update the Answer Center by the following day. In a very important way, the operators may "reexperience" that which has already been experienced, and the knowledge is shared throughout the corporation.[13]

Experience also holds value for the critical understanding it adds to a new situation. Nissan Motor, for example, will place test drivers in specific countries to gain a sense of local driving conditions, driving styles, customs, values, and lifestyles. When Nissan is developing a new product, that experience becomes invaluable, providing insight and direction. The test drivers also share their observations on the best ways to introduce the product vis-à-vis the competition.[14]

Truth

Knowledge conveys how things truly are. It is an expression of events as they really occur. It is an attempt to see the environment with objective reality. Although a manager may wave his or her hand and say, "Make it so," the worker often has the most accurate understanding of the effort required to get the job done. This is the truth element of knowledge—the critical understanding that bridges the gap between objectives and results. In the process of new product development, truth often holds great value. For example:

▶ Market researchers for Cheerios were surprised to find that breakfast was not the main purpose for consumers' buying the cereal. Instead, parents with small children valued the product because they could bag it, carry it, and portion it out to their kids anywhere.

▶ The brand manager for a spray-on cooking oil saw his neighbor coating his lawn mower blades with the product. It prevented the grass clippings from sticking to the mower, explained the neighbor, and it didn't harm the grass.

▶ Designers visiting the homes of Kimberly-Clark customers noted the pleasure parents got out of having their kids wear increasingly "mature" clothing. Pull-on diapers were especially appealing to parents, making them feel that the toddler was taking a step toward "grownup" dress. Huggies Pull-Ups were introduced in 1991, and by the time the competition could catch on, Kimberly Clark was selling $400 million worth of pull-ups annually.

▶ A new product developer from Hewlett-Packard spent the day watching a surgeon at work. The surgeon was performing the operation with the aid of a television monitor, which magnified the area being worked on. Periodically, nurses obstructed the surgeon's view of the screen as they walked by. Although no one complained, the designer saw an opportunity for improvement and a new product. She developed a lightweight helmet with an internal projection system. The surgeon gained an enhanced view of the operable area and was no longer disturbed by operating room movement.

▶ Consultants developing the design for new cellular phones studied the habits of pager users. They found that people were inventing special codes for their close friends and relatives so they could screen pages. Using this insight, the consultants recommended screening capabilities for the phones.[15]

Judgment

Karl Weick calls judgment, or sense making, a process of creating a contextual reality. It is neither neat nor easily attained, but judgment allows people to make decisions in situations of extreme uncertainty. In a world of rapid change, says Weick,

> Wise people know that they don't fully understand what is happening at a given moment, because what is happening is unique to that time. They avoid extreme confidence and extreme caution, knowing that either can destroy what organizations need most in changing times, namely, curiosity, openness, and the ability to sense complex problems. The overconfident shun curiosity because they think they know what they need to know. The overcautious shun curiosity for fear it will only deepen their uncertainties.[16]

Good judgment, as a component of knowledge, is the ability to make sense of a situation that is completely unfamiliar. Poor judgment, conversely, occurs when we lose our ability to reconstitute the reality of a situation, as was the case on a hot August day in Montana, 1959.

The fire at Mann Gulch probably began on August 4 when lightning set a small fire in a dead tree. The temperature reached 97 degrees the next day and produced a fire danger rating of 74 out of a possible 100, indicating the potential for the fire to spread uncontrollably. When the fire was spotted by a lookout on a mountain 30 miles away, 16 smoke jumpers were sent at 2:30 from Missoula, Montana, in a C-47 transport plane. (One man became ill and didn't make the jump.) A forest ranger posted in the next canyon, Jim Harrison, was already on the scene trying to fight the fire on his own.

Wind conditions that day were turbulent, so the smoke jumpers and their cargo were dropped from 2,000 feet rather than the usual 1,200. The parachute connected to their radio failed to open, and the radio was pulverized as it hit the ground. But the remaining crew and supplies landed safely in Mann Gulch by 4:10. The smoke jumpers then collected their supplies, which had scattered widely, and grabbed a quick bite to eat.

While the crew ate, foreman Wagner Dodge met up with ranger Harrison. They scouted the fire and came back concerned that the thick forest near which they had landed could become a "death trap." Dodge told the second-in-command, William Hellman, to take the crew across to the north side of the gulch, away from the fire, and march along its flank toward the river at the bottom of the gulch. While Hellman did this, Dodge and Harrison ate a quick meal. Dodge rejoined the crew at 5:40 and took his position at the head of the line moving toward the river. He could see flames flapping back and forth on the south slope as he looked to his left. Then Dodge saw that the fire had suddenly crossed the gulch about 200 yards ahead and was moving toward them. He yelled at the crew to run from the fire and began angling up the steep hill toward the bare ridge of rock.

The crew was soon moving through slippery grasses two and a half feet high but was quickly losing ground to the flames—eventually towering at a height of 30 feet, rushing toward them at a rate that probably reached a speed of 660 feet per minute. Sensing that the crew was in serious danger, Dodge yelled at them to drop their tools. Two minutes later, to everyone's astonishment, he lit a fire in front of the men and motioned to them to lie down in the area it had burned. No one did. Instead, they ran for the ridge and what they hoped would be safety.

Two firefighters, Robert Sallee and Walter Rumsey, made it through a crevice in the ridge unburned. Dodge survived by lying down in the ashes of his escape fire. The other 13 perished. The fire caught up with them at 5:56—the time at which the hands on Harrison's watch melted in place.[17]

What happened at Mann's Gulch can easily be labeled a horrible case of misfortune and poor decision making. Most fundamentally, however, the firefighting crew at Mann Gulch lost its ability to make sense of reality. The crew members lost their powers of judgment. Few managers would admit that this example does not parallel situations in the corporation. Managers must routinely use their judgment to make decisions in times of uncertainty or danger. The process involves asking questions that seem vague and dealing with answers that are equally as vague. In the case of the fire at Mann Gulch, there was in fact little effort to reduce uncertainty. On the plane ride to the fire, the crew members did not speak to one another, and other than the short lunch, the entire crew never had an opportunity to discuss issues of basic strategy. When change escalated to a life-threatening level, the firefighters become so disconnected from the reality of their present situation that they rushed past the one solution to their problems, the escape fire that their foreman had built. In organizations, says Weick, judgment allows the organization to ask questions, "bringing to the surface, testing, and restructuring one's intuitive understandings of phenomena on the spot, at a time when actions can still make a difference."[18] Thus, judgment is an integral element of knowledge because it allows organizations to fight fires, if possible, or devise a new plan of attack if the situation becomes too hot.

Intuition

Some call it instinct, others call it gut feelings, rules of thumb, or business sense. By whichever name, intuition, that unconscious decision maker born of experience and refined through trial and error, is a critical element of knowledge. It guides the knower in the face of changing circumstances and through unfamiliar territory. It is the source of speed, because the knower does not have to relearn elements of a new situation. If they are familiar, then learning is instantaneous. In action, intuition is familiar to most. Consider the following instances:

> Don Dietz, operations director for Allied Signal, defines intuition as a compilation of facts, along with one's experiences and skills.
> "I think it develops over a number of years of learning, dealing with people and business experiences," he said. "Some people, because of the way they think and the way they go about doing business, may be better at it than others. But a lot of it is learned."
> Mr. Dietz also uses intuition when hiring new employees.

"First, of course, is their skills, which is more fact-based," he said. "But then you look at their personality, their philosophy. You have a feeling for how they will mesh with other people in the group, whether they bring a diversity with them that will help the group expand and look at new horizons."

Dennis Moreno, senior vice president of sales and marketing at Cornish and Carey Residential Real Estate, defines intuition as an inner sense.

"If an issue arises that feels odd, sounds odd, looks odd, or my stomach gets upset, I want to back off immediately," he said. "When something doesn't feel good inside, your inner sense is telling you something is wrong, and you have to listen."

"It's that little voice that wakes you up at 3:30 a.m.," he added. "You've got something on your mind, and you can't shake it. Your inner self is saying, 'This is an unresolved issue and you need to act on it.' "

Howard Pruitt, director of human resources at Compass Design Automation, said he relies a great deal on intuition in his business decisions.

"A lot depends on the environment, but even as a kid I tended to look at things and say, 'This feels right to me,' " he said.

Mr. Pruitt said with his decision style, 40 percent to 50 percent of the available information is enough for him to take action.

"If it doesn't work, you can always clean it up or fix it later," he said. "But at least you're not sitting there going, 'I wonder if we have enough information to do something.' "[19]

Values

Values are the lenses through which we view the world and, subsequently, one of the main guides when gathering knowledge. Values dictate the ways in which we determine what is important and test actions. The story of Masura Ibuka, the founder of Sony, illustrates the enduring power of values to guide a company. In 1945, Ibuka launched Sony with just $1,600 in savings and seven employees. He ran the company out of the telephone operator's room in an all-but-destroyed department store in downtown Tokyo. On May 7, 1946, just 10 months later, and after several failed product launches, he felt it necessary to codify Sony's guiding ideology. He wrote the following "Purposes of Incorporation":

▶ To establish a place of work where engineers can feel the joy of techno-logical innovation, be aware of their mission to society, and work to their hearts' content.

▶ To pursue dynamic activities in technology and production for the recon-struction of Japan and the elevation of the nation's culture.

▶ To apply advanced technology to the life of the general public.[20]

It is remarkable to note that Ibuka penned this statement in the face of utter ruin. Although he barely had enough cash to keep the doors of his company open, he felt it was needed to guide the evolution of Sony. More than 40 years later, and after rapid growth, Sony's CEO, Akio Morita, rephrased the ideology.

> Sony is a pioneer and never intends to follow others. Through progress, Sony wants to serve the whole world. It shall be always a seeker of the unknown. . . . Sony has a principle of respecting and encouraging one's ability . . . and always tries to bring out the best in a person. This is a vital force in Sony.[21]

Lest the reader think of corporate value statements as sentimental pieces of prose that simply hang in the corporate lobby, the Sony example shows that Ibuka's "Purposes of Incorporation" and Morita's "Pioneer-ing Spirit" had real impact on the functioning of the company. Compared with its Japanese competitors, Sony did not rely on traditional market research techniques, and in some cases it flouted them, adopting a more "crusading" attitude. The company as a whole was intent on bringing quality technological products to market and then educating consumers on their need and value. This attitude paid off as Sony introduced a series of products for which market research had indicated little customer demand, such as the first magnetic tape recorder in Japan (1950), the first all-transistor radio (1957), the first home-use videotape recorder (1964), and the first portable cassette player, the Sony Walkman (1979).[22]

Collins and Porras documented the core ideologies of the world's most successful companies in *Built to Last*. Reading how strongly they are articulated and knowing the lengths these companies go to commu-nicate their importance (Johnson & Johnson CEO Jim Burke estimated he spent 40% of his time communicating the J&J credo throughout the company), one gets a deeper appreciation for how values may guide the actions of a company in the following examples.

Company	Guiding Value
3M	▶ Innovation: "Thou shalt not kill a new product idea."
American Express	▶ Heroic customer service
Merck	▶ We are in the business of preserving and improving human life. All of our actions must be measured by our success in achieving this goal.
Motorola	▶ Continual improvement in all that the company does—in ideas, in quality, in customer satisfaction.
Wal-Mart	▶ We exist to provide value to our customers—to make their lives better via lower prices and greater selection; all else is secondary.[23]

"Whereas at one time the decisive factor of production was land, and later capital . . . today the decisive factor is increasingly man himself, that is, his knowledge."[24] Those words did not come from an economist, academic, or seer of the information age. Pope John Paul II wrote them in his 1991 encyclical *Centesimus Annus*. This was not the first time that a learned man had noted the value of knowledge. In 1962, Princeton University economist Fritz Machlup estimated that knowledge production accounted for 34.5% of the U.S. gross domestic product (GDP). In 1977, Marc Porat, later the CEO of software company General Magic, wrote in his Ph.D. dissertation that the information sector of the economy represented 25.1% of the GDP and generated 43% of all corporate profits. Although these studies certainly generated interest, few executives in the classic corporations of 1950 to 1980 would have dwelled very long on the importance of knowledge as a corporate asset. Today, however, the value of knowledge, once a conceptual thing that appealed to intuition, has become explicit. Today, as never before, we can see the value of knowledge in almost every facet of the economy and every corner of the corporation's activities.

KNOWLEDGE: THE LATEST STORE OF ECONOMIC VALUE

In 1993, the editors of *Fortune* magazine grappled with an editorial problem. Should Microsoft Corporation be listed under the annual *Fortune* 500 list for manufacturing companies or service companies? It certainly is not a manufacturer, the reasoning must have gone, because the only objects it produces are intangible lines of computer code. And it's not a service provider because once you buy the software, you're on your own to make it produce. As a matter of fact, what does Microsoft do besides come up with great ideas? As a matter of fact, that is exactly what the software giant does: It sells the best ideas its employees can come up with. *Fortune* decided to print just one *Fortune 500* list in 1993, merging the traditional categories of manufacturers and service providers. With that step, the magazine unceremoniously acknowledged that the traditional lines with which it used to divide the economy were no longer applicable in a new economy where information and knowledge have equal value.[25]

One year later, on November 7, 1994, *Business Week* made this implication explicit when it ran a cover story titled, "The Spawning of a Third Sector: Information." In that issue, the magazine proposed basing economic data on three sectors: manufacturing, service, and information. Although the new classification glossed over its own inconsistencies—for example, education was listed as a service, publishing as information—*Business Week* again recognized knowledge as a significant source of economic value.[26] Beyond the academic value of being smart and the political value of knowing more than the next guy, knowledge has increasingly gained real, discernible, and measurable value for this economy and for corporations.

The rest of this chapter will examine the value of knowledge as

1. a corporate asset,
2. a competitive advantage, and
3. a manager of change.

KNOWLEDGE AS A CORPORATE ASSET

On June 5, 1995, International Business Machines made history. For the first time, IBM made a hostile takeover bid. The target was a growing company in Massachusetts called Lotus Development Corporation. At the time, Lotus was known for its spreadsheet application Lotus 1-2-3 and its e-mail program cc:Mail. The prize of the Lotus acquisition, however, was none of these. As far as Big Blue was concerned, it was an exciting software package called Notes, the leading product in the "groupware" market (software that creates an environment for collaboration, information storage and retrieval, and communication over a corporate network). Lou Gerstner, IBM's chief, set the bid price for Lotus at $3.5 billion; 14 times Lotus's book valuation of $250 million. Clearly, IBM was paying for more than Lotus's software, sales, and market share.[27] As the story unfolded, it turned out that IBM sought to purchase a stake in the future of enterprise computing, and part of that price tag included paying for the knowledge that Lotus held in its corporate mind.

IBM made its hostile bid for Lotus for all the reasons one may expect. First of all, the software was valuable. *Fortune* described the technology in 1994 by saying, "Notes takes the processors and electrical connections of a computer network and makes them work like synapses in a vast collective brain."[28] More than e-mail and databases, Notes acts as a backbone for group information sharing and collaboration over an electronic network.

> Imagine being a salesperson on the road, consulting a database you share with hundreds of co-workers. You dial in from your hotel room and download whatever Notes files you need. Then you tap away at your laptop, adding comments and modifying numbers. Meanwhile scores of your colleagues may be working at their machines, making similar changes.
>
> What happens when you log back into the server and your work flows back into the database, now much altered by your fellows? Notes reconciles all that material, no matter how complex. The program works in part by consulting people when it's confused. If two users revise the same document in different ways, for example, the system will ask which version to keep, or whether to keep them both.[28]

After its introduction, it became a demanded product for corporations that needed to unify far-flung operations and workers on the move. Chase Manhattan, General Motors, Hewlett-Packard, and 3M are counted among the champions of Notes. Andersen Consulting and Price Waterhouse were two of the world's largest users of Notes in 1994. Each has nearly 40,000 employees using the software.

Most important, the product delivered on its productivity promise. Ann Polermo, an analyst for International Data Corporation, conducted a study on the value of Notes and concluded that it was "revolutionary." Even with conservative calculations, Polermo found that companies got an average 179% return on their Notes investment within three years after installation. In service businesses, she found, the rate of returns averaged 351%.[29]

Second, IBM went after Lotus because it was clearly the dominant player in a promising groupware market. Initially, there was some tension between IBM executives and Lotus CEO Jim Manzi. IBM software chief John Thompson looked at a company called Attachmate, which produced a Notes-like product called Open Mind. Ultimately, however, Thompson recommended to Gerstner that he go after Notes.[30] At the time of the acquisition, Lotus's share of the entire groupware market was approaching 70%,[31] with an installed base of 1.5 million users.[32]

Third, and perhaps most significant, IBM went after Lotus because it scared Bill Gates. It bothers Lou Gerstner to no end that people often refer to Microsoft as the world's largest software maker. In fact, IBM sells twice as much software as Microsoft—$11 billion worth every year. Ask anyone who seems to control the future of software, however, and the answer is likely to be Microsoft. Jim Moore, a strategy consultant said in 1995, "In the Sixties and Seventies people talked about IBM not as a member of the industry but as the environment. Now Microsoft has become the environment."[33] Despite huge sales, two thirds of IBM's software sales are associated with running Big Blue's mainframe systems, a technology with thin margins and a dim future. Microsoft's Windows, on the other hand, is the operating system for more than 80% of the home computers in the United States, and Microsoft leads the pack in application software with Excel, Word, and PowerPoint.

Microsoft's dominance in the computing industry is not based on superior revenues. In fact, on the eve of the Lotus acquisition, IBM's annual revenues were more than 10 times that of Microsoft. In spite of this, Microsoft's market capitalization is roughly equal to that of IBM. As Jim Moore's comment bears out, Microsoft's products have become omnipresent and thus synonymous with the concept of desktop computing. Four of five computers ran Windows, a platform from which Microsoft launched (and continues to launch) its attacks on software competitors.

In the summer of 1995, however, it became apparent that the next wave in the evolution of computing would not take place on the desktop. It would take place on the network, and Lotus Development, a company battle-scarred from past competition with Microsoft (its Lotus 1-2-3 was the winning spreadsheet program that helped popularize PCs in the 1980s), was already leading the pack of contenders for Microsoft's mantle in the world of networked software. IBM saw in Lotus the only way to take from Microsoft that elusive prominent spot on the consumer's desktop. Like Microsoft, Lotus Development had thousands of companies building software to complement its own—more than 6,700 in all. Even though Bill Gates belittled Notes as "basically just a bad operating system," one did get the sense that the mighty Microsoft saw a threat in Notes. By the end of 1994, it had yet to deliver on its answer to Notes—a groupware equivalent called Exchange—and even its executive in charge of business systems, Jim Allchin, admitted that Exchange could not match Notes's performance.[34] This was the opportunity IBM saw in Lotus.

Unfortunately, to turn promise into profit, IBM would have to overcome its own history of poor marketing of PC software.

- ▶ After spending $2 billion developing and marketing its OS/2 operating system, launched in 1988, IBM has made but the smallest dent in Microsoft's dominance in the PC OS market.[35]
- ▶ IBM's Prodigy online service continues to be dwarfed by competitors America Online, CompuServe, and, while it lasted, Microsoft Network.[36]
- ▶ IBM sought to capture a slice of the lucrative Edutainment software market in 1996, by producing a game to accompany the release of Disney's *Jungle Book* movie. By the time the software hit the market, the movie had been playing for more than 6 months.[37]

Of all IBM's acquisition blunders, none was more prominent in public memory than IBM's 1984 purchase of the Silicon Valley firm, Rolm Corporation. That acquisition paralleled the Lotus purchase exactly. Rolm was the market leader in what was considered a "sure-bet" technology for the future: private branch exchanges (PBXs), telephone switching devices that could combine the transmission of data and voice over a single system. As was also the case with the Lotus deal, IBM saw great promise in the future of this technology but acknowledged it did not have the expertise or time to bring it to market. Most significantly, Rolm, a Silicon Valley-based company, had a culture distinctly different from the button-down style at IBM. This is where the similarities of the acquisition of Rolm and Lotus end. Within four years, IBM lost $300 million on the deal, as PBX technology got passed over by local area networks. More fundamentally, however, the problem with the IBM and Rolm union was based on culture. When Armonk met the Valley it turned out that white-shirted engineers and sandaled whiz kids did not coexist well. IBM sold off most of Rolm in 1988 to German communications giant, Siemens, and got rid of the rest by 1992. Three years later, and with a new chief at the helm, IBM's June 1995 acquisition of Lotus would test the efficacy of IBM's corporate memory. Days after the deal was announced, Aberdeen Group analyst Bob Sakekeeny warned, "Lotus's wealth is in the brains of its workers, and if they walk it doesn't matter what's left."[38]

If IBM's exponential markup on the value of Lotus Development was not enough to indicate hidden value, then its actions after the acquisition proved that Big Blue would do everything it could to safeguard the real value in its prize: Lotus's knowledge. Even before the sale, some key developers had left the company to start their own ventures, in effect taking their precious brains with them. Eric Hahn, for example, was the general manager of the division that launched cc:Mail, Lotus's best-selling e-mail program. He left Lotus before the IBM purchase to start Collabra Software in Mountain View, California. Just two months after IBM acquired Lotus, Netscape Communications purchased Hahn's company in an effort to go head-to-head with IBM for a share of the groupware market.

With lessons learned from the Rolm fiasco and quite familiar with the transience typical of the software industry, IBM closed the Lotus deal prepared to do whatever it took to protect its investment. Big Blue was not interested in Lotus's management talent, as evident by its unwillingness to give Lotus CEO Jim Manzi the hefty corporate responsibilities he wanted at IBM. (Manzi left within 60 days after the deal was sealed.)[39] What IBM wanted, quite literally, was Ray Ozzie's head.

It took Ray Ozzie 10 years and $500 million to build Notes. In 1981, Ozzie was 25 years old and a student at the University of Illinois. He got the idea for Notes when he left the university and lost his access to an Internet-like environment called Plato, a network of universities on which people traded e-mail and held online discussions. He decided to create software that would emulate the sense of community he had experienced using Plato. At the time, few people saw computers as anything but powerful calculators and word processors. Ozzie foresaw the day when networks of computers would unite people. Most venture capitalists passed on funding the development because it was too radical. Finally, in 1984, Mitch Kapor gave Ozzie some start-up funds. Ozzie moved his development team into a farmhouse in Littleton, Massachusetts, and spent the next five years developing Notes. Not until 1989, when there were enough PCs to form a real demand for network software, did Ozzie put the product on the market. At the heart of Notes's innovation is a procedure Ozzie called *replication*—a procedure some say made machines "telepathic." Essentially, replication enables one computer to know what each of the others in a network knows, making global collaboration possible. That one feature, replication, is what took Ozzie so long to perfect, and it represents the edge Lotus had over any company that purported to make groupware, Microsoft included. Asked whether he worried about Microsoft's Exchange program, Ozzie replied in 1994, "You won't hear me get defensive about Exchange, because I know from personal experience how difficult it is to do what we've done."[40]

For all the promise of the groupware market, IBM's purchase of Lotus came down to two words that Ozzie could say with confidence: I know. And if he knew how to innovate 10 years before, he would know how to innovate 10 years hence, extending IBM's dominance in this market. So after the acquisition, IBM showed through a series of symbolic actions that it had learned from the Rolm fiasco. It did whatever it could to ensure that Ozzie's understanding and all other stores of knowledge at Lotus would continue to grow unfettered.

Just after the purchase, Scott McCreedy, an industry analyst with International Data Group, foretold the moral of this story. "As much as Notes is a great product, and cc:Mail has a bright future, I'd be looking to use Lotus more than anything as a cultural model. That would be worth a couple of billion to IBM. Lotus is the culture you need to develop great software."[41] As will be discussed in later chapters, culture is one of the most powerful stores of knowledge in a corporation. By nurturing the culture that made Lotus successfully thrive, IBM ensured the growth of its knowledge investment.

The management and programmers at Lotus had reason to fear the effects of coming into Big Blue's fold. They initially worried that the giant corporation's conservative management approach and slow decision making would quash the fast-paced entrepreneurial style prevalent at Lotus. In fact, this turned out not to be the case. In one action after another, IBM showed that it really was not interested in absorbing Lotus, soul and all. The first sign of this came after Manzi's resignation. Top management at Lotus worried that IBM would appoint a chairman from within its own ranks. But 24 hours after the fact, IBM named Jefferey Papows and Michael Zisman to share the office of the president. The two men, both top managers at Lotus, felt the gesture was symbolic and extremely important to the future of the company. Said Papows, "They announced it publicly, before the employees had time to ponder, 'Oh my god, what happens now?' "42

That was the first in a series of actions that confirmed IBM's commitment to allowing Lotus's culture to flourish within its new home. Soon after the merger, Zisman and Papows brought a radical proposal to Gerstner and Thompson, IBM head of software. As a preemptive strike to Microsoft's release of Exchange, they wanted to cut the price on Notes in half. After just one hour of discussion, Gerstner and Thompson ceded, "If you feel real strongly about it—we've got to bet on your understanding of the marketplace—do what you need to do." Considering IBM's reputation for legendary bureaucracy and analysis paralysis, the quick decision impressed the new presidents immensely and had a powerful effect among Lotus employees. Said Papows, "That kind of hallway rumor whips through this organization faster than our e-mail."42 Now feeling more confident with its new owner, Lotus again brought forward a bold proposal typical of an entrepreneurial company. It wanted to increase its advertising budget by 40% to $200 million. IBM agreed, but when Notes commercials began to appear, they didn't have the look of IBM. They were edgy—like Lotus was. Perhaps most significant of all its initiatives, IBM put stock programs in place to "re-create that dream factor" for Lotus employees. As part of the buyout, thousands of Lotus employees who had stock options were paid off in full. Making that dream come true seemed to foretell a massive exodus of key programmers after the purchase. Lotus executives were successful in persuading their new bosses of the importance of continuing the incentives. The new stock options, tied to IBM performance, did not excite many Lotus employees at first. But since then, the stock has doubled, driving the Lotus employee turnover rate down to 6%, half what it was before the IBM purchase and 60% lower than the industry norm. Finally, Lotus discovered that there were some pretty strong advantages to being allied with IBM. Gerstner himself went on the road to sell Notes to the CEOs of the *Fortune* 500, closing sales with U.S. West, Chrysler, Coca-Cola, Mobil, and Prudential.43

IBM's investment in knowledge has paid off in full. Notes is still the industry leader in groupware and is expanding. By the end of 1997, Lotus had 18 million Notes users, up from 9.5 million in 1996 and 4.5 million in 1995. It continues to dominate the groupware market with three times the installed base of its closest competitor, Microsoft Exchange. The company has added 1,000 jobs a year for the past two years and began a $30 million engineering lab in Westford, Massachusetts. Although IBM does not report Notes sales separately, Merrill Lynch analyst Bruce Smith estimated in July 1997 that sales were approaching $1 billion. Notes has become a welcome complement to IBM's products and services. For every dollar of Notes sold, IBM brings in an additional four in consulting fees and hardware sales.[44]

Of course, software is the prototypical knowledge industry, so this example really relates only to like industries, right? Wrong. Knowledge, in the form of relationships, know-how, and experience, has become an asset that corporations will fight for to the end.

It is difficult to imagine how thieves might steal knowledge as they would a valuable piece of machinery, until one considers just how pervasive knowledge can be to individuals of great importance to an organization. Knowledge, as valuable to a corporation as any tangible assets—such as a powerful laser, mainframe computer, or state-of-the art manufacturing facility—has increasingly come under the protection of the law. Written into law in 1996, the Economic Espionage Act (EEA) defines "trade secret" as most define knowledge:

> All forms and types of financial, business, scientific, technical, economic, or engineering information, including patterns, plans, compilations, program devices, formulas, designs, prototypes, methods, techniques, processes, procedures, programs, or codes, whether tangible or intangible, and whether or not stored, compiled, or memorialized physically, electronically, graphically, photographically, or in writing if: (A) the owner thereof has taken reasonable measures to keep such information secret; and (B) the information derives independent economic value, actual or potential, from not being generally known to, and not being readily ascertainable through proper means by, the public.[45]

In case after case, legal battles among companies confirm that they value knowledge as an integral corporate asset and will fight to the bitter end if they feel they have been robbed.

One of the most celebrated cases in recent history concerned José Ignacio Lopez de Arriortua, a Spanish national and vice president for General Motors. In 1993, Lopez left GM to accept the number-two spot at Volkswagen. His brilliant career ended abruptly, however, when German officials discovered that Lopez had left GM with confidential documents, including price lists for car parts and the plans for an experimental factory. Volkswagen, apparently unaware of Lopez's actions, and embarrassed by the incident, paid GM $100 million in cash and agreed to purchase $1 billion in parts over seven years to settle civil disputes.[46]

Dow embarrassed itself by suing General Electric for allegedly stealing its trade secrets for producing plastic instrument panels for cars. By hiring away 14 of its top engineers, said Dow, GE intended to set up a "mini-Dow within GE." The crux of Dow's case lay in evidence that one of the engineers had in his possession marketing plans that he could have gotten only while working at Dow. In fact, this was the case, but he had acquired the information from a public presentation made by GE officials.

In one particularly unfortunate case, an executive at Campbell's found out that the knowledge in his head belonged to the company. Daniel J. O'Neill was heading Campbell's U.S. soup operations when Heinz offered him a job running all of its North American operations and parts of South America, too. O'Neill jumped at the opportunity, quickly giving notice at Campbell's. At that point, the soup giant reminded O'Neill that he was bound by a noncompete agreement that barred him from working for Heinz. O'Neill knew too much about the soup operations, went Campbell's reasoning. O'Neill agreed that his knowledge would put Heinz at an unfair advantage and proposed that he redefine his job so that no soup duties were involved. That was not good enough for Campbell's, which contended that because O'Neill had attended board meetings and had access to top executives, he knew too much about the general strategy of the entire company. Following much negotiation, the two companies worked out a compromise. After a nine-month period of inactivity (during which his knowledge of Campbell's activities would be presumed to have gone stale), O'Neill would be allowed to work in those divisions of Heinz that were not in direct competition with Campbell's. He couldn't be the head of North America or of South America or of beans, mustard, pickles, or soups; O'Neill was limited to heading just two brands. His knowledge was considered so dangerous he was banished to dog food and tuna.[47]

If the trends of intellectual capital protection and theft are any indication, the value of knowledge has been growing exponentially for the past 20 years. Consider the following:

- ▶ Between 1983 and 1989, Congress passed 14 laws to protect a company's intellectual property.
- ▶ The number of lawsuits over intellectual property increased by nearly two thirds between 1980 and 1988.[48]
- ▶ "The American Society for Industrial Security reports that electronic security breaches rose from fewer than 1 every three months before 1980 to more than 30 per month in 1995."
- ▶ According to Management Analytics, an Ohio information security firm, computer crime accounts for an estimated $10 billion of losses every year.[49]
- ▶ FBI Director Louis Freeh estimates that $24 billion in proprietary information is stolen every year by as many as 23 foreign countries.[50]

KNOWLEDGE AS A COMPETITIVE ADVANTAGE

Recall the story of Japan's successful challenge to the U.S. automobile industry, for it vividly illustrates the power of knowledge as a competitive advantage. At the end of World War II, Japan was in ruins.[51] Yet out of this rubble rose a Japanese manufacturing juggernaut, the first country to unseat the dominance of Detroit's Big Three. Contrary to popular belief, the Japanese did not beat the United States through superior innovation or technology. Rather, the Japanese won the car war through superior management technique—that is, better developed knowledge.

Ironically, the same management techniques that Japan used to lead the world in manufacturing were invented in the United States by men like W. Edwards Demming and Joseph Juran. German economist Kurt Singer noted in the 1950s,

> They [the Japanese] invent few things, receive passionately, and excel in the art of adapting, adjusting, fitting. They are exceptionally shrewd in sifting and excluding. What they have chosen to undertake is often reduced in scale or scope but within these limits is carried to perfection.[52]

In the 1950s, when Kurt Singer wrote these words, the Japanese corporations were in the midst of 2,000 technology transfer arrangements with U.S. and European firms. Even the concepts of zero defect and total quality management were American management inventions, adapted to Japanese needs. Lean manufacturing provides a perfect example of the Japanese way.

Taichi Ohno had a goal for Toyota Motor Company in 1947. He wanted to eliminate all waste and perfect quality in the manufacturing process. Ohno's production technique defied the intuitive logic of the time. Efficiency, he believed, could be achieved through short runs of a variety of products. To realize such gains, workers would need quick access to a variety of tools. Ohno overcame these early challenges by keeping the worker's tools on the factory floor rather than in centralized bins. His tinkering yielded fantastic results; by 1960, the time it took to change a tool dropped from up to 3 hours to less than 3 minutes. This hurdle cleared, Ohno's plants were capable of handling the diverse product manufacturing he had originally envisioned. To do so, however, required a change not just in the technique of the workers but in the systems of the company's suppliers as well. Faced with this problem, Ohno developed the Kanban system. Ohno described the origin of his system:

> *Kanban* [is] an idea I got from American supermarkets. . . . In 1956, I toured U.S. production plants at General Motors, Ford and other machinery companies. But my strongest impression was the extent of the supermarket's prevalence in America. The reason for this was that by the late 1940s, at Toyota's machine shop that I managed, we were already studying the U.S. supermarket and applying its methods to our work. . . We made a connection between supermarkets and the just-in-time system. . .
>
> A supermarket is where a customer can get (1) what is needed, (2) at the time needed, (3) in the amount needed. . . . From the supermarket we got the idea of viewing the earlier processes in the production line as a kind of store. The later process (customer) goes to the earlier process (supermarket) to acquire the required parts (commodities) at the time and in the quantity needed. The earlier process immediately produces quantity just taken (restocking the shelves).[53]

American manufacturing systems of the 1950s are sarcastically remembered as "just in case," when compared with the Japanese Kanban or "just-in-time" system. As opposed to the American way, which kept extra parts and inventory on hand in the event that they would be needed, Kanban streamlined the production process to include only that which was necessary. Basically, it works this way: A lot of parts move down the assembly line with a Kanban card attached to it. When workers need more parts, they remove the card and send it upstream to a worker who produces the needed parts. The relationship works in the same way with suppliers outside Toyota, many of whom are located close to the plant. The Kanban card acts as a purchase order and as a bill from the supplier. The power of Kanban is its simplicity.

Ohno's reliance on developing the best way to manufacture cars was an investment in knowledge. His systems relied less on technology or economic power, the roots of American industrial dominance, than on a fundamental relationship between the worker, the manager, and the company.

> At the core of the [lean manufacturing] were two premises. . . . The first was that the average worker is motivated by the desire to do a job that enhances his sense of self-worth and that earns the respect of other workers. The second premise was that the worker is inspired by an employer who places value in the worker's input. Under the system in Japan, every worker is encouraged to think—to use brainpower to find ways of improving products and processes and eliminating wastes—and is rewarded for improvements.[54]

Compare this with a description of management at a General Motors plant.

> The workers wanted to do their jobs well, wanted to be competitive, but all too often they were fighting against unbeatable odds to get the job done. Every problem became a confrontation; since there was a basic mistrust between labor and management, it was hard to establish a cooperative environment where problems could be solved. . . . Workers operated in a vacuum; they did the job they were told to do without relating it to the final outcome. . . . [It] was an environment where workers were not partners in the task of building cars. Often they did not know how their jobs related to the total picture. Not knowing, there was no incentive to strive for quality—what did quality even mean as it related to a bracket whose function you did not understand? Workers were held accountable through a system of intimidation: Do your job and your supervisor won't yell at you.[55]

KNOWLEDGE AS A MANAGER OF CHANGE

Between 1990 and 1993, Microsoft tripled its sales to $3.8 billion and practically tripled its employee count to 14,000. At roughly the same time, between 1991 and 1994, another entity tripled in size: the Internet. The number of commercial sites on the World Wide Web grew from 9,000 to 21,700. In the fall of 1995, 20 million people were surfing the Net, and they weren't using any of Bill Gates's software to do it. The story of how Microsoft finally took notice of the market opportunity they were missing on the Internet and realigned themselves to vie for dominance shows how knowledge may act as an effective pivot point for companies in the midst of great change.

In February 1994, Steven Sinofsky, Bill Gates's technical assistant, returned to his Alma Mater, Cornell University, on a recruiting trip. That's where Microsoft's Internet strategy began, on a snowy campus in Ithaca, New York, when Sinofsky saw students logging onto university computers to check e-mail and download course materials. He sent an e-mail to Gates and the senior technical staff with the subject heading, "Cornell is WIRED!" The response from Redmond lacked luster. A staff member directed Sinofsky to a programmer in networking, J. Allard, the only employee at Microsoft at the time with the word *Internet* on his business card.

Allard had run an unsanctioned project early in 1993, directed to developing Microsoft's first Internet file server. He made it to distribute solutions to bugs in Microsoft programs and, for a while, it was one of the top 10 most visited sites on the Internet. Despite his frequent e-mails and memos to upper management, no one took notice of Allard's call to arms—that is, until Sinofsky weighed in. In the spring of 1994, Gates held a retreat at the Shumway Mansion in nearby Kirkland, Washington, to discuss Internet strategy. Coming out of the retreat and after a subsequent think week (Gates's equivalent of a vacation during which he goes into isolation with stacks of technology briefings, magazines, and industry studies), Gates released a memo on March 16 expressing his will to make Microsoft a "leader in Internet support." It was a first step, but as board member David F. Marquart recalls, a measured one. "His view was the Internet was free. There's no money to be made there. Why is that an interesting business?" says Marquart, a Silicon Valley investor.

Even if Microsoft was not convinced, several companies were perfectly willing to jump at the Internet opportunity. The day before the retreat at the Shumway Mansion, on March 4, 1994, a start-up company called Netscape Communications (originally called Mosaic) was founded. A little more than a year later, Netscape held a hugely successful IPO (initial public offering), with shares jumping up to 75 on the first day before closing at 58. As Microsoft mulled over what to do, Netscape's browser had become for the Internet what Windows was for the desktop. By this time, Gates was no longer tentative. In May 1995, he issued a memo titled "The Internet Tidal Wave," in which he assured the company, "I have gone through several stages of increasing my views of its [the Internet's] importance. Now, I assign the Internet the highest level."[56] The Internet was, Gates said, "the single most important innovation in computing" since the IBM PC. Gates sounded the alarm. What remained to be seen was whether the company could reverse its previous ambivalence toward the Internet. Already, some observers were questioning Microsoft's long-term vision. On November 16, 1995, for example, Goldman Sachs & Company removed Microsoft stock from its "recommended for purchase" list because of concerns about Internet strategy.

On December 7, 1995, Bill Gates held an all-day press conference to convince the world that Microsoft viewed the Internet as its most important focus. Although products would not arrive for many months, Microsoft did begin a turnaround in orientation that was described by former Disney studio chief Jefferey Katzenberg as "breathtaking."

- ▶ The company's Internet Platform & Tools Division grew from 800 to 2,500 workers, more than the total of Netscape, Yahoo, and the next five largest start-ups combined.
- ▶ Gates launched Microsoft into content development creating *Slate,* an on-line magazine, and MSNBC, a 24-hour television channel/Internet news site.
- ▶ Microsoft licensed Sun Microsystems's Java programming language, a versatile and powerful technology for Internet development.
- ▶ America Online (AOL) made Microsoft's Internet Explorer the primary web browser for its customers' desktops.
- ▶ On February 12, 1996, Microsoft released the Internet Information Server for free, a direct challenge to Netscape's hegemony in web servers.

Since the day Microsoft reoriented itself toward the Internet, as Gates said, there is "not one product we have where [the Internet] is not at the center."[56] Still, it is one thing for the senior executives to say so and quite another for 20,000 employees to fall in line. That is exactly what happened, however, and it is worthwhile to take a look at what enabled Microsoft to turn itself around so quickly.

Oh, our eyes have seen the glory of the coming of the Net,
We are ramping up our market share, objectives will be met.
Soon our browser will be everywhere, you ain't seen nothin'
  yet
We embrace and we extend!

Our competitors were laughing, said our network was a fake.
Saw the Internet economy as simply theirs to take.
They'll regret the fateful day
The sleeping giant did awake
We embrace and we extend!

Glory, glory to the vision,
Though Netscape treats us with derision,
But soon will come the hour
When their stock price starts to sour,
We embrace and we extend!

Battle Hymn of the Reorg—Anonymous Microsoft
employee in MicroNews, the in-house newsletter[57]

There is a critical element that will turn an executive's directive into a platitude if it is missing or into a holy war if it is present: culture. Infused with the right experience and values (both elements of knowledge), culture can act as a call to arms for a company. This was the case with Microsoft. Paul Marizt, the Microsoft vice president who organized the December 7 Internet summit, said, "The thing that really motivates us is paranoia and competition." Throughout the reorganization, Microsoft employees were given plenty of both. In 1995 and 1996, memos were circulated throughout the company saying of Netscape,

> ▷ "This is not about browsers. Our competitors are trying to make an alternative platform to Windows. They are smart, aggressive and have a big lead. This is not Novell or IBM we are competing with."

▶ "Netscape/Java is using the browser to create a virtual operating system. Windows will become devalued, eventually replaceable."[58]

Strategy at Microsoft begins with Bill Gates, but management does its job to ensure that employees know their marching orders. The December 7 Internet Summit was broadcast throughout the Redmond campus via closed-circuit television. Speeches from the event were circulated, and later, videotape copies were sent to all employees. Said Chris Peters, a Microsoft vice president, "If the chairman says success is defined as that, you will get a lot of that!"[59]

Microsoft makes a particularly appropriate example for this book, because it stands in such stark comparison with the modes of the classic corporation. Whereas the classic corporation sought men and women of mediocre intelligence to run its machines and offices, Microsoft wants only the "supersmart" within its ranks. Gates is blunt on this point: "There is no way of getting around the fact that, in terms of IQ, you've got to be very elitist in picking people who deserve to write software."[60] Microsoft receives more than 120,000 resumes every year from which it picks "others among the smartest."[61] The rationale for picking only the best is not exactly what one might expect. Certainly, it takes a brilliant mind to program software. But the mind Microsoft wants is one well suited to the nature of this industry. Gates told his software developers in 1993, "There's not a single line of code here today that will have value in, say, four or five years."[62] Therefore, employees must have the ability to quickly reorient their thinking, acquire new skills, and excel in their new capacity—exactly what was expected of them when Microsoft embraced the Internet opportunity.

The leaps these companies have made are leaps of the mind. Through knowledge, a company may re-create itself to excel in its marketplace. We call such companies knowledge organizations.

PART

III

THE FUTURE AS EPILOGUE

CHARTING THE KNOWLEDGE PATH
A Survey of America's Largest Companies

The improvement of the understanding is for two ends; first, our own increase of knowledge; secondly, to enable us to deliver that knowledge to others.

—John Locke

n January 1998, the Annenberg Center for Communication at the University of Southern California released its study, "Knowledge Organizations: Their Emergence and Impact on Corporate Education and Training." (The authors were the principal investigators of the research.) The results of that study, which was undertaken with Chicago-based market researcher OmniTech Consulting Group, indicate that the notion of a knowledge organization is just beginning to take hold in American corporations.

This chapter will focus on our major research findings. Although presenting such information may seem to threaten the long-term vitality of this work, it is a necessary step. Research must set a point in time and in the evolution of a concept so that future progress may be tracked. We hope that our research combined with the practical advice that follows will effectively move the pursuit of the knowledge organization forward.

KNOWLEDGE ORGANIZATION: WHAT DOES IT MEAN?

The term *knowledge organization* meant different things to different respondents, yet there are some areas of consensus (see Figure 7.1). Of respondents, 48% believe that to be a knowledge organization, there must be continuous learning, ongoing improvement, and evolution. The company learns from experiences and mistakes and unlearns things that are not working. These respondents all agree on one thing: Learning never stops. It is a lifelong process that helps a company continually adapt in order to remain strategically competitive in its marketplace. Commentary on the term was telling:

▶ "A culture where no one has made it so much that they know everything they need to know." (Finance/Insurance)
▶ "An organization that learns from mistakes. Risk taking is acceptable, and open communication and analysis is encouraged. There is company growth because of this." (Manufacturing)
▶ "An organization that is always searching for improved ways of disseminating and applying knowledge." (Finance/Insurance)
▶ "The idea of a continuous learning environment. The broad view includes experience, colleague interaction, and transmission to other projects." (Technology/Information Systems [IS])
▶ "Continually taking pieces of knowledge and changes into account to stay ahead of the competition and looking at where your organization can go." (Retail/Wholesale)

One quarter (25%) of respondents see a knowledge organization as a place in which knowledge is shared. There is information exchange across all levels of an organization. Ideas and best practices are shared globally. The logic behind gathering and sharing best-practice informa-

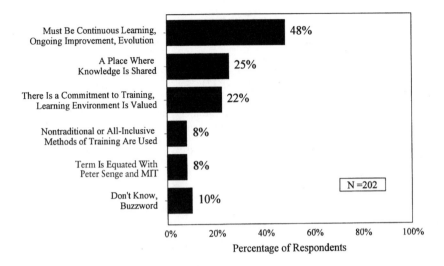

Figure 7.1. Knowledge Organization Definitions

tion is that once captured, practices can be widely understood and successfully reused.

▶ "Free-flowing learning that can be spontaneous or semistructured. Valuing it, sharing it, and integrating it within a company." (Retail/Wholesale)

▶ "A systems approach to transfer learning and leverage learning across the whole company." (Finance/Insurance)

▶ "A learning organization shares best practices at all levels. There is continual focus on improving and sharing best practices at a global level." (Manufacturing)

▶ "A learning organization is a company that knows some of its best information resources are renewable if captured." (Finance/Insurance)

Of respondents, 22% see the organization as playing an integral role in the facilitation of the knowledge organization concept. They believe that in a true knowledge organization there is a commitment to training and that value is placed on the learning environment. These respondents feel that the organization must take responsibility for learning and provide the tools, support, and resources to foster training and education. Some respondents describe this as a financial commitment; others describe it as a training ground with a specific structure.

> ▷ "Empowering the individual with professional and personal development and providing them with the tools in order to do that." (Transportation)
> ▷ "A knowledge organization puts financial commitment and human resource commitment behind the development of employees." (Services)
> ▷ "The company embraces employee and corporate development in a proactive manner using cutting-edge learning methods in support of employee growth." (Finance/Insurance)
> ▷ "In a learning organization, high value is given to the ongoing education of top management as well as lower echelons." (Manufacturing)

Other meanings were also cited, although heard less often. Of respondents, 8% think a knowledge organization implies nontraditional or all-inclusive methods of learning. Employees are challenged to stay current and keep up with the trends by using different forms of media and taking advantage of coaching and mentoring rather than traditional educational methods.

> ▷ "A knowledge organization looks at moving away from traditional education to coworker coaching, mentoring learning, and learning logs for learning technology." (Services)
> ▷ "To be a knowledge organization means to be on the cutting edge, moving toward different media." (Finance/Insurance)
> ▷ "In a knowledge organization, there are a variety of ways to get information. There is persistent and consistent learning throughout one's career. Learning occurs on the job." (Retail/Wholesale)

An additional 8% of respondents equate the term *knowledge organization* with Peter Senge and the Massachusetts Institute of Technology. Respondents point out different aspects of Mr. Senge's ideas. Some equate the term with information sharing, others stress unlearning of unsuccessful practices, and others focus on the strategic value of learning for continuous improvement.

> ▷ "The five parameters of Mr. Senge. An organization that continuously improves and uses learning as a strategic weapon." (Utilities)

▶ "The term is framed in Peter Senge's model. There is an unlearning of things that aren't working." (Retail/Wholesale)

▶ "Peter Senge's book *The Fifth Discipline.* An organization that relies on the sharing of information and values, and needs the incoming of new information." (Retail/Wholesale)

There is a small group of respondents for whom the term *knowledge organization* means little. Of respondents, 10% do not know what a knowledge organization is or feel that there is no clear definition of it. Several of these respondents indicate that it is just a buzzword.

The knowledge organization concept means different things to different people. But nearly half of respondents believe a knowledge organization involves continuous learning, ongoing improvement, and evolution. To move forward with this discussion, we have narrowed our definition of a knowledge organization to three criteria. The rationale for choosing each of these will be discussed in following sections. A knowledge organization is one that

1. values and acknowledges knowledge as its primary competitive advantage,
2. encourages continual learning, and
3. actively manages its intellectual capital.

We understand that there are likely many more aspects of a company that make it knowledge intensive—such as reasoned use of information systems or acceptance of change. The intent of this chapter, however, is to provide corporations with "markers" by which to judge their proximity to a true knowledge organization. It is therefore necessary to focus on criteria that are uniformly recognized and practiced in corporations.

Valuing Knowledge as a Primary Competitive Advantage

Not enough can be said about the importance of the right mental model when implementing knowledge systems. Among her "Characteristics of Continuously Renewing Organizations," Harvard's Dorothy Leonard-Barton lists an enthusiasm for knowledge as the first criterion. Managers must recognize and respect the knowledge inherent in employees and throughout the organization.

The managers respect and encourage the accumulation of knowledge as a legitimate undertaking and one for which they are responsible. This love of learning is woven throughout the organization, whether the activity be problem solving across internal boundaries, creating knowledge through experimentation, importing it from the outside, or transferring it to other sites and nations.[1]

Leonard-Barton goes so far as to say that for some companies, the building of knowledge is not simply good business sense but also fun. For example, Chaparral Steel, one of the world's top minimills, has embraced an attitude of constantly advancing knowledge. According to Production Manager Paul Wilson,

In other companies, the word is, Don't Rock the boat. Here we rock the hell out of the boat. We don't know the factory's limits. We want it to change, to evolve. . . . You don't have to have credit for particular ideas to be thought good at your job. Lots of innovations take more than one good idea. They go through a gestation period, and lots of people figure out how to make sense of it. The point is to focus on the good of the whole. That's why we don't have suggestion boxes, where you hide ideas so someone else won't steal them.[2]

The element of group experimentation and knowledge building prevalent at Chaparral Steel, a company of 1,000 employees, is also strongly present at America's largest companies. (Respondents were asked to rate the degree to which they agree or disagree with the following and other statements on a scale of 1 to 4, in which 1 is *do not agree at all* and 4 is *completely agree.*)

> ▶ *In my company, top-level management believes training and education contribute to the organization's financial success.*

Nearly three quarters (72%) of all respondents agree with this statement, assigning ratings of 3 or 4. Across all respondents, 32% completely agree. There is a relationship between the existence of a corporate university and agreement levels as well as the scope of training provided and the extent to which respondents are in accordance with this statement.

Not surprisingly, significantly more respondents in companies with a corporate university than those without one agree completely with this statement. Whereas 42% of corporate university respondents assign ratings of 4, only 24% of respondents without a corporate university give this rating. If top management believes training and education contribute to the organization's financial success, it follows that they will be more willing to spend the time and money to establish and run a corporate university.

The correlation between the level of agreement with this statement and the scope of training provided by a company is also not surprising. More respondents who provide training on an international basis give ratings of 4, indicating that they agree completely. Whereas 48% of international trainers give ratings of 4, only 24% of national trainers and 25% of regional trainers do the same.[3]

Interestingly, we found that very few companies consider themselves to be knowledge or learning organizations. Looking across all respondents, the majority of respondents do not consider their companies knowledge organizations. Using a 4-point scale in which 1 is *not at all* and 4 is *completely,* 67% of respondents rate their companies a 1 or 2. The mean score across all respondents is 2.2.

Certain types of respondents consider their companies to be closer than others to a true knowledge organization. Respondents who provide training internationally view their companies as more of a knowledge organization than do respondents who provide training regionally or nationally. Approximately half (49%) of international trainers rate their companies a 3 or 4 on the knowledge organization scale compared with 26% of regional trainers and 24% of national trainers.

Respondents who currently do not consider their companies to be knowledge organizations (those respondents giving ratings of a 1 or 2) were asked if they feel their companies are moving toward becoming this type of organization. Of the 134 respondents who do not currently view their companies on the forefront of knowledge, the large majority (78%) answered "yes," they feel their companies are becoming knowledge organizations.

KNOWLEDGE ORGANIZATIONS AND CONTINUAL LEARNING

The age-old concept of learning—that is, the one-way passage of knowledge from an expert to a student—is rapidly being replaced by a new learning paradigm. Learning, as Senge would say, is now the process by which corporations check their visions against reality. Learning systems are thus geared to making employees more attuned to changes in their internal and external business environments. Leonard-Barton has said that companies may learn by creating "porous boundaries."

> Managers need to expose their companies to a bombardment of new ideas from outside in order to challenge core rigidities, encourage inventive serendipity, and check technological trajectories for vector and speed versus competitors. An amazing amount of knowledge exists in the public domain. If a company has antennae out into the world community and encourages employees to collect and disseminate that information internally, that knowledge is a treasure trove.[4]

Our research indicates that corporate America perceives a knowledge imperative in today's economy and is adapting its notions of learning to keep ahead of change. The majority of respondents (62%) believe the knowledge organization concept has had an impact on training and development at their companies. When these respondents were asked the question, "How has the knowledge organization concept affected training and development at your company?" several explanations were given. Not surprisingly, the explanations given are implementations of the very ideas conveyed in the definition of a knowledge organization.

For example, 22% of the respondents who believe the concept has had an impact explain that a learning environment has been created, fostering continuous learning. This environment promotes shared knowledge and best practices. A few of these respondents mention a switch from more traditional learning and training to just-in-time training. Several of these respondents emphasize that learning occurs more spontaneously. Individuals become more self-reliant and have some responsibility for their own learning, with the help of resources supplied by the company.

> ▶ "There has been a conceptual leap from training and development to learning. Our structure is decentralized with each area providing learning. Employees are more self-reliant. They will be searching out learning, and it is the corporation's responsibility to have that learning available." (Utilities)

- ▶ "We're encouraging managers not to see traditional methods of training as the only interventions of choice. They are beginning to see that there are more opportunities for learning in less conventional ways, such as at the moment of need, on the job." (Manufacturing)
- ▶ "We're experiencing a switch from classroom training to just-in-time training. This helps our employees acquire skills immediately, and thereby, production is increased." (Manufacturing)
- ▶ "We are moving away from a training mentality to organizational development. We are moving toward an individualized pull strategy, developing individual abilities rather than a push strategy of training blocks of employees with a predetermined curriculum." (Finance/Insurance)

Of respondents perceiving an impact, 13% say there is more awareness and understanding of the knowledge organization concept across their organizations. This, in turn, brings an awareness and understanding of the need to implement this type of environment within their organizations. One respondent describes a heightened interest in training, which has accompanied awareness.

- ▶ "The concept has definitely piqued employee interest in training." (Manufacturing)
- ▶ "More senior managers understand the concept." (Finance/Insurance)
- ▶ "The heightened awareness of the need for it has probably expanded customer base." (Manufacturing)
- ▶ "People see learning as being a necessity rather than being an add-on part of the job." (Manufacturing)

An additional 13% state that a corporate university, a specialized department, or a structured training program has been established to further the knowledge organization concept within their organizations.

- ▶ "We've taken a really formal approach to training. We've put in place a much more structured program, and we've developed a stricter budget for training." (Manufacturing)
- ▶ "Change from training to having a corporate university with a curriculum for job progression." (Retail/Wholesale)
- ▶ "We've created an organized learning structure." (Services)
- ▶ "We are now trying to structure and standardize our training." (Transportation)

Another 13% cite that the knowledge organization concept has become a strategic initiative or corporate philosophy. The concept has gained management support and is often part of a company's value statement.

▶ "It has pushed learning and education into the forefront of our organization." (Utilities)

▶ "Our company is only one year old. It is part of our corporate value statement." (Manufacturing)

▶ "Having a knowledge organization as a major strategy is a tenet of policy of the worldwide supply chain, which employs three quarters of the company's personnel." (Manufacturing)

Of respondents perceiving an impact, 11% describe an increased commitment to training. Companies have added resources such as more staff or more money. Whether obtained from internal or external sources, training initiatives and programs have increased.

▶ "It has developed to a greater extent our own internal training. We have also started using and paying for outside source training." (Finance/Insurance)

▶ "Focus on the concept has affected our training budget and increased it." (Retail/Wholesale)

▶ "We have corporate training, and a training initiative." (Services)

Another 11% say the knowledge organization concept has refocused or redefined training and development. Companies are reorganizing training around the concept and changing the way training is delivered to and thought about by employees.

▶ "We have become much more focused on specific business needs." (Manufacturing)

▶ "It's part of a total reengineering effort wherein we are going from a traditional training department to a constancy to the company." (Finance/Insurance)

▶ "It has focused training and development, changing the way people think of training." (Manufacturing)

The concept of a knowledge organization has caused 10% of respondent companies to reassess or reevaluate their practices to ensure facilitation of the learning process. Specific actions taken include extended analyses, needs assessments, and feedback systems.

> ▶ "Primarily, we've done assessments of our needs and evaluated and restructured the curriculum so that it is aligned with the company's strategic business plans. The company's goals are built into the curriculum and drive the learning process." (Utilities)
> ▶ "Feedback systems are in place now." (Finance/Insurance)
> ▶ "We've undergone a one-year analysis of our company." (Services)

Of respondents who perceive an impact, 8% say that the knowledge organization concept has had an impact on the training curriculum. Several respondents are introducing new courses into their programs.

> ▶ "It impacts the types of curriculum being developed. Opportunities to learn are increasing." (Finance/Insurance)
> ▶ "We're developing a new series of courses for higher leadership. They're the next level of management courses." (Entertainment)

An additional 8% say supervisors, mentors, and peers are responsible for much of the training that was once handled through a centralized organization. Several describe the existence of supervisory or mentor-related training roles as opposed to traditional facilitator-led instruction.

> ▶ "We're looking at non-facilitator-led training and mentor-related programs." (Finance/Insurance)
> ▶ "Supervisors and peers provide sustained training." (Retail/Wholesale)

Figure 7.2 shows the impact of the knowledge organization concept on training and development.

KNOWLEDGE ORGANIZATIONS MANAGE THEIR INTELLECTUAL CAPITAL

As a starting point, we have defined the practice of managing intellectual capital as a three-part process:

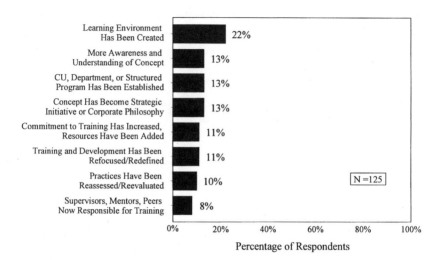

Figure 7.2. Concept Impacts on Training and Development
NOTE: All respondents state that the knowledge organization concept has had an impact on training and development. A variety of ways the concept has affected training and development are cited.

1. Knowledge generation

2. Knowledge measurement

3. Knowledge allocation

By implication, companies that do not make express efforts to manage their intellectual capital are not knowledge organizations, for their actions do not indicate that they place a premium on knowledge as an organizational asset.

Knowledge Generation

The challenge for corporations thus becomes constructing methods by which its most talented and experienced employees may describe what they know. This is the essence of knowledge generation: to turn tacit into explicit. Our research has indicated that companies are committed to capturing their knowledge, skills, best and worst practices—all forms of tacit intellectual capital—for the benefit of the organization.

▶ The majority of respondents (66%) say their organizations currently have programs or systems in place to capture knowledge, skills, and best or worst practices. Although the existence of knowledge-capturing programs and systems is fairly common among respondents, the types of knowledge-capturing programs or systems vary. When asked to describe their systems, respondents spoke of many kinds of programs. Judging from the diversity of the answers, it looks like companies have many options or ways to capture knowledge, skills, and best and worst practices.

▶ Of the respondents with systems, performance reviews or evaluations are the most frequently cited program (24%). These reviews may encompass skills inventories and assessments.

▶ The second most frequently cited program, mentioned by 19%, is benchmarking. Some companies do internal benchmarks. Others benchmark themselves against industry leaders. Benchmarking methods also vary; they include committees, studies, consortiums, and contacts. Regardless of the specific method, benchmarking is one way in which companies capture knowledge and best and worst practices.

▶ Seventeen percent say their companies have online systems, such as databases or Lotus Notes, in which best practices can be submitted and to which employees can refer.

▶ Of respondents with a system, 13% use employee and customer feedback to capture best and worst practices. Specific tools are surveys and focus groups.

▶ Eleven percent say their companies have a best-practice organization or quality assurance team that collects, evaluates, and shares best and worst practices.

▶ Of respondents with systems, 9% cite meetings, forums, conference calls, and study groups as ways to review and increase awareness of best and worst practices.

▶ An additional 9% explain that practices are documented or recorded in books, magazines, newsletters, or on videotapes and audiotapes so that employees can refer to them at any time.

Knowledge Measurement

Our research shows that intellectual capital accounting has not caught on in corporate America. A very small percentage of the population currently has a human capital accounting system.

- ▶ Only 15% of all companies have some system to quantify human capital. Human capital accounting systems are not more likely to be found in any one particular industry or company size, type, and so on.
- ▶ Of the 84% of respondents who do not currently have a human capital accounting system, only 24% say they will in the future. Human capital accounting does not appear to be a "must have" system for most respondents.
- ▶ Assuming that all respondents who currently have a system in place will also have a system in the future, only 35% of respondents will have some form of human capital accounting.

Knowledge Allocation

When Jack Welsh created the General Electric Work-Out in 1991, the company had 298,000 employees, more people than live in Tampa, Florida; St. Paul, Minnesota; or Newark, New Jersey. The company's sales growth, $3.8 billion, was greater than the total sales for all but 126 of the Fortune 500 industrial companies. General Electric manages more credit cards than American Express, refrigerates 36% of American's food, and entertains one in five families with its television sets. As *Fortune* magazine noted, "Calling General Electric just a company is like calling California just a state."[6] Welch wanted to run this company like a small business, extracting from its ranks the techniques that would make it number one or two in every one of its business enterprises. The Work-Outs were needed to trim organizational procedures of unnecessary bureaucracy. In a typical Work-Out, 40 to 100 employees, representing various levels and capabilities within a GE unit, will take a three-day retreat at a local hotel or conference center. Working as a facilitator, the unit chief helps the employees develop an agenda and then leaves for the next two days. During that time, the group lists complaints, debates solutions, and prepares presentations for the final day. In the final day of Work-Out, the employees make presentations to their supervisor with their specific recommendations on how to proceed. The supervisor may respond in one of three ways: yes, no, or decision postponed for a specified period of time. When Armand Lauzon, head of plant services at the GE Aircraft Engine factory in Lynn, Massachusetts, reentered the Work-Out room on the third day, he was presented with 108 proposals. And his employees strategically positioned his chair to force a decision. "I couldn't make eye contact with my boss without turning around, which would show everyone in the room that I was chickensh-t." Lauzon accepted 100 of the 108 proposals, including one for endorsing an employee-designed protective machine shield. The design, made by an hourly worker on the back of a brown paper lunch bag, saved the unit $80,000.[7]

GE's Work-Out represents a commitment to growing collective knowledge. We have found that companies are not only committed to this pursuit, they have the baseline level of respect among employees to make it a reality. When we asked the senior human resources executives to respond to the following statements, we found that a large portion of corporate America has the core values underlying a knowledge organization—trust, acceptance of failure, and high value placed on learning.

> ▶ *In my company, increasing the collective knowledge of the organization as a whole is more important than increasing the knowledge of individuals.*
>
> On the whole, respondents do not show strong agreement or disagreement with this statement. The majority (79%) fall in the middle of the scale, giving ratings of 2 or 3. There do not appear to be any differences in responses across different types of respondents.

> ▶ *My company has an atmosphere of trust and respect, where people listen to what others are saying.*
>
> Nearly three quarters of all respondents (71%) agree with this statement, giving ratings of 3 or 4. Only 4% indicate they do not agree at all that their companies have an atmosphere of trust and respect.
>
> Respondents in the retail/wholesale industry show higher agreement than manufacturing, utilities, and finance/insurance respondents. Of retail/wholesale respondents, 40% completely agree with this statement, whereas only 9% of manufacturing, 12% of utilities, and 11% of finance/insurance agree completely.

> ▶ *My company accepts failures, learns from them, and does not try to assess blame.*
>
> In general, there does not appear to be strong agreement or disagreement with this statement. The majority of all respondents (79%) give ratings of

2 or 3, but agreement levels are not equal among all types of respondents. Respondents in different industries have different levels of agreement. Retail/wholesale respondents show higher agreement than manufacturing, utilities, and finance/insurance respondents. Of respondents in the retail/ wholesale industry, 29% completely agree, compared with 8% of manufacturing respondents, 6% of utilities respondents, and 9% of finance/ insurance respondents.

DEGREES OF KNOWLEDGE ORGANIZATIONS

Companies have embraced the concept of a knowledge organization to varying degrees. For some, the term is merely a buzzword and has little meaning. For others, it is a concept that plays an integral part in a company's assessment of its value.

There are several dimensions to being a knowledge organization, and there are different degrees to which a company incorporates these dimensions into its day-to-day activities. To gain greater insight into the knowledge organization phenomenon, this study examined corporate atmospheres, employee attitudes, systems/processes, and current/future practices. Specifically, respondents' views of their companies' atmosphere and the attitude of leadership were assessed. Questions were asked regarding the existence of systems and processes to assess employee morale and to capture and disseminate knowledge. Finally, respondents were asked whether some form of human capital accounting is or will be in place at their companies.

Although very few respondents completely agree that their companies are knowledge organizations, some respondents appear closer than others to being a true knowledge organization. Based on responses to statements identified in Table 7.1, respondents were grouped into five tiers according to respondents' perceptions of themselves as knowledge organizations.

Based on both subjective and objective measures related to company atmosphere, attitudes, systems, and required training, a small percentage of respondents (14%) appear to be currently embracing the knowledge organization model, whereas the majority of respondent companies (57%) are far from being true knowledge organizations. Within the small percentage currently embracing the knowledge organization model, a select group (2%) seems to be embracing the concept to the fullest extent,

TABLE 7.1 Knowledge Organization Attitude Statements, by Tier[a]

	Tier 1 (Closest) N = 4		Tier 2 N = 25		Tier 3 N = 57		Tier 4 N = 69		Tier 5 (Farthest) N = 47	
	Mean	Top Box (%)	Mean	Top Box (%)	Mean	Top Box (%)	Mean	Top Box (%)	Mean	Top Box (%)
Extent to which company is considered a knowledge organization	3.3	25	3.2	28	2.6	4	2.0	0	1.6	0
Increasing collective knowledge more important than increasing individual knowledge	4.0	100	3.0	21	2.7	11	2.5	10	2.2	2
Company has atmosphere of trust and respect	3.5	50	3.4	40	3.0	25	2.8	10	2.5	6
Company accepts failures	3.3	25	3.3	40	2.7	18	2.5	4	2.2	9
Management believes training and education contribute to financial success	3.8	75	3.7	76	3.3	46	2.8	19	2.4	6

a. Statements rated on a 4-point scale. Top box indicates the percentage of respondents who gave the statement the highest possible rating.

modeling their internal practices and modifying their corporate atmosphere to be true knowledge organizations.

▶ *Tier 5 (47 respondents):* Tier 5 respondents do not consider their companies to be knowledge organizations. Of Tier 5 respondents, 44% consider their companies to be "not at all" a knowledge organization. No respondents in this group currently have a human capital accounting system. A very small percentage (approximately 14%) of Tier 5 respondents assess employee morale annually or have systems or programs in place to capture knowledge. Slightly more than one third (34%) require training on an annual basis. Coupled with their lack of systems and programs, Tier 5 respondents also do not view their companies as having an atmosphere indicative of a knowledge organization.

▶ *Tier 4 (69 respondents):* Tier 4 also includes respondents who do not consider their companies to be knowledge organizations; however, the majority (78%) rate themselves a 2 on a 4-point scale, whereas only 10% rate themselves a 1 or "not at all" as a knowledge organization. Like Tier 5 respondents, Tier 4 respondents do not believe their companies have an atmosphere that reflects a true knowledge organization. Yet three times as many Tier 4 respondents (39%) assess employee morale yearly compared with Tier 5 respondents (13%). In addition, the majority of Tier 4 respondents (68%) currently have programs or systems in place to capture knowledge and best practices.

▶ *Tier 3 (57 respondents):* No Tier 3 respondents consider their companies to be "not at all" knowledge organizations. Nearly half (48%) rate themselves a 3 on a 4-point knowledge organization scale, whereas the same percentage rate themselves a 2. Different from Tier 4, nearly half of Tier 3 respondents (46%) completely agree that their management believes training and education contribute to financial success. Eighty-eight percent have programs or systems in place to capture knowledge and best practices and approximately one in every four (24%) has a human capital accounting system.

▶ *Tier 2 (25 respondents):* Tier 2 respondents show nearly all aspects of being a knowledge organization. Sixty-four percent rate themselves a 3 on a 4-point knowledge organization scale, whereas an additional 28% rate themselves a 4. All currently have programs or systems in place to capture knowledge and best practices. The majority (84%) assess employee morale at least once a year. In addition, 40% of Tier 2 respondents completely agree that their companies have an atmosphere of trust and respect, and the same percentage (40%) completely agree that failures are accepted without blame assessment. Furthermore, three quarters (76%) completely agree that management believes training and education contribute to financial success; however, only three quarters (76%) require some sort of training yearly. Less than one third (32%) currently have a human capital accounting system in place.

▶ *Tier 1 (4 respondents):* Among all 202 respondents only 4 can be classified as Tier 1 companies. These four exemplar companies may be considered true knowledge organizations. All four annually assess employee morale, require yearly training, and have programs in place to capture knowledge and best practices. What separates this group from Tier 2 is that in addition to the above, all have a human capital accounting system. Tier 1 respondents currently consider their companies to be knowledge organizations, giving ratings of 3 or 4 on a 4-point scale. Tier 1 respondents also agree that their companies have the atmosphere of a knowledge organization.

It may be surprising that all four respondents in Tier 1 do not completely consider their companies to be knowledge organizations; however, respondents' definitions of a knowledge organization lend credence to this observation. Many respondents believe that a knowledge organization is one in which there is continual, ongoing learning and growth. In the spirit of this definition, a true knowledge organization is continually striving and evolving. Companies coming closest to fully embracing this concept might rate themselves a 3, feeling there is always more they can do to be a true knowledge organization.

TIER 1: FOUR DISTINCT EXEMPLARS

True knowledge organizations do not appear to come in the same or even similar packages. Apparently, no particular industry or type of company fully embraces the knowledge organization concept. Furthermore, those closest to true knowledge organizations approach corporate education and training differently.

Each of the four companies in Tier 1, those truly embracing the knowledge organization concept, comes from a different corner of corporate America (see Table 7.2). They represent four different indus-

TABLE 7.2 Profiles of Four Distinct Exemplars

	Exemplar 1	Exemplar 2	Exemplar 3	Exemplar 4
Industry	Manufacturing	Finance/Insurance	Services	Retail/Wholesale
Revenue	$2.8 billion	$4.2 billion	$1.3 billion	$1.3 billion
Employees	6,000	48,000	17,000	3,800
1997 training budget	$2.2 million	$1 to 9 million	$0.5 million	$0.7 million
Training via computer	20%	75%	0%	30%
Outsourcing (% of budget)	60%	DK	40%	10%

NOTE: Each of the four companies identified as completely embracing the knowledge organization concept comes from a different corner of corporate America and approaches training differently.

tries: manufacturing, finance/insurance, services, and retail/wholesale. Their revenues range greatly from $1.3 billion to $4.2 billion. They employ 3,800 to 48,000 employees. Training budgets vary greatly among these four companies, ranging in 1997 from $0.5 million to $2.2 million.

The method by which employees receive training at these companies also varies greatly. Two of the companies have corporate universities; the other two do not. Training via computer makes up 0% to 75% of total available training hours. Likewise, classroom training makes up 5% to 70% of total available training hours.

By the year 2000, these companies might be closer to each other in terms of the way training hours are allocated across delivery methods. In 2000, training via computer is expected to compose between 30% and 75% of total available hours, and classroom training between 5% and 55%. With these four companies (as with many others in corporate America) there is a predicted increase in the future availability of computer-based training as the availability of classroom training declines.

Although all four companies outsource a portion of their training, each does so to a different degree. Between 10% and 60% of training budgets are spent on outside sources among the four Tier 1 companies. All four companies partner with outside consultants or private vendors; however, only three partner with universities.

There is not even consensus on the value of an MBA or executive MBA, either now or in the future. One of the four companies currently does not reimburse for an MBA and sees the value of the MBA degree declining in 2000. The other three companies believe an MBA degree is and will continue to be extremely valuable. These three companies currently reimburse for an MBA degree.

There are only two items on which the four companies appear similar: (a) who is receiving the bulk of training and (b) what training topics will be provided in 2000. All four companies spend the large majority of training and education hours delivering to nonmanagement personnel (80% to 95% of training and education hours). This is not likely to change in 2000, when a similar proportion of training and education hours will be delivered to nonmanagement personnel (75% to 95% of training and education hours).

In 2000, all four companies anticipate providing training in all of the topics evaluated.[8] These topics span the areas of management, soft skills training, and technical skills training. All employees might not receive training in each area, but at least some will.

Is it surprising that these four companies fund, source, and deliver education and training differently? Not according to respondents' definitions of a knowledge organization. When asked what the term *knowledge organization* means, respondents do not specify a particular budget size, source of training, or delivery method. They do stress continual learning and sharing of information. How information is shared or skills are taught does not seem to be a defining characteristic of a knowledge organization. What we would expect is that the bulk of employees (i.e., nonmanagement personnel) receive training on a breadth of topics—and this is the case.

CONCLUSION

In her examination of manufacturing-based knowledge organizations, *Wellsprings of Knowledge,* Dorothy Leonard-Barton discusses the concept of *higher-order learning.* Behind every action, she says, managers must see a potential for knowledge building.

> So, for instance, when they sign a travel voucher for an employee to visit a customer site, they think about the use of knowledge thus engendered. How will it be leveraged beyond the use by one individual? What mechanisms exist to share that information? How widespread is such

travel? For every activity, the manager asks, What is the potential knowledge-building import of this action?[9]

For most companies, efforts to become a knowledge organization have begun in the training room, the traditional site of knowledge generation. As the higher-order learning that Leonard-Barton speaks of continues to have an impact on the nature of learning itself, however, those in charge of generating knowledge within corporations will continue to reassess the methods by which the organization generates and disseminates knowledge.

INTELLECTUAL CAPITAL ACCOUNTING

When a man's knowledge is not in order, the more of it he has the greater his confusion.

—Herbert Spencer

J ust as there are hard assets of varying worth and durability, knowledge has differing levels of value to the organization. A knowledge organization, according to New York University business professor William Starbuck, must possess knowledge that is out of the ordinary. He says, "Exceptional expertise must make an important contribution. One should not label a firm as knowledge-intensive unless exceptional and valuable expertise dominates commonplace knowledge."[1] The ability to recognize, measure, and allocate valuable knowledge within a company differentiates a knowledge organization from a corporation that is simply laden with intellectual capital (IC). Knowledge has three levels of value.

1. *Public knowledge* is not specific to any one company or industry. Someone who can type 60 words per minute is worth roughly the same amount to any number of companies in various industries.

2. *Industry knowledge* is necessary to make a company truly competitive, but it is not sufficient on its own. Total quality, fanatical drive, or top-notch information management, for example, may be required for companies to compete in the world economy, but something more is needed to triumph.

3. *Company knowledge* builds over time and cannot be copied easily by competition. Company knowledge is that which distinguishes the company from its competitors. It is the result of accumulated experience and a keen sense of self-awareness at all levels, from individual to largest unit.

Undoubtedly, every corporation in the world, past and present, has possessed some degree of company knowledge. Those companies with a greater proportion of such knowledge have prospered, whereas those based on public knowledge have fallen by the wayside. In the emerging economy, where knowledge is every bit as valuable as, if not more valuable than, tangible assets, companies must be able to continually build their company knowledge. A chief financial officer who earnestly claims at the end of the fiscal year, "I know there's tremendous value in this company, I just can't show where it's held," would be promptly shown to the door. Similarly, tomorrow's managers must be able to locate, measure, and allocate the organization's knowledge assets. It is an imperative, and it is the defining characteristic of all knowledge organizations.

As the term *knowledge organization* continues to spread through academic research units and boardrooms of corporate America alike, it is essential that managers understand this critical point: To be a knowledge organization, you must expend tremendous effort generating, measuring, and allocating the company's knowledge assets. Knowledge will never generate itself; technology alone is all but useless when it comes to generating knowledge. The managers' greatest strength in building a knowledge organization will be to know valuable knowledge for what it is.

MILL VALLEY: KNOWLEDGE ACCOUNTING GAINS MOMENTUM

In July 1994, a group from industry, academia, and policy research met in Mill Valley, California, to address some fundamental questions:

▶ Does the existing management language value knowledge as an essential resource for creating value and wealth?

▶ What are the meaningful predictors of a company's future prosperity?

▶ How shall we value and measure IC?

The meeting in Mill Valley captured an important truth about today's economy: The very notion of value has changed. The measures of an organization's productivity or an economy's wealth have long been intimately tied to the most highly valued assets of the time. Walter Wriston, retired chairman of Citicorp remembers, "When I was a kid in the bank, the most important economic indicator we looked at was freight car loadings. Who the hell cares about them now?"[2] In an age when tangible assets were the focus of corporate wealth, such an indicator made sense. In the information economy, new indicators are called for.

Traditional accounting techniques do not do an adequate job of measuring the value of IC. According to a company's ledgers, tangible acquisitions such as computers, real estate, and machinery are listed as company assets. Knowledge-building expenditures such as training, research, and development are treated as costs. Still, it is the latter that consistently develop new wealth for the company. American Airlines, for example, values its airplanes as assets. But Sabre, its proprietary electronic reservation system, which analysts say makes more money from licensing than the jetliners do, does not on the balance sheet.[3]

Some of the most discriminating arbiters of value, venture capitalists, have begun to note the shortcomings of measures that fail to account for a company's knowledge assets. Says Ann Winblad, partner of Silicon Valley's Hummer Winblad Venture Partners, "The P&E is just people. They have no factories, no inventories. The assets walk out of the door at night." One of Winblad's criteria for funding a company is whether it has "the ability to attract excellence. Without IC, you're nothing."[4] Harry Kellogg, executive vice president of Silicon Valley Bank, wishes there were some way to quantify IC.

We understand the value of intangible and intellectual property. But we can't put a dollar amount on it because the accounting firms don't show that in financial statements. And bank regulators, even if we told them what an intangible asset's worth, wouldn't give us any value there either. It's really something we know is there and that we know is valuable.[5]

Critics of IC accounting tend to shy away from the obscure, "soft" concept of knowledge as a valued asset, gravitating to the more established notion of value as something you can hold in your hands, take to the bank, or save for a rainy day. Research has shown, however, that the market does value IC. Zantout and Tsetsekos announced in the *Journal of Financial Research* their research on the relationship between announcements of research and development (R&D) expenditures and stock price. They examined 114 announcements of plans to increase R&D spending made between June 1979 and December 1990. The 71 firms that made these announcements were listed on the New York Stock Exchange and the American Stock Exchange. Not only did firms see a .742% increase in stock price after the announcement of increased R&D spending, but rival companies suffered a .563% decrease in stock price.[6] Remembering the Mill Valley meeting in his 1997 book, Leif Edvinsson says,

> At the heart of this group's work was the belief that most, if not all, of a company's Intellectual Capital could be visualized in some way. In particular, the right empirical indicators *could* be identified and measured, and the right presentation format found, such that Intellectual Capital could be put on the same strong, objective, and comparative base as financial capital.[7]

THE VISION-GUIDED INTELLECTUAL CAPITAL REPORT

Managers are justified in approaching this topic with a wary eye, because most of the talk about the high value of knowledge has had no numbers associated with it. We will provide some empirical ways to measure knowledge, but we don't provide a universal set of formulas to measure knowledge in organizations. We take this position for two reasons. First of all, the numbers that one assigns to IC are inherently tied to the reason the company is collecting the information. Therefore, companies must measure their knowledge assets within some context. Annie Brooking, a British IC consultant, describes the problem with most generic IC audits:

> In the generic intellectual capital audit we would look at all the intangible assets in the company and document their existence, current state and maybe their value. For employees we would document their education,

put each one through a set of psychometric and personality tests to discover the potential of every employee. We would discover who could think critically, sell products and services, provide dexterity skills and work in teams. . . . It would also be necessary to look at all intellectual property rights, all trademarks and all know-how. The end result would be an immense amount of knowledge about intangible assets. . . . In short, it would help us to generate statistics which may or may not be useful information. The problem with a generic audit is that because we are dealing with intangibles, notably humans, the process would never ever conclude.[8]

Devising an IC auditing system, Brooking concludes, must be intimately tied to the goals of conducting such an audit. For example, there is a difference between corporate performance measurements taken for management decision purposes and shareholder reporting purposes. Although they may describe the same aspect of the company, the measures are tailored to the intent of measurement. In their landmark series of articles on *The Balanced Scorecard,* an intangible asset accounting system, Robert Kaplan and David Norton underscore the importance of finding appropriate measures for intangible corporate assets.

Today's managers recognize the impact that measures have on performance. But they rarely think of measurement as an essential part of their strategy. For example, executives may introduce new strategies and innovative operating processes intended to achieve breakthrough performance, then continue to use the same short-term financial indicators they have used for decades, measures like return on investment, sales growth, and operating income. These managers fail not only to introduce new measures to monitor new goals and processes but also to question whether or not their old measures are relevant to the new initiatives.[9]

Thus, Kaplan and Norton present an IC accounting system whose measures are defined by the company itself. "The balanced scorecard," they wrote, "demands that managers translate their general mission statement on customer service into specific measures that reflect the factors that really matter to customers." The authors seem to say that every company must decide for itself which IC matters and which does not. Electronic Circuits, Inc. (ECI), the fictional name for a semiconductor company Kaplan and Norton based their theory on, "established general goals for customer performance: get standard products to market sooner, improve customers' time to market, become customers' supplier of choice through partnerships with them, and develop innovative products tailored to customer needs."[10] Then ECI developed its own measurements. "To track the specific goal of providing a continuous stream of attractive solutions, ECI measured the percentage of sales from new products and the percentage of sales from proprietary products."[11]

Ultimately, what matters most is that companies make the effort to track the creation and flow of IC in their organization. Hugh McDonald, of ICL, a British computer manufacturer, made this point when he said, "It almost doesn't matter what the bloody metrics are, so long as you can know that this thing, whatever it is, is getting better or worse. If you don't keep your intellectual capital refreshed, it will erode."[12] A generic IC accounting system, although useful for comparing companies, would fail to capture information useful in managerial decision making.

The second reason for not promoting a set of formulas for IC accounting is succinctly stated by Thomas Stewart of *Fortune* magazine: "The field of intellectual capital is too new for cookbooks."[13] Although Stewart is one of the leading writers on IC, he says his aim is to inspire chefs (corporate executives) to come up with their own inventive recipes for IC management.[14] In December 1997, Stewart published a lengthy "knowledge quiz" in *Fortune,* asking businesspeople a variety of questions on how they would value IC. Here are some of the questions he posed:

> ▶ Where have you learned the skills and knowledge that are most important to doing your job well? Rank in order, with 1 being most important, 5 least important.
>
> ___ Academic experience
>
> ___ Training provided by employer or a previous employer
>
> ___ Yourself (independent research or your own experience in the job)
>
> ___ Your colleagues
>
> ___ The people who use what you do (customers or "internal customers")
>
> ▶ You're part of a cross-functional, geographically dispersed team working on a project of considerable importance to your company. Your work will be faster and better if you have easy access to corporate data and can share all information fully. However, there is a chance that sensitive information will leak. Under these circumstances, will your company:

    __ Err on the side of openness, running the risk of a leak?

    __ Err on the side of security, running the risk that your work will be slower and less complete?

Do you agree with the decision you think your company would make? Why or why not?

▷ At home one night, you have an idea for a new product, even a whole new line of business for your company. The more you think about it, the better it seems. What do you do?

    __ Tell your spouse about it and forget about it.

    __ Tell your boss and let him forget about it.

    __ Tell your boss and hope she remembers to give you credit.

    __ Tell the people who are most likely to act on the idea, but send a copy to your boss to cover your butt.

    __ Copy your Rolodex and start phoning venture capitalists.

At the end of the quiz, Stewart writes, "How to score: You don't. These questions are an informal diagnostic tool, fingers poking at various pressure points related to intellectual capital management. The questions should be the basis for discussion and the discussion the basis for an agenda."[15]

Does this mean knowledge is, after all this, an asset that managers must value on faith but never learn how to use in decision making? In this chapter, we will describe where to look for knowledge in an organization and how to measure it. The discussion is based largely on the world's first IC annual report from the Swedish financial services firm, Skandia. Skandia's 1994 report—*Visualizing Intellectual Capital*—and its subsequent reports are coherent first attempts to express the intangible value in a corporation. The chief architect of Skandia's IC measurement, Leif Edvinsson, readily acknowledges in his book, *Intellectual Capital: Realizing Your Company's True Value by Finding Its Hidden Brainpower,* that his work is pioneering and thus open to scrutiny and appraisal.[16] As we examine the Skandia report, and the measures that Edvinsson's team has chosen to reflect IC, it is particularly interesting to discuss the assumptions that support the use of these measurements. For example, consider the three metrics of IC shown in Table 8.1 and the assumptions that support their use.

Our intent here is to point out that every company possesses a unique understanding of what intangible assets are truly valuable to the organi-

TABLE 8.1 Skandia Report Information

Metric	Assumption	Possible Interpretation
Average years of service with company (#)	Employee turnover, especially in the core group of the company, is a threat to sustained organizational capital value.[17]	Some would argue that intellectual capital is actually hampered by ingrained mental models gained from working in one place for too long. What about the value of new ideas?
Customer information technology (IT) literacy (%)	Most companies are so focused on their own IT prowess that they forget that their customers must also reach a certain IT competence threshold to remain successful customers.[18]	Would this apply to a grocery store or some other retail outlet that is not so dependent on the technological sophistication of its customers?
Direct communications to customer/year (#)	Measures how often the company actually communicates (newsletter, direct contact, magazines, press releases, and so forth) per year.[19]	Within this list of communications, there are varying degrees of success and intimacy. Mass communication does not always translate into quality communication, but it would be assigned a higher value according to this measure.

zation and therefore which measures to use. Standards for measuring IC among companies and across industries may be a long time in coming, but to begin, Skandia's example provides a taxonomy for classifying the organization's knowledge assets and a series of metrics to measure them. The rest—experimenting with these and other metrics—is up to you.

INTELLECTUAL CAPITAL ACCOUNTING

IC theorists generally agree that there are three major stores of knowledge in a corporation: customer capital, structural capital, and human capital.

Customer Capital

Customer capital is the value a company gains from an ongoing relationship with its customers. The value of such relationships is intuitive. After all, customers pay the company's bills. But the dollar value of customer capital is also very real. Ford Motor Company believes that every percentage point of increased customer loyalty—a measure of repeat orders—translates into $100 million in profits. MBNA, the credit card issuer, estimates that it can increase the lifetime profitability of the average customer by 125% if it decreases its customer defect rate by 5%.[20] Of the three forms of IC, customer capital is the most familiar to managers and is already widely measured. Market share, customer retention/defection rates, and per-customer profitability are all well-accepted measures of customer capital.[21] Although these measures are critical, they do not completely reflect a company's true customer capital, primarily because the very nature of customers has changed. Edvinsson and Malone have noted,

> The consumer of 1997, having enjoyed a decade of growing control over the purchase process, expects to personally define the product or service to match his or her needs. The modern consumer also expects to be fully trained in the product's use, wants it to never break down—or if it does to have a service rep quickly on-site, on the phone, or on-line—and assumes there will be a smooth software, if not hardware, upgrade path when the next generation of the product appears in a year or so. The modern consumer wants immediate, customized, flawless delivery, be it from a drive-thru restaurant or a datalog.[22]

In the days when companies sought to attract as many customers as they could, with as little product variety as possible, one metric sufficed to describe the company's customer capital: How many? In their celebrated book *The One to One Future,* Don Peppers and Martha Rogers say that market share is no longer an accurate measure of a company's success.[23] Customers expect the vendor to get involved with them, and they expect the company to collaborate.

> As a customer, you can already see this beginning to happen. Marketing companies are asking you to collaborate with them in the selling process—whether it's your long distance company asking you to specify what 20 phone numbers you'd most like to receive discounts on, or a

bank asking you to complete your money transfers at the ATM machine or via touch-tone phone, or an automobile company asking you to complete a survey and rate its dealer's service department or make a wish list of the options you'd like on your next car. . . . Instead of measuring the success of your marketing program by how many sales transactions occur across an entire market during a particular period, as a 1:1 marketer, you will gauge success by the projected increase or decrease in a customer's expected future value to your company. The true measure of your success, one customer at a time, will not be market share, but share of a customer.[24]

Rogers and Peppers don't merely point out that customers have changed. They show that the very relationship that companies have with their customers has changed. Today, it is not enough for companies to simply meet customer demand. Even world-class customer service is not enough to maintain a competitive advantage. Instead, companies must be able to anticipate customers' demands. Edvinsson and Malone describe the relationship between the company and customer as *codestiny*. The seller, manufacturer, supplier, retail outlet, and, of course, the customer become bound together to make sure the customer succeeds (i.e., realizes an unfulfilled need). But, say Edvinsson and Malone, "With customer success comes responsibilities. . . . The customer must divulge critical information in order that the product can be 'mass customized' for his or her specific desires."[25] Leonard-Barton illustrated the lengths Thermos went to when it created a new electric grill:

> The Lifestyle team not only set up the traditional focus groups, but team members visited people's homes and videotaped barbecues. To their surprise, it wasn't always Dad slaving over the grill; increasingly, it was Mom. Moreover, many cookers were getting very weary of the mess, smell, and smoke associated with charcoal, and they wanted something attractive (not just functional) to put on their expensive patio decks. When the team returned to Thermos headquarters, its product concept was very different from products the company currently had on the market. Team members' observations of real people in real usage environments caused them to focus on the customer instead of the product— and that focus made the difference between another me-too black iron box with a gas grill built in and a very novel, handsome electric product.[26]

Truth, an element of knowledge discussed in Chapter 5, is ingrained in Thermos's customer capital. But this value is not reflected in market share. The role for IC accounting is to accurately reflect the wealth that a company holds in its customer capital. In *Intellectual Capital,* Edvinsson and Malone describe five new indicators of customer capital:

> ▶ *Customer type.* What is the profile of a typical customer for the company's product, today and into the future?
> ▶ *Customer duration.* How long do customers remain loyal to the firm?
> ▶ *Customer role.* Where does the customer fit in the value chain?
> ▶ *Customer support.* How does the company ensure customer satisfaction?
> ▶ *Customer success.* Do the company's products or services help the customer achieve what they want to?[27]

Skandia's metrics to measure its customer assets are as follows:[28]

1. Market share (%). Skandia uses market share as an indication of customer satisfaction.
2. Number of accounts (#).
3. Customers lost (#). Says Edvinsson, "In an era where there will be fewer and fewer available and good potential new customers, the loss of even a single current one is a singular defeat for the company. It represents the loss of years of time and money invested in developing that customer, and even more years of lost revenues."
4. Telephone accessibility (%). Defined as "the number of calls answered within three signals."[29]
5. Policies without surrender (%).
6. Customer rating (%). Skandia uses several indices to measure the quality of its relationship with its customers. They capture intangible elements such as daily interaction with the company, customer frustration, and overall satisfaction.
7. Customer visits to the company (#).
8. Days spent visiting the customer (#). This and the previous measure together indicate the level of the company's personal interaction with its customers. Separately, the metrics reveal how customer contact is weighted.
9. Market coverage (%). This is referred to as an "opportunity index" for Skandia to reach its potential customer base.[30]
10. Vacancy rate (%). Used primarily by the Real Estate division of Skandia, vacancy rate is an indicator of property management performance.
11. Gross rental income/employee ($).
12. Number of contracts (#).

13. Saving/contact ($).
14. Points of sale (#).
15. Number of funds (#).
16. Number of fund managers (#).
17. Number of internal IT [information technology] customers (#).
18. Number of external IT customers (#).
19. Number of contracts/IT-employee (#). Although the rationale for including items 17 through 19 is not clearly explained in any of Skandia's intellectual capital annual report, Edvinsson says that the value of technology is to "increase both the 'transparency' (that is, ease of using) and the packing of knowledge, as well as the communications systems needed to share that knowledge."[31]
20. Customer IT literacy (%). Skandia believes that to be successful, its customers must attain a certain level of IT proficiency.

Skandia also maintains a system for its aircraft insurance division (see Box 8.1).

Structural Capital

Edvinsson has defined structural capital as all the value that remains when the lights are turned out at 5:00 p.m.[32] This definition gives a hint, but it may be too esoteric to fully grasp the value of structural capital. What if two widget factories each had machines, desks, secretaries, managers, and all the necessary elements of a business, but one is more successful than the other. In addition to the skill and intellect of the people involved, the elements of an organization that have become institutionalized through procedures, lessons learned, best practices, culture, and proprietary technology are also the roots of success and primary elements of structural capital. Says Stewart, "McKinsey is *the* strategy consulting firm, the University of Chicago has *the* economics department, Ritz-Carlton is *the* expert in hotel management."[33] Clearly, it could not be solely the people that work there. Otherwise, these companies would lose their status with the changing of staff. Companies that lead with knowledge make deep investments in their structural capital, developing systems and processes that will sustain their competitive advantages despite unforeseen disruptions. Of course, the necessary first step to making that investment is to know what structural capital exists in the organization.

BOX 8.1

**From the pages of Skandia's *Customer Value*,
a supplement to the 1996 annual report**

In the report on Skandia Aviation, an airline insurance division, Skandia reported:

"One of the aviation department's unique resources is the MARIA database. In addition to market information on insurance premiums and claims, it includes information on the world's jet aircraft fleet: the size, age and sum insured, the number of take-offs and landings for each individual plane, and so on."[34]

Skandia uses the following structural capital metrics, which they refer to as their "process focus."[35] (Bear in mind that Skandia is a financial services firm and is therefore highly dependent on information technology as its primary source of structural capital.)

1. Administrative expense/managed assets (#).
2. Administrative expense/total revenues (#).
3. Cost of administrative error/management revenues (%). Edvinsson admits, "publishing this figure takes management courage."[36]
4. Total yield compared with index (%).
5. Processing time, outpayments (#).
6. Contracts filed without error (#).
7. Function points/employee-month (#).
8. PCs/employee (#).
9. Laptops/employee (#).
10. Administrative expense/employee ($).
11. IT expense/employee ($).
12. IT expense/administrative expense (%).

Numbers 8 through 12 reveal the degree of technology penetration in the organization as a ratio of the company's administrative expenditures, the assumption being that this is an efficiency ratio.

13. IT staff/total staff (%).

14. Administrative expense/gross premium (%).

15. IT capacity (CPU [central processing unit] and DASD [data access storage device]) (#).

16. Change in IT inventory ($).

17. Employees working at home/total employees (%). This metric helps Skandia track its telecommuting program and the integrity of its IT network.

18. IT literacy of employees (#). An indication of how well Skandia employees use the IT system.

In addition, Skandia reports gains in customer capital (see Box 8.2).

Human Capital

Many CEOs have confided in visitors to their companies, "Our employees are our greatest asset." That has never been truer than it is today, and research is beginning to emerge that proves it. The National Center on the Educational Quality of the Workforce (EQW) studied the relationship between education and productivity at 3,100 U.S. workplaces. A 10% increase in worker education, the EQW said in its 1995 report, will result in an 8.6% gain in productivity. Alternately, a 10% rise in capital stock (the value of equipment) increased productivity by just 3.4%.[37] Human capital is the sum of the workers' skills, experience, capabilities, and innate knowledge.[38]

Measuring a company's knowledge assets may remind you of the short-lived practice of human resource accounting (HRA). The theory first appeared in the late 1960s, the product of business professors R. Lee Brummet and Eric Flamholtz. The basic premise of HRA is that an employee's cost and value to an organization may be measured and budgeted using traditional accounting methods.[39] By holding training expenses and performance records up to company goals, for example, the accounting department could make budgeting decisions. The roots of HRA's demise were part methodological and part public perception.

Riel Miller, a veteran HRA researcher for the Organization for Economic Cooperation and Development, said in his 1996 book *Measuring What People Know* that early HRA theories did not pay close enough attention to knowledge-creating activities outside of the class-

Box 8.2

From the pages of Skandia's *Customer Value,* a supplement to the 1996 annual report[40]

In the report on Skandia Life UK, the following mentions the following gains in customer capital.

▶ **Five-Star Award for Customer Service.** In 1996 Skandia Life was voted "Best Company of the Year" in an annual survey of insurance companies' level of service conducted by the British magazine *Financial Planner.*

▶ Continuous Relationship Improvement. **Skandia Life recently launched Clearly First, a company-wide programme aimed at further improving the quality of its customer care.**

▶ **Skandia Life Cowes Week.** Since 1995, in an effort to strengthen the bond with brokers and increase awareness about the Skandia trademark, Skandia Life has been a main sponsor of Cowes Week, the world's largest sailing regatta and one of the four key events in the UK's social calendar, alongside Wimbledon, Ascot, and Henley.[41]

room.[42] Perhaps more damaging to HRA was the implication, intended or not, that human beings were assets—that is, units that could be owned and manipulated by the corporation. "You look at [HRA] and say, you know, I can't really attach a value to human resources—that went out with slavery," says Dave Wildon, national director of education for accounting firm Arthur Little.[43] In fact, no company may ever own a person's IC. At best, they may rent it. Stewart suggests assuming a different mind-set when measuring human IC: Think of human capital as an investment, not a cost.[44]

Unfortunately, this does not make the task any easier. Like customer capital, the very nature of a person's role within the corporation has changed. Malone and Edvinsson call them *The New Workers.*[45] They are the men and women who staff, manage, and run the corporations that would seem unrecognizable compared with their classic corporation predecessors. The virtual corporation has replaced towering bureaucracies and in the process redefined the very notion of a job.

▶ *Office Goers.* Although initially there doesn't seem to be anything new about someone who travels to the company for a day of work, consider the effects of downsizing and other changes on the workplace. Not only are fewer employees expected to do more, they have to do it faster than ever before.

▶ *Telecommuters.* Working in the spare bedroom with a company computer and fax line, these employees make up an increasingly large amount of the labor pool. The Bureau of Labor Statistics estimates that 30% of the U.S. workforce spends an average of 6 to 8 hours per week telecommuting. Employees of information-intensive companies such as banks or insurance agencies spend an average of 30 to 40 hours at home per week.[46]

▶ *Road Warriors.* Spending weeks, if not months, on the road, these corporate executives and managers are "in the paradoxical situation of being detached from the company while still being at the very center of its operations and value creation."[47]

▶ *Corporate Gypsies.* The parallel rise of outsourcing and management consulting has given rise to a new breed of employees: ones who don't work for the firm. Nonetheless, these people still create value, generate new knowledge, and contribute to the company's competitive advantage.

We could add to this list executives for hire, interns, and other types of outsourced intelligence, such as market researchers. The point here, however, is not to be exhaustive so much as illustrative. There are myriad sources of human IC in the organization, ones that knowledge managers must know as well if not better than tangible sources of value.

Here are the metrics Skandia uses to measure its human capital:

1. Leadership index (%).
2. Motivation index (%). This and the preceding metric are the result of the FLINK index, a measure of quality developed in 1992 at SkandiaLink, an insurance and investment unit. FLINK measures the following aspects of the operation:
   ▶ Satisfied customers
   ▶ Satisfied salespersons
   ▶ Motivated and competent staff
   ▶ Quality-assured and effective administration[48]
3. Empowerment index (of 1,000) (#). Again, Skandia developed its own index, with the aid of the Swedish Institute of Public Opinion Research (SIFO). The SIFO survey looked at:
   ▶ Motivation
   ▶ Support with the organization

- ► Awareness of quality demands
- ► Responsibility versus authority to act
- ► Competence[49]

4. Number of employees (#).
5. Number of employees/number of employees in alliances (%).
6. Employee turnover (%).
7. Average years of service with company (#). Edvinsson considers excessive turnover a threat to the organization's cumulative human capital value.
8. Number of managers (#).
9. Number of women managers (#). This is not, says Edvinsson, the result of political correctness. Instead, he says, "the new corporation, with its diverse management needs, will require personality types, life experiences, and management styles that are unprecedented in middle corporate ranks."[50]
10. Training expense/employee ($).
11. Average age of employees (#).
12. Share of employees under age 40 (%). Together with 11, this metric shows how well the company renews its talent pool.
13. Time in training (days/year) (#).

Skandia also provides information on the value of knowledge sharing (see Box 8.3).

HOW SKANDIA DEVELOPED ITS
INTELLECTUAL CAPITAL REPORT

We will conclude this chapter by looking at how Skandia conceived of and implemented the world's first public IC annual report. First, we should say that Skandia is neither the first nor the only company in the world to establish systems to manage its knowledge. Knowledge organization theorist Karl Sveiby reports that W-M Data, one of Sweden's largest software companies, has been reporting on its IC since 1989.[51] And Gordon Petrash, head of Dow Chemical's R&D, in 1992 became a pioneer knowledge manager when he devised a system to manage the company's rich store of patents.[52]

Monsanto has a management position called "Director, Knowledge Management,"[53] and organizational charts across the corporate spectrum

BOX 8.3

**From the pages of Skandia's *Value Creating Processes*,
a supplement to the 1995 annual report**

In the report on Vesta, an insurance division, a section appeared on the Work Methods, Support Systems and IT. The following, the report said, will "lead to a more impactive work form and greater opportunities for knowledge sharing.

► Routine handbooks that describe work procedures for sales, customer care, customer renewal, operations and claims handling have been produced.

► Benchmarking of business processes has been implemented and deviation analyses have been carried out—internally between different units as well in comparison with other companies.

► Competence development of the staff is carried out continuously. Further education is conducted through the Division's own educational institute, which conducted a total of 750-course days in 1995."[54]

have begun to include titles such as chief learning officer, chief knowledge officer, and director, IC. Although Skandia may not be the original or the sole pioneer in this trend, it has made the most concerted effort to develop systems for IC accounting and reporting that may be shared across industries and throughout the world.

In the early 1980s, Skandia's CEO Bjorn Wolrath and top executive Jan Carendi (who would go on to become head of the Skandia Assurance & Financial Services or AFS division) began to discuss how traditional management and accounting theories did not apply well to Skandia's situation. For service businesses, particularly knowledge-intensive ones such as Skandia, wealth did not reside in equipment and inventory as much as it did in talent, competence, and industry relationships. Wolrath had been wrestling with this issue for several years along with Leif Edvinsson, then director of the Swedish Coalition of Service Industries. Beginning in 1985, the coalition issued a series of reports describing new ways to value service companies and introducing the concept of developing and nurturing the organization's nonfinancial elements. In 1991,

Skandia created an IC management function for its AFS business unit and named Edvinsson its director. He recalls,

> The chart of the Skandia AFS IC function was to grow and develop the company's intellectual capital as a visible, lasting value that would complement the balance sheet. The operation was also to forge a link between other company functions, such as business development, human resources, and information technology. In the process, it was to develop new measurement tools and metrics as well as implement new programs to speed knowledge sharing in the organization.[55]

Wolrath and Carendi say they did not view IC reporting as a way to add perceptual value to the organization. Wrote Wolrath in the 1994 Annual Report, "This supplement should be viewed as a way of describing the otherwise intangible dimensions of the operations, and not as an attempt to create value added in the likes of the emperor's new clothes."[56] Wolrath sought, and Edvinsson would ultimately deliver, a tool that management could use internally to make decisions and externally to describe the company's knowledge assets to shareholders.

These efforts came just in time for rapid growth of the AFS division. At the time Edvinsson joined Skandia, AFS distributed its long-term savings products through more than 26,000 brokers and 10,000 bank offices worldwide. AFS served more than 500,000 contracts and employed 1,100 employees. By 1995, the AFS federation had grown to include 50,000 alliances and would eventually swell to 65,000. The employee count went up to 2,000 in this time. Although this was positive growth for the division, traditional reporting failed to convey its true meaning. Says Edvinsson, "The growth of alliances is very much visible from an organizational reporting standpoint. What is seen is the 2,000 current employees but not the leveraging resources of the 65,000 alliances—a thirty-times impact per employee."[57] Edvinsson set to work devising a system that would accurately reflect this application of IC.

In May 1995, the IC team, now including a full-time IC controller responsible for all reporting, issued the world's first public IC annual report. Titled "Visualizing Intellectual Capital in Skandia," it was distributed as a supplement to the company's traditional financial report. Several months later, Edvinsson says, 500 corporations had contacted him, wanting to develop IC reports of their own. In retrospect, Edvinsson recalls, to get to this point, he and his team went through six phases. We share these points to give the reader a sense of what it might entail to prepare your organization to account for its IC.

1. *Missionary.* A few pioneers identify the value of IC and the need to measure and manage it effectively. Through the use of metaphor and some simple metrics, these individuals must convince enough of the organization that this is a worthwhile effort.

2. *Measurement.* The IC team develops metrics for measuring IC and taxonomy for organizing the report. They must also devise a way to marry IC measurement with the company's standing accounting system.

3. *Leadership.* At this phase, leaders at various levels within the organization must incorporate the new thinking.

4. *Technology.* The organization must develop technologies that allow for the "transparent" packaging and sharing of knowledge.

5. *Capitalizing.* The company must capture the ways it packages organizational technology—databases, for example—into IC.

6. *Futurizing.* Skandia did not take this last step until 1996, when it created the company's first Future Center, a step that should nurture the ongoing development of IC.[58]

The one element of the Skandia experience that undoubtedly applies to all industries is the ever-present need for leadership in these activities. In the next chapter, we will look at how leadership into the next century will become defined by its ability to shepherd the organization through the change that knowledge measurement and management will bring.

CONCEPTUALIZING AND LEVERAGING KNOWLEDGE

If a man empties his purse into his head, no one can take it away from him. An investment in knowledge always pays the best interest.

—Benjamin Franklin

n this chapter, we set forth a model for conceptualizing and leveraging knowledge. The model grew out of our review of what has been written about knowledge, conversations with professionals who deal on a daily basis with knowledge issues, and the results of our national survey.

At the heart of the model is vision. A clear vision is the major prerequisite to understanding and implementing the four phases of the model. Understanding the value of a knowledge organization requires a different mind-set, a different set of values, and a different way of measuring performance. We will have more to say regarding vision in Chapter 10, "Leading with Knowledge."

Stability is no longer a factor in conducting business, and knowledge issues have in many cases replaced tangible assets as the new organizational wealth. Conceptually moving toward becoming a knowledge organization might be easier with a reference point, hence the model (see Figure 9.1).

PHASE 1: IDENTIFYING AND CAPTURING KNOWLEDGE

There is an aspect of knowledge that makes this process difficult: Much of the knowledge in the corporation is tacit. The knowledge is not only intangible but also frequently inexpressible. Although the knower may swear there is a reason he or she can perform a task well, that person cannot easily explain the technique, let alone teach a colleague how to do it. We are intuitively familiar with tacit knowledge, although we are rarely asked to document it for the benefit of others. Hungarian philosopher Michael Polanyi is widely credited with first articulating the concept of tacit knowledge. In a chapter titled "The Tacit Dimension," he wrote,

> I shall reconsider human knowledge by starting from the fact that we can know more than we can tell. This fact seems obvious enough; but it is not easy to say exactly what it means. Take an example. We know a person's face, and can recognize it among a thousand, indeed among a million. Yet we usually cannot tell how we recognize a face we know. So most of this knowledge cannot be put into words. But the police have recently introduced a method by which we can communicate this knowledge. They have made a large collection of pictures showing noses, mouths, and other features. From these the witness selects the particulars of the face he knows, and the pieces can then be put together to form a reasonably good likeness of the face.[1]

The challenge for corporations thus becomes constructing methods by which its most talented and experienced employees may describe what they know. Our research has indicated that companies—66% of the respondents to our survey—are committed to capturing their knowledge, skills, best and worst practices—all forms of tacit intellectual capital (IC)—for the benefit of the organization.

Thomas Stewart of *Fortune* magazine, made an insightful commentary on the nature of capturing knowledge when he said, "Knowledge grows so fast that any attempt to codify it is ridiculous; but the identities of in-house experts change slowly."[2] Herein lies a potential solution to capturing relevant knowledge. Rather than trying to quantify and express

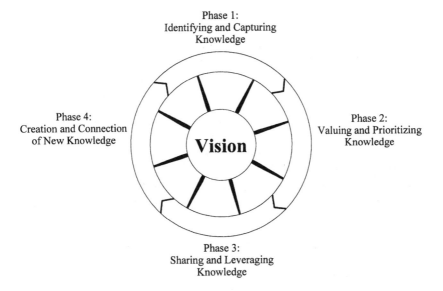

Phase 1:
Identifying and Capturing
Knowledge

Phase 4:
Creation and Connection
of New Knowledge

Vision

Phase 2:
Valuing and Prioritizing
Knowledge

Phase 3:
Sharing and Leveraging
Knowledge

Figure 9.1. A Strategic Model for Conceptualizing and Leveraging Knowledge
SOURCE: Copyright © 1999 by Richard C. Huseman, Ph.D., and Jon P. Goodman, Ph.D.

all the tacit knowledge that lies in people's minds, a knowledge organization will get much better return on its time investment by locating vessels of knowledge and constructing what Davenport and Prusak call "Knowledge Maps."[3]

Knowledge Mapping

A knowledge map—which may take the form of a "corporate yellow pages," an online database, or even an actual map—points to the stores of knowledge that exist throughout an organization. These may include particularly valuable proposals, databases, or, as Ernst & Young consultant Patricia Seeman calls them, *Rudis.*

While working at pharmaceutical company Hoffman-LaRoche, Seeman was part of a project to shorten the time required to obtain regulatory approval for new drugs. She created a corporate yellow pages that listed individuals according to their knowledge. There was a section for the person who knew what the clinical trial requirements were for new drugs in the United States and another for the person who knew the

German requirements. As Seeman worked her way through the organization, cataloging people's expertise, she encountered an individual named Rudi. "I sort of help people out," Rudi told Seeman, when asked what he did at the pharmaceutical giant. Seeman went on to meet other Rudis, people who acted as guides for corporate knowledge. Said Seeman, "The Rudis are the gray mice, whom senior management never notices—people who not only know something, but take the time to share and are very good storytellers."[4]

Assembling a corporate knowledge map starts with the individual knowledge maps of the company's Rudis. Some companies will actually survey their employees on a regular basis to find out what they know. From there, the company may patch together the individual maps into a larger, corporate-wide one.

PHASE 2: VALUING AND PRIORITIZING KNOWLEDGE

The word *manage* is defined in the *American Heritage Dictionary* as follows: "to direct or control the use of."[5] In corporations, managers are those individuals who control or direct the allocation and deployment of a company's assets. Money managers control investment decisions. Operation managers direct the use of machines or systems. And division managers control employees' time, what has been termed *human resources*. We have established that knowledge is a valuable asset to corporations. Yet despite the pioneering efforts of some exemplary companies, such as Skandia, few companies exist today that manage their knowledge assets with the same degree of sophistication as they do their hard assets. This is partly because knowledge management is an immature practice, but largely because managing knowledge assets is very difficult work. The money manager may produce a convincing algorithm to describe the future value of an investment. An operations manager may scientifically evaluate the declining productivity of a machine, but how can a knowledge manager predict the intellectual output of a human being? To date, the task has been largely avoided.

Clearly, every company generates knowledge, much of it proprietary. However, the ability to manage an asset, allocate its value, and leverage its worth starts with the ability to identify, value, and prioritize it. As

Larry Prusak, head of Knowledge Management Consulting for IBM, professes, "If I can find it I can measure it, and if I can measure it I can manage it."[6] Efforts to quantify knowledge have been called human capital accounting and, more recently, IC reporting. The intent of both practices is to give managers some formulas by which they can "count" the knowledge assets of their organization to later allocate those assets or use the data for reporting purposes. More important than quantifying IC, however, Phase 2 allows the organization to design a yardstick for its knowledge. As the company changes, it may refer to past performance and future expectations in the realm of knowledge.

Our research data show that IC accounting has not caught on in corporate America. Only 15% of the companies we surveyed have some system to quantify human capital. IC accounting is a provocative practice. Steven Wallman, commissioner of the Securities and Exchange Commission, said in 1997 that he saw great potential in IC accounting for the future of corporate performance reporting. Although Wallman did not endorse all aspects of IC accounting, he did point out that the practice does reveal value in corporations that has been heretofore hidden in traditional financial reports.

> One clear driver of wealth production in a company is customer satisfaction. People have found that if you have higher levels of customer satisfaction, you have higher retention level, you can also charge more, and you've got more loyalty. Lots of things flow through high levels of customer satisfaction. Firms like J. D. Power and others are capable of measuring that in surveys.
>
> Employee satisfaction measures are also starting to come to the fore. People are starting to feel reasonably comfortable with a number of those. These can be anything from very objective, simple measures, like how many days of absenteeism are there, to measures that relate more psychologically gratifying issues of how happy people are at work and things like that.[7]

Wallman embraces the controversial nature of what he proposes by underscoring that stakeholders in a corporation are increasingly valuing different aspects of the enterprise. He even foresees a day when financial statements would be dynamic, indicating value that resides in the eye of the beholder.

You as an investor, might value employee satisfaction or customer satisfaction. I might value brand integrity and patents. Another person might value the financial incentive of managers as defined by the number of options they hold and the strike price. I might value intangible assets more highly than you might, or less highly, or not at all. But at least I would have access to it, and be able to place it into my own grid and assign some multiple that made sense to me.[8]

Forbes columnist John Rutledge, who holds a Ph.D. in economics and is the chairman of a merchant banking firm in Connecticut, calls such ideas "At best useless. At worst, 'stakeholder' meddling."[9] The most troubling aspect of IC reporting, Rutledge says, "is to tinker with financial statements, so companies full of smart people who don't make profits look more attractive to investors. . . . Anyone who has ever attended a Mensa meeting can see the fallacy of this idea. There is a big difference between smart and effective, and I'll take an effective person over a smart one any day."[10] Rutledge contends that the most significant challenge to knowledge organizations is not reporting IC—it is managing it.

There may be a middle ground between Wallman's and Rutledge's arguments. Perfecting IC accounting will likely take many years, but at this point, the process—and the public debate—of what intangible assets matter to a company is of most import. At the very least (and this is no small matter), it encourages managers to pay attention to the stores of competency in their organizations that contain value.

PHASE 3: SHARING AND LEVERAGING KNOWLEDGE

I read somewhere that everybody on this planet is separated by only six people. Six degrees of separation. Between us and everybody else on this planet. The president of the United States. A gondolier in Venice. Fill in the name. . . . [But] you have to find the right six people to make the connection.

—John Guare, Playwright[11]

Whether managers get involved or not, employees will transfer knowledge between themselves. Over the cubicle wall, at the water-cooler, or after work, people exchange the know-how that is the source of a company's competitive advantage. However, these exchanges are local and imperfect. We will gather knowledge from our neighbor because he or she is close by, not necessarily because that person is the best source. In the same way, we go to friends for workplace advice because it's more comfortable than talking to a stranger. But what if that stranger happens to be the foremost expert in the needed realm of knowledge? How does an organization ensure that its employees' knowledge is leveraged throughout the firm, particularly if the firm spans the globe?

As corporations increasingly recognize knowledge as their most valuable source of competitive advantage, they must devise systems for the fast and efficient transfer of knowledge. It is not enough for a company to generate mountains of knowledge if it has no means of knowing what it knows. Monsanto discovered this axiom in 1995, when it lost a major contract to a competitor. After the loss, the company's leadership learned that a sales representative had heard a rumor that Monsanto's customer was close to signing with the competitor. Unfortunately, he was located halfway around the world and due to time differences and organizational boundaries, he was not able to pass the information on to the account representatives.[12] Without architecture for transferring even this small bit of knowledge, Monsanto's competitive advantage slipped.

Disseminating knowledge entails applying the right knowledge to the right situation in a timely fashion. For many organizations, this can be the most daunting aspect of knowledge management because it has to overcome several barriers:

- ▶ *Distance:* Separate divisions may benefit from each other but are so far removed that knowledge allocation becomes difficult.
- ▶ *Hierarchy:* Corporations with rigid hierarchies and avenues of communication may find that employees do not see any opportunity to share what they know.
- ▶ *Culture:* In many corporations, knowledge is power, so sharing what one knows must reap some reward.

This is just a short list of obstacles managers must overcome to effectively allocate what employees know and to determine what knowledge is embedded in the organization. The problem is compounded in large organizations.

There is no *right* way to transfer knowledge. It could be training, coffee breaks, or Internet-distributed databases, depending on the unique cultural and systematic factors at work in the organization. Davenport and Prusak tell the story of when companies started to move away from mainframe computers. IBM suddenly needed to reinvent itself, and employees were thrust into a time of great change. Then-chairman John Akers upbraided employees in a memo to stop congregating at water-coolers and to get back to work. In fact, the workers were exchanging knowledge, trying to come up with means for making the transition.[13]

In Japan, most knowledge transfer takes place after hours and off-site. Company dinners and visits to nightclubs are firmly entrenched as part of the Japanese knowledge-sharing culture. Many Japanese firms have even built "talk rooms" where employees may drink tea and engage in informal discussions.[14]

The idiosyncratic truth about knowledge is that if it is forced into too narrow a structure, it will lose its distinctive qualities. The best an organization can do in these circumstances is to foster the circumstances in which knowledge is best transferred. Toward the end of this chapter, we will look at some techniques companies are using to transfer knowledge, but first a look at how knowledge flows through an organization.

Nonaka and Takeuchi describe four ways in which knowledge passes from individual to individual within an organization.[15] Each of the four ways assumes that there are two kinds of knowledge: (a) tacit, that which is known but not easily described, and (b) explicit, that which is known and can be codified in a tangible form, such as a document or story.

Socialization: From Tacit to Tacit

Socialization is the process by which employees share the experiences that form "know-how." Frequently, it is through observation, imitation, and practice rather than direct communication that we gather new knowledge. The craftsman-apprentice relationship is indicative of socialization. Cook and Yanow explored the nature of socialization in their study of the three finest flutemakers in the world.[16] All located around Boston, the workshops of the Wm. S. Haynes Company, Vernes Q. Powell Flutes, Inc., and Brannen Brothers—Flutemakers, Inc., are renowned worldwide as producers of the most enduring and acoustically perfect flutes. Although flutes from each of these shops are of arguably comparable excellence, the processes that go into their construction are highly unique. A flutemaker from Haynes, for example, cannot walk into a Powell workshop and make a Powell flute. The expertise that each of the shops possesses is so specialized that the masters cannot even explain what goes into the process. "In describing why a piece might need to be reworked, a flutemaker would typically make only cryptic remarks, such as, 'It doesn't feel right' or 'This doesn't look quite right.' " Thus, the only way for the flutemakers to transfer knowledge to a new hire is through socialization.

> Apprentices have typically been trained by sitting at a workbench to do one of the steps of manufacture as would any other flutemaker. As an apprentice finished a piece of work, he would show it to a master-craftsman who would judge it, just as she would judge the work of any other flutemaker: If it did not feel right or look right, it would be handed back to the apprentice to be reworked until it did.[17]

Chaparral Steel has developed a 3.5-year-long apprenticeship program with the Bureau of Apprenticeship and Training in the U.S. Department of Labor. The program allows apprentices to attain the position of operator/craftsman by completing 7,280 hours of training on the job and through formal education. Foremen from various units track the performance of apprentices throughout the program and evaluate them. Chaparral also employs a socialization technique known as "vicing."

In most factories, when a supervisor is absent, the supervisor from the previous shift is asked to stay on for overtime. At Chaparral, the supervisor is expected to work the overtime, but not as a supervisor. Instead, the senior operator assumes the position of vice supervisor for that shift, which provides the opportunity to learn from the supervisor's experience. According to CEO Gordon Forward, "Expertise must be in the hands of the people that make the product."[18]

Combination: From Explicit to Explicit

Combination is the most familiar form of knowledge transfer. Knowledge that has been codified in a report, job description, or client proposal is handed from one individual to another. Hiring a recently graduated MBA is a form of combination. The MBA comes to the company with certain knowledge sets that have been gleaned from university research and experience.

Internalization: From Explicit to Tacit

Internalization, also known as "learning by doing," occurs when an individual takes explicit knowledge provided by the organization, such as a procedure manual, and turns it into personalized, tacit knowledge. General Electric's Answer Center, discussed in Chapter 6, is an example of an organization's effort to internalize knowledge in its customer service representatives. Past solutions to customer complaints are made explicit and included in a database. When a customer service representative encounters a similar problem, she accesses the solution from the database and internalizes it.

Externalization: From Tacit to Explicit

Externalization is the process by which an individual expresses through metaphor, analogy, or image the tacit knowledge in his or her head. Managers may lie awake at night in vain, wondering how they are going to transfer "Jenny's knowledge into Jack's head." The fact of the matter is that it is nearly impossible to actively manage the process of externalization. Instead, knowledge managers should seek to create an environment and systems whereby people may most easily engage in storytelling and other forms of externalization.

Collaborative technologies have been widely used as platforms for the transfer of corporate knowledge. In this next section, we will focus on two of the most widely used technologies for this purpose: intranets and Lotus Notes. Although we acknowledge that other technologies, such as artificial intelligence, case-based reasoning, workflow automation, and data mining, have been used effectively for knowledge management, these tools are relatively more specialized in their application; some are considerably more recent, and there is less reliable information.

Technology as a Platform for Knowledge Transfer

Since their inception, electronic networks have promised corporations interoperability, savings in terms of workflow automation, and integration. Up until recently, this promise went largely unfulfilled as information technicians struggled to reconcile incompatible operating systems, unwieldy customized databases, and an overall infrastructure that was simply not friendly to growth. Intranets—internal, private applications of the more popular Internet—have given corporate America a glimpse at true interoperability. In 1996, Forrester Research found that 96% of 50 companies from the *Fortune* 1,000 had an intranet or were planning on building one in the near future. The Gartner Group estimates that more than 50% of large corporations in the United States will deploy web technology internally by 1998.[19]

One gets the sense that an intranet is a very recent application by the wide variety of definitions it holds. There seems to be some consensus among the people who actually build intranets, however. According to Greg Hubbard, systems architect for SHL Systemshouse in Dallas, Texas, an intranet is an "Internet tool(s) among family."[20] More literally, John Dubiel of Boston Edison says "the Intranet is the Internet in a bottle."[21] Finally, Mark Dodge, telecom manager for United Parcel Service declares, "the Intranet is an organism that creates joy for users, concern for marketing and sheer terror for telecom."[22] This last statement gets to the root strength of an intranet: It is an infinitely expandable phenomenon that may encompass any function of business operations. By its very architecture, an intranet is designed to accommodate varied information forms, operating systems, and computer platforms.

Even in its elemental stage of development, intranets have given many companies reason to consider their full potential. According to a study by International Data Corporation (IDC), a company that creates intranets stands to recoup 1,000% of its investment within 6 to 12 weeks. The study "The Intranet: Slashing the Cost of Business"[23] was based on several companies in the United States, three years after they first implemented their intranets. Many of the applications garnering such savings for corporate America concern the dissemination of knowledge assets. Consider the following examples.

Merging Cultures

In 1995, Lockheed merged with Martin Marietta to create Lockheed Martin Corporation, one of the world's largest defense contractors. By 1996, the merged companies had together acquired or merged with 80 other businesses. This degree of combining visions, cultures, and structural links within an organization created havoc. In the case of Martin Marietta, the company had deep-rooted policies and procedures for everything from vacation policy to the steps taken in a government contract bid. Of course, for the larger Lockheed Martin to maintain forward momentum, these cultural and procedural inconsistencies would have to be surmounted.

Lockheed Martin created Enterprise Information Systems (EIS), a division spread throughout the company that had the task of unifying knowledge assets. When EIS decided to launch an intranet for the policies and procedures, a wave of information conversion ensued. Millions of lines of line of code were run from a mainframe computer through an HTML filter. Hard copy manuals were optically scanned for their information and converted to HTML. Soon, policy coordinators were submitting their protocols to EIS for inclusion on the intranet. With the "open architecture" of the intranet, organizations outside the corporation, such as contractors, were able to keep up with information on policies and procedures. Three groups now guide the content creation on the corporate intranet:

1. *The Network Governing Council* acts as an overall monitor of the intranet's development. It addresses issues of protection of proprietary knowledge, growth of the intranet, and appropriate business uses of the intranet.
2. *WebServ.EIS* manages and implements intranet initiatives such as a dedicated help desk.
3. *Lockheed Martin Web Authors Guild* includes content providers from across the organization. The group works on all issues that affect the creators and consumers of knowledge on the intranet.[24]

Knowledge Sharing

Douglas Aircraft Company, a division of Boeing Corporation, delivers aircraft service bulletins—industry advisories that give critical information on how to modify and service the company's aircraft. The average length of each bulletin is 25 pages. Every customer receives four or five of these advisories every year, accounting for 4 million printed pages. Transferring the process from print and mail to an electronic format housed on a corporate intranet helped Douglas and its clients on three points. Because 65% of the company's customers are international, it took too long for the time-sensitive documentation to arrive in hard copy form. The documentation went from being in a "dead" format (i.e., written on paper) to a "live one" (i.e., in an electronic format that the end user could manipulate). Finally, the electronic dissemination of information also makes storage easier. Douglas is currently working on putting maintenance manuals on the web, which can run 45,000 to 50,000 pages long.[25]

Distributed Training

Northern Telecom's intranet links 280 locations and 63,000 employees in 15 different time zones. On October 21, 1996, Nortel held a one-day worldwide technology exposition that gave its 17,000 technology employees an opportunity to share their projects and ideas via demonstrations, Web sites, and videoconferences. The exposition was held entirely on the company's intranet of 40 Web sites. Eight weeks prior to the event, a Tech Expo '96 site went on-line, providing employees with a place to register their demonstrations, search for other sites, and view video feeds previewing the Expo. On the day of the Tech Expo, more than 140,000 visits were recorded to the Nortel site.[26]

Sales Support

Cadence Design Systems, Inc., sells electronic design automation software and professional services for the design of computer systems, consumer electronics, and semiconductors. In 1995, the Cadence leadership noticed that its customers wanted software and consulting support for the design process rather than tools specifically geared to solving a particular problem. To manage the change, the sales department would have to interact more closely with the customer throughout the entire development process. Sales reps had to understand Cadence's line of 1,000 products and services. It was equally important for the reps to have an understanding of the client's business so Cadence could provide consulting services matched to the client's needs. The sales process now encompassed six elements: qualification, study, proposal, commitment, implementation, and assessment. Any solution had to fall within computability parameters. Cadence employees worked on hardware including Macintosh, PC, and Unix. In addition, the system would have to support native languages, including Japanese. Lotus Notes was considered initially, then passed over for an intranet architecture because the reps needed to integrate information external to the organization.

Early in 1996, Cadence launched OnTrack. The system uses a home page with links to other informational sites and custom applications to draw out each phase of the sales process with ample supporting information. Based on the company's intranet, OnTrack shifts its content dynamically, depending on the location of the client company. For example, when a user logs on to OnTrack, he or she may choose from a worldwide view. Each region chosen may modify the sales process according to its local geography, economy, and so on. OnTrack includes a workflow tool. Information on a customer is made available through an outside news provider. Customer presentations, forms, and sample letter templates are also available to speed the sales process. Members of the sales force, marketing department, and managers all have the right to contribute content to OnTrack. A corporate information submission process, which includes HTML forms, guides them.[27]

Many corporate networks have based their network collaboration and knowledge sharing on Lotus Notes, the technology discussed in Chapter 6. Although Notes, which is based on a proprietary architecture, has been criticized by some information technology (IT) professionals for being too cumbersome and expensive, it is currently widely used by large corporations seeking order for their IC.

But knowledge managers should approach technologies cautiously for their IC management projects. As Stewart points out, the point of knowledge management technology is not the technology.

> To be sure, using high-speed microprocessors, intranets, and whizzy search-engines, you can automate, spiff up, and turbocharge the apparatus. You can preserve what might otherwise deteriorate, catalog what might otherwise disappear. But the sixty-four-bit question remains: If you build it, will they come? Will they bother to make the connection, and can they find what they are looking for?[28]

Unfortunately, the answer to Stewart's question is frequently "No." Although some research has indicated that Notes can increase productivity, other studies show that the technology may fail even before it is implemented. Managers who do not first consider the complexities of their organizations' technology implementation may look like children trying to ram a square peg through a round hole.

Wanda Orlikowski, a professor at MIT's Sloan School of Management, conducted an in-depth analysis of the implementation of Notes at a management consulting firm she calls *Alpha*.[29] "The career structure within Alpha is hierarchical," reported Orlikowski, "the four primary milestones being staff consultant, senior consultant, manager, and principal." Alpha's chief information officer was hired in the late 1980s to increase the firm's effective use of technology. One of his first actions was to buy site licenses for Lotus Notes, which he described as "breakthrough technology," and distribute the software throughout the company (worldwide). The CIO lobbied principals and managers at local and national meetings to adopt the technology, which they did rapidly. The actual use of Notes, however, did not progress at the same rate of implementation. When Orlikowski conducted her research at Alpha, she discovered that one of the greatest barriers to mass use of the system was simply a matter of awareness. Although the principles and managers of the firm liked the idea of Notes, that enthusiasm did not trickle down to the consultants' level, where much of the firm's knowledge was held. Many consultants found out about the Notes implementation by reading it in trade journals. Some found out when it was installed on their computers by a technologist. By and large, many employees at Alpha were unaware of what Notes was and why the firm had purchased it. Some comments from Alpha consultants illustrate this point:

> ▶ "I know absolutely nothing about Notes. I don't know what it is supposed to do."
> ▶ "It's big email."
> ▶ "I've heard that it's a hard copy of email—but I am not very clear about what it is exactly."
> ▶ "It has something to do with communications."
> ▶ "I believe Notes is putting word processing power into spreadsheets."[30]

Even more daunting than overcoming a barrier of ignorance, Alpha had to overcome a culture that seemed antithetical to the mission of Notes: sharing. Competition at management consulting firms can be fierce. Such organizations are characterized by an "up-or-out" culture in which the lower-level employees work hard for the few promotions handed out every year. In such a climate, and such a business, where a consultant's intellectual ability is all that may distinguish him or her from a colleague, it is not surprising that employees did not rush to populate the Notes knowledge archive. In a separate study on knowledge sharing in the management consulting industry, *Consultant's News* found that the greatest concern among executives at management consulting firms was "devising new ways to convince their consultants to willingly and consistently share more information, knowledge, and insights with each other."[31] Alpha employees seemed to corroborate this need:

> "Usually managers work alone because of the competitiveness among the managers. There is a lot of one-upmanship against each other. Their life dream is to become a principal in Alpha, and they'll do anything to get there."

> "I'm trying to develop an area of expertise that makes me stand out. If I shared that with you, you'd get the credit, not me. . . . It's really a cut-throat environment."

> "Power in this firm is your client base and technical ability. . . . It is definitely a function of consulting firms. Now if you put all this information in a Notes database, you lose power. There will be nothing that's privy to you, so you will lose power. It's important that I am selling something that no one else has. When I hear people talk about the importance of sharing expertise in the firm, I say, 'Reality is a nice construct.' "[32]

The third aspect of Alpha that went unexamined prior to the Notes rollout was its policies and procedures. If knowledge-sharing technology seems to clash with preexisting corporate policies (official or unofficial), management must clearly delineate the pecking order of priorities. Otherwise, as Alpha found out, the employees will decide for themselves which is more important.

> "Security is a concern for me. . . . We need to worry about who is seeing the data. . . . Managers should not be able to access all the information even if it is useful [such as] financial information to clients, because they leave and may go and work for competitors. So there should be prohibitions on information access."

> "I would be careful what I put out on Notes though. I like to retain personal control so that when people call me I can tell them not to use it for such and such. But there is no such control within Notes."

▶ "I'd be more fearful that I'd put something out there and it was wrong and somebody would catch it."[33]

At the time that Orlikowski examined Notes usage at Alpha, the implementation was new and, clearly, several barriers had to be overcome before any benefit would be realized. Some firms have managed to do so by implementing very structured protocols for populating their Notes databases. However, this brings up another problem: making a distinction between knowledge management and information management. One of the authors has examined the Notes databases for a consulting firm on par with Alpha. The problem at this firm is not one of too little activity; it is one of too much. Consultants have entered so much information, much of it unstructured and poorly classified, that the database has become unruly. Every consultant in this particular unit of the firm has the ability to enter whatever information he or she pleases, without any regard for its value to the organization. Some of the companies participating in the *Consulting News* survey described systems of submission and review that would avoid the problem of knowledge databases cluttered with information.

▶ At KPMG Peat Marwick, consultants are encouraged to create folders of potential best practices that are then screened by competency leaders in one of 11 areas, ranging from electronic data interchange (EDI) and technology management to mobile computing. The competency leader articulates the knowledge management environment for each area and ensures that a process is in place to standardize the best practices that are contributed; then an administrative staffer maintains the information in a centralized place.

▶ Gemini Consulting has adopted a different process, relying on a combination of full-time knowledge editors and part-time consultants linked to each of the firm's 40 centers of excellence, according to John Bateson, senior vice president in charge of innovation and knowledge management. These editors "make an arbitration" but have no formal criteria to guide their selection. "We encourage each of them to use their judgement and to ask questions like, 'Is (this practice) truly different? Is this transferable? And to make judgments such as 'This is great. This is new. But they haven't really pushed the envelope.' "[34]

▶ Andersen Consulting focuses these efforts around the firm's "communities of practice" by industry and appears to have among the most formal of processes for collecting best practices in the consulting industry. Three levels of consultants are involved in the capturing, screening, and selection, according to Charles Paulk, the firm's chief information officer. Best practices are reviewed from a "strategy, process, and technology standpoint." The partner responsible for each industry area acts as a "knowledge sponsor," providing "a big picture view of how that area wants to serve clients and identifying overall approaches." With that direction, a "knowledge integrator" focuses on defining the content of each practice submitted for inclusion in the firm's database. And "knowledge developers" are the consultants who actually contribute the content, with the help of part-time technical support staff.[35]

▶ Ernst & Young manages knowledge, worldwide, through its Center for Business Knowledge. This unit undertakes the formidable task of identifying, collecting, and purifying knowledge across enormous boundaries and categories. The output can be anything from specialized knowledge about a geographic region to licensing requirements.[36]

PHASE 4: KNOWLEDGE CREATION AND CONNECTION

Would that creating new knowledge were as simple as filling a room with smart people and then giving them some time to come up with revenue-generating innovations. If this were the case, history would not be filled with stories of brilliant ideas that never made it to market and industry veterans who led their companies astray. Knowledge that is useful to the organization must be intimately responsive to market realities, closely aligned with the company's strategic direction, and uniquely suited to the competencies of the workforce. To generate such knowledge, Nonaka and Takeuchi enumerate five enabling conditions organizations must meet.[37]

1. *Intention.* Loosely defined as the organization's goals, intention guides individuals as they generate new knowledge, helping them discern that which will bring the organization closer to its stated vision of success.

2. *Autonomy.* At the individual level, autonomy gives employees the time and space needed to develop new knowledge. Autonomous people feel

free to think about remote possibilities and creative ideas that are the wellsprings of a company's innovation.

3. *Redundancy.* Although it connotes a replication, redundancy actually refers to a common language and overlapping experience in businesses. For members of teams to generate a solution to a problem, they must be able to agree on what the problem is even if they approach it from varying perspectives. Redundancy allows this to happen.

4. *Requisite variety.* An organization's internal diversity must match the complexity of the environment in which the company exists. Requisite variety exists when people have quick access to needed information. When the opposite occurs, insularity clouds the organization's view of the real market situation and the organization's knowledge needs.

5. *Fluctuation.* Also referred to as "creative chaos," fluctuation in an organization counteracts knowledge-inhibiting roles, routines, and mental models. In response to fluctuation, which often appears as a crisis, organizations usually devise their most productive new knowledge.

The notion of fluctuation makes a perfect starting point to discuss the most immediate way in which organizations generate knowledge: through shared problem solving.

In Search of Conflict

While it is difficult to change a company that is struggling, it is next to impossible to change a company that is showing all the outward signs of success. Without the spur of a crisis or a period of great stress, most organizations—like most people—are incapable of changing habits and attitudes of a lifetime.

—John F. McDonnell,
McDonnell Douglas Corporation[38]

Ironically, that which makes companies so strong—their core competencies—are generally the sources of their failure. What Dorothy Leonard-Barton refers to as *core rigidities,* in her book *Wellsprings of Knowledge,*[39] have spelled the demise of entire industries. For example, Leonard-Barton writes how Sam Walton said in his autobiography that Sears lost its dominance because it would not acknowledge the threat that Wal-Mart and K-Mart posed. Instead, it continued to rely on its tried retailing and purchasing techniques while the competition gained ground. Not until the end of the 1980s did Sears' position papers even mention Wal-Mart. A former executive at Sears recounts that the company issued "bulletins" to senior management prescribing solutions to corporate problems. "God forbid there should be a problem that comes up for which there isn't a bulletin," the executive said.[40]

In another example, the Japanese auto industry lost its advantage over the United States by relying too heavily on the strengths that had helped it unseat Detroit in the first place. In 1980s, the world's eyes were focused on the Japanese production systems that allowed it to design and develop automobiles a year faster than the average American or European company. Just-in-time systems, small-lot production, and total quality management made the Japanese factory the envy of manufacturers around the world. By the early 1990s, however, the United States had emulated many of these innovations and narrowed the gap between Japanese and American production time to tolerable levels. Industry experts have noted that the American "catch-up" was not the only reason the Japanese lost their lead. In addition, Japanese design became "fat." Too wide a variety of designs and too many model changes and unnecessary options were evidence that the Japanese advantage had become a liability. Although "lean" production systems may have put Honda, Nissan, and Toyota in the same class as the American Big Three, "overspecialization" threatened to destroy their competitive advantage.[41]

Individuals are no different when it comes to core rigidities. People tend to develop specialized skills and then rely exclusively on them as they approach problems. The self-described "marketing guys," "techies," or "numbers persons" reveal the skills they use to identify themselves. Although these skills may have brought them success in the past, when it comes to new knowledge generation these personalized skills might become obstacles. As Leonard-Barton observes, "innovation occurs at the boundaries between mind-sets, not within the provincial territory of one knowledge and skill base."[42] To shake people and organizations out of the insularity of their personal knowledge and core rigidities, organizations must create conflict.

> Business is conflict. That's the creative process. You don't get excellence by saying yes. You get love, but you don't get excellence. Simon & Schuster is a company that raised the hurdles on excellence every bloody day.
>
> —Richard Snyder, Former CEO, Simon & Schuster[43]

When individuals come together to solve a problem, they bring with them their unique perspectives, tools, and personalized skills. The conflict that ensues, observes Gerald Hirshberg, director of Nissan Design International, may create knowledge. He calls the energy created by such conflict, *creative abrasion*. It has the power to create rather than destroy, Hirshberg says, to synthesize rather than fragment.

> Multiple disciplines in the same studio, fighting over radio stations and modes of dress and work hours and what's perceived as work . . . , all of that I saw as a rich yeasty opportunity for a kind of abrasion that I wanted to turn into light rather than heat.[44]

There are companies, such as Interval Research, a think tank for new media innovation, that thrive on such conflict of styles. Says Interval President and CEO David Liddle, the company needs both "nerds and hippies."

> Hippies are people who care about doing the right thing, and once they have done the right thing, they kind of let getting it finished up be left to somebody else. Nerds are people who care about doing things right, and they don't worry too much about the big, broad, flexible outlook and all that sort of stuff. They are very, very proud of their execution and quantitative aspects of what they have gotten done and so on.[45]

Interval constantly seeks to maintain a mix of cognitive styles—nerds and hippies—that will generate new ideas. Nissan Design also actively manages such complexity. New hires take "personalysis" tests to ascertain their probable temperament in a group setting. Hirshberg is quick to acknowledge that the tests are not some form of psychoanalysis, but they do prove useful for managers when creating work teams. The test, he says, "works beautifully in helping us to be open about the fact that each one of us is quite different, and there are some tremendous opportunities to alleviate some of the tensions we are experiencing by acknowledging openly those differences."[46] Some Nissan Design employees even go so far as to display a color-coded sign of their cognitive style on their desktops. Although such displays may seem to counter the intention of the initiative (people may prejudge certain personality types, etc.), managers may guard against this by making sure that group decision making focuses on the problem at hand, not on the presenters.[47]

Such is the case at Intel, the microprocessor giant, where soon-to-retire Chairman and CEO Andrew Grove has long espoused a management style he calls "constructive confrontation." Grove developed this style as a young manager when he found himself drawn into a battle between one quality and one operations engineer. Every day, each one would come into Grove's office to complain about the other. Finally, Grove stopped one of the engineers in midcomplaint and asked the other engineer to join them in the argument. The confrontation that ensued was embarrassing and somewhat halting, Grove recalls, but after years of practice, this management style has become synonymous with working at Intel.[48] Constructive confrontation at Intel is defined by two characteristics: (a) open debate, irrespective of rank or seniority, is encouraged to explore issues, and (b) the debates are focused on finding what's best for the company, not the individual. Grove describes a meeting that took place at Intel that exemplifies the utility of constructive conflict.

> "I just don't understand how your new way of measuring things around here will help us at all," the plant manager said, grimacing. Others at the meeting merely looked puzzled. The vice president of manufacturing, the plant manager's direct superior, had just finished vigorously urging the use of a particular statistical indicator to determine whether the company's plants were delivering products on time. Faced with the plant manager's incredulity, the vice president redoubled his efforts, trying again to win over everyone in the room.
>
> The plant manager remained unconvinced. His colleagues then jumped into the fray. Arguments generated rebuttals, numbers collided with other numbers. New ideas began to surface, most of them to be immediately rejected, until eventually the heated exchanges dissipated. The still-animated group of people in the room suddenly realized, with considerable satisfaction, that they had now come up with the right statistical measure.
>
> As the meeting ended, the vice president shook his head in mock dismay. "It's too bad," he said, "that you people are so reticent." He put away his papers somewhat ruefully—his hours of preparation for the meeting had not resulted in his proposal being adopted. But he also knew that what had finally been agreed upon was better than his original idea.[49]

Nonaka and Takeuchi describe a case in which Matsushita, the Japanese electronics and appliance manufacturer, deliberately introduced an environment of chaos to generate new knowledge. In May

1983, Matsushita faced a declining home market for home appliances and increased competition from companies in newly industrialized countries. It launched an initiative to improve its competitiveness in these markets and to thrust itself into new markets traditionally dominated by IBM, NEC, and Hitachi. The company combined three "problem children," divisions that produced goods for practically mature markets. These included the Rice-Cooker Division, the Heating Appliances Division, and the Rotation Division that made food processors. The focus of this integration was to capitalize on a trend one market researcher had noted in America: "More working women, increasingly simplified home cooking, and poorer diets."[50] The newly formed Cooking Appliances Division soon came up with a slogan to guide their development efforts: Easy & Rich. The idea was to create products that would enable simple cooking of high-quality food. The first product to come to market, a home bakery, was a success, but only because Matsushita was able to first introduce creative chaos (the melding of three divisions) and then foster a common language among the new co-workers. To introduce *redundancy,* the company organized a three-day retreat for 13 middle managers from the various divisions. In addition, the personnel department produced an in-house newspaper called "Hot-Line."[51]

Creative conflict and shared problem solving are means for generating knowledge that the organization needs immediately. What about knowledge the organization may need in the future? In this case, the organization must actively engage in experimentation.

Experimentation

So long as enough of the economy's indicators do not change, the organization may paint a reasonable vision of what is to be. When new technologies, markets, and competitors regularly disrupt the traditional logic of the marketplace, managers are hard-pressed to find any milestones by which to judge their future, let alone their present situations. Of course, this does not relieve managers of their responsibility to maintain forward momentum. The question thus becomes, How? Experimentation creates options for the company in the middle of enormous uncertainty. Experimentation satisfies Nonaka and Takeuchi's "requisite variety": the precondition for knowledge generation that internal diversity must match market chaos. In short, companies must mimic all the uncertainty and rapid change inside the organization that occurs outside.

In his 1984 book *Three Degrees Above Zero,* Jeremy Bernstein described Bell Laboratories as a place where scientists were comfortably sheltered from the tumult of the marketplace, free to ponder fundamental technical and scientific problems.[52] Corporate research laboratories—such as the celebrated Xerox Palo Alto Research Center (PARC)—have come under a considerable amount of scrutiny for not producing "hard returns" on dollars invested in their intellectual pursuits. Any student of computer history knows the story of PARC's invention of the graphical user interface that was subsequently commercialized by Steven Jobs in the Macintosh because the scientists at PARC did not see the value of their invention.

In today's age of rapid change, much of corporate America has moved away from this model of experimentation and is increasingly supporting research that is closely aligned with the company's strategic direction. At Alcoa, for example, research is tightly linked to the needs of individual business units. Teams are assembled from the business units to consider sponsoring current research projects. In one case, a business unit asked a team of researchers to visit a customer site. The researchers quickly recognized a way the client could reduce manufacturing costs by using new alloys.[53]

MCI Communications has taken this trend to its extreme by eliminating its central research lab entirely. Instead, the company's 12,000 researchers develop technologies that have been licensed from other laboratories. This trend has caused some to worry. California Institute of Technology physicist Michael L. Roukes asks, "With corporate labs becoming users rather than creators of new frontiers, where will the new frontiers come from?"[54]

Bill Gates is bucking the prevailing trend in corporate America to outsource large-scale research and development. He has hired 245 scientific researchers from around the world to staff Microsoft's research laboratory. Microsoft Research is headed by Nathan Myhrvold, who graduated from high school at age 14, earned his master's in geophysics from UCLA at age 19, and earned his Ph.D. in mathematical and theoretical physics from Princeton at age 23. Myhrvold, Microsoft's chief technology officer, also earned a degree in mathematical economics along the way. After leaving a fellowship with Steven Hawkin, Myhrvold started a software company that Microsoft acquired in 1986. By 1991, he was running the company's advanced developments unit, a group whose job was "doing things others agree are theoretically possible but have not been done before." In that year, Myhrvold proposed to the board of directors a research lab that would pursue projects that "only the investigator thinks is possible." The overriding culture of such a lab, Myhrvold insisted, would be like a dinner party at which you don't "interrupt the conversations and tell people what they should be saying and thinking. If you pick the right people to convene, more and better things happen than you could have planned."[55] If Microsoft Research is a dinner party, guests must be prepared to sit with an intellectually exclusive crowd. Researchers at Microsoft include the following:

- Gary Starkweather, inventor of the laser printer
- Gordon Bell, father of the VAX microcomputer
- Chuck Thacker, co-inventor of Ethernet
- Alvy Ray Smith, founder of Pixar, the computer animation company that made *Toy Story*

Remarkably, however, Microsoft Research supports scientists whose work does not even intuitively relate to computing. Jennifer Tour Chayes and her husband, Christian Borgs, for example, are statistical physicists researching the "behavior of gases, liquids, solids, and other states of matter from the underlying microscopic world of molecules, atoms, and electrons." The research is supported on the premise that if the company wants to discover the next strategic technology, it must develop it internally. Gates initially balked at hiring Chayes and Borgs, but six months after their hire, researchers from another group—cryptography—discovered the physicists and began an inquiry. The cryptographers were interested in Chayes and Borgs's statistical insights into phase transitions—when a gas turns into a liquid for example—that could help them devise an "organic" code that would change at certain points, rendering it unbreakable. The two research groups regularly compare notes to see where their work may intersect.[56]

Of course, not every company will invest the millions of dollars needed to build a laboratory of Microsoft's caliber. But research and experimentation can take place throughout the organization because it is a mind-set and a discipline as well as a place and a budget item. For example, the prevailing attitude at 3M is that innovation may come from anywhere in the company, including the shop floor. The well-documented inventions of scotch tape and Post-it Notes were the result of managers who experimented with a new idea and then championed it until product delivery.[57] Experiments such as these are frequently unremarkable at first, perhaps even irrelevant, but they have the power to rejuvenate the entire company.

In 1972, Hewlett-Packard introduced the HP-35 scientific calculator, the first portable calculator to perform trigonometric, logarithmic, and exponential functions. Bill Hewlett championed the design of this product because he wanted such a tool for his own personal use. Marketing research indicated that the company would be able to sell only 5,000 calculators, but within three years of the product launch, HP sold more than 300,000, and by 1989, the company controlled a significant portion of the $2.23 billion industry.[58]

Managers may create a climate for experimentation with one important first step: They must embrace the knowledge-building capacity of intelligent failure. Obviously, failures exist that do not benefit the organization—what comedian John Cleese calls "true copper-bottomed mistakes like wearing a black bra under a white blouse, or, to take a more masculine example, starting a land war in Asia."[59] Intelligent failure, on the other hand, results from risk taking.

Although it sometimes sounds as if Silicon Valley is the home of only good ideas, industry watcher Michael Malone says, "In truth, it is a graveyard. Failure is Silicon Valley's greatest strength. Every failed product or enterprise is a lesson stored in the collective memory of the country."[60] Tom Peters credits failure as the critical learning experience for legendary entrepreneurs like Richard Branson of the Virgin Group, Les Wexner of the Limited, and Anita Roddick of Body Shop International.[61] When these people, like people in any organization, question why things are the way they are and experiment with new methods, the results, successful or failed, constitute new knowledge.

Embodying Knowledge

The third form of knowledge generation involves the processes, techniques, and technologies a company employs in its operations. When a company purchases a new tool or implements a new procedure, the people who implement it will invest their personal knowledge and often create new knowledge to maximize its benefit. At Chaparral Steel, for example, new tools are constantly pushed to the limits of their productivity. Managers operate under the assumption that every tool has the potential to be improved. When Chaparral acquired steel-rolling equipment, the vendor said the tool could produce 8-inch slabs. Eventually, Chaparral modified the tool to produce 14-inch slabs, at which point the vendor asked to buy the design for this improvement. Chaparral's electric arc furnaces, which initially melted steel at the rate of 250,000 and 500,000 tons per year, now melt 600,000 and 1 million tons per year, respectively.[62] Employees of Chaparral had literally embedded their knowledge in the machines and increased the value of the tool to the organization.

To manage this knowledge-generative process, managers must involve the right people in implementing the tool or system. To begin the selection process, they must answer the following questions:

> ▶ *What knowledge must the users possess to develop new knowledge effectively?*[63]
>
> When assigning tasks, managers must remain aware of the understanding that the task will require. If the users do not possess the requisite understanding, such as how to work a machine or complete a task, they will not be able to create new knowledge.

> ▶ *What type of knowledge should the users possess to implement the tool or system?*
>
> For example, do the users have to be expert in the area of human resource management to develop a new benefits package calculator? Alternately, should the users represent the people who actually use such a tool? Each of these user types possesses specific knowledge and will generate unique knowledge for the organization.

> ▶ *Are the users representative of the situations in which the tools will be used?*
>
> If a new tool is to be used on one site by a well-defined group of individuals, then the user pool should reflect that group. If the tool is being developed for use across multiple sites, however, the manager must ensure that users representative of the entire organizations invest their knowledge in the tool. For example, researchers found that a company implementing software at three of its plants was experiencing hazards at two of the sites

because the third was used as the implementation prototype. Idiosyncrasies must be taken into account.

▶ *Are the users willing to invest their knowledge in the tool or system?*
The feedback and suggestions users give when implementing a new tool or system are the foundations of new knowledge. If a user is unwilling to share such knowledge, the manager must find users who are.

Importing Knowledge

There are times when an organization that does not possess certain knowledge internally and does not have the skills to find it through experimentation must look outside its own boundaries. A firm's mastery of innovation depends on its ability to recognize its capability gaps and to fill them with knowledge external to the organization. Sources of external knowledge are numerous. They include, but are not limited to, the following:

Consortia of Competitive Firms. Sensitivity to monopolies limited the number of joint ventures in the United States, but it was a concern for the country's competitiveness that led to the passage of the National Cooperative Research Act (NCRA) of 1984. The legislation was meant to counteract Article 7 of the Clayton Act that prohibited two or more firms from contracting to cooperate for a specific business objective. Under NCRA protection, companies filed for 609 R&D joint ventures between 1985 and 1996, translating into 53 joint ventures filed annually. In comparison, between 1976 and 1979, only 21 joint ventures were filed, or 7 annually.[64] According to another study, research among competitive firms yields a rate of return 150% greater than research done by the firm independently. IBM, Motorola, and Apple, for example, banded together to develop the PowerPC chip. Detroit's Big Three auto manufacturers have come together to improve designs of crash test dummies and electronic vehicle batteries.[65]

Universities. Universities have become prolific sources of new knowledge. According to a study by the Association of University Technology Managers (AUTM), in 1995, academic institutions in North America collected $592 million in royalties and licenses from their research, a 167% increase from 1991. University patents rose from fewer than 250 in 1979 to more than 2,741 in 1996. AUTM estimates the market value of these patents at $25 billion. The flood of lucrative licensing deals is thanks in large part to the 1980 Bayh-Dole act that enabled universities to own and patent inventions made under federally funded research initiatives. Prior to Bayh-Dole, universities filed fewer than 250 patents per year.[66]

Among universities, Stanford is a frequently cited model for industry-academe cooperative research. Much of the credit for Stanford's almost symbiotic relationship with Silicon Valley has been given to the late Frederick Emmons Terman. In the late 1930s, Terman was an engineering professor with a couple of promising students. He encouraged them to turn their graduate thesis into a commercial product and thus was born Hewlett-Packard. Terman championed the Stanford Research Park, one of the world's first industrial parks, which served as William Hewlett and David Packard's second home after the famous Palo Alto garage where they launched their business. Terman accurately predicted that the U.S. government would direct a great deal of research monies into science and technology after World War II. His vision was to turn the pastoral stretch of land where Stanford sits into a community of knowledge that would rival Oxford and Bologna.

Between 1960 and 1990, companies spawned by Stanford graduates created 250,000 jobs.[67] In the 1980s, three start-up companies emerged from Stanford's Margaret Jacks Hall, then home of the computer science department. These companies now have a combined market value of $50 billion.

> On the second floor, a professor named Jim Clark was working on a project that would become Silicon Graphics. On the fourth, Andy Bechtolsheim, then a Ph.D. candidate, was building a prototype workstation for the Stanford University Network, or Sun, which would become Sun Microsystems. In the basement, a research computing director named Len Bosack, together with Sandy Lerner, his wife and a counterpart at the business school, were coming up with ways to link the various computer networks woven throughout the campus, an effort that became Cisco Systems.[68]

Stanford is not the only university to graduate successful high-tech entrepreneurs. University of California, Berkeley, has Gordon Moore and Andrew Grove of Intel as distinguished alumni. But at Stanford, it is *de rigeur* for academics to work in the Valley and for executives to share their experiences with students about to enter the job market. Stanford's current engineering dean, John Hennesey, developed RISC (reduced instruction set computer) chip technology in the early 1980s, took a sabbatical to start a company called MIPS computing, and then returned in 1985 to continue teaching.[69] Indeed, Terman's legacy is institutionalized at Stanford. There is the Yahoo! Professorship, Paul G. Allen Center for Integrated Systems, classrooms with the names Toshiba, NEC, Mitsubishi, and of course, Hewlett-Packard hanging above the door.[70]

Complementary Industries. Leonard-Barton explains how General Motors' Electronic Data Systems Corporation is leveraging knowledge held by noncompetitive companies to enter new markets.

> [It] is experimenting with interactive media by allying itself with a wide variety of partners—an in-room, hotel-movie venture with Spectradyne; a gambling venture with Video Lottery Technologies; an agreement with USTravel to explore automated machines dispensing tickets for airline or Broadway show seats; a CD-ROM home-shopping experiment with Apple; and a home-banking service with USWest and France Telecom. Each of these partners is expected to provide some expertise that EDS neither has in-house nor intends to develop.[71]

Managing the import of knowledge sometimes requires overcoming a tendency among individuals to reject knowledge that is not their own. When it comes to generating knowledge, however, being original is less important than being effective. The stories of how the Japanese implemented the American concept of total quality management to their advantage should prove this point. British Petroleum encourages its employees to adopt useful knowledge despite its origin by presenting the "Thief of the Year" award to the individual who steals the best idea for an application. Texas Instruments has a similar honor called, "Not Invented Here, but I Did It Anyway."[72] Another way to overcome "Not Invented Here" mentality is to support what Leonard-Barton calls "knowledge gatekeepers," those individuals who maintain ties outside the organization with industry groups, clubs, and conferences.[73] Managers should encourage these gatekeepers, for they will continually renew the company's store of new knowledge.

The most effective way to unblock the path to external knowledge is to instill a sense of urgency. By stressing the importance of an immediate and highly effective solution, employees will naturally look to existing sources of such knowledge before building the knowledge themselves. In fact, it is management's job to guide all knowledge generative activities—whether they involve problem solving, experimentation, process development, or import—by creating a need for knowledge and then proving the means to fill that need.

Never Knowledge for Its Own Sake

> The role of top management is to give employees a sense of crisis as well as a lofty ideal.
>
> —Ryuzaburo Kaku, Chairman of Cannon[74]

According to MIT's Peter Senge, workers feel a certain pressure when they are presented with a vision of where the company is going compared with its present state. He calls it *creative tension,* and it is the source of much of a company's knowledge generation.[75] For without that vision of the end goal, employees are incapable of grasping what knowledge matters and what does not. Knowledge generation must be pursued under the direction of what Senge calls the company's *shared vision.* At its simplest level, a shared vision is the answer to the question, "What do we want to create?" Just as people carry personal visions as pictures or images in their heads and hearts, people throughout an organization carry shared visions. They create a sense of commonality that permeates the organization and gives coherence to diverse activities.

> A vision is truly shared when you and I have a similar picture and are committed to one another having it, not just each of us, individually, having it. When people truly share a vision they are connected, bound together by a common aspiration. Personal visions derive their power from a common caring. In fact, we have come to believe that one of the reasons people seek to build shared visions is their desire to be connected in an important undertaking.[76]

When Ford Motor brought together 400 people for the 1994 "Team Mustang," the group needed a shared vision to guide its knowledge creation. With so many perspectives on such a complicated product as a car, each person holding his or her own personal vision of what the customer would want, the team needed a shared vision to guide the execution of details. The first image the team developed was "Rambo," a muscle-bound warrior. Then the team considered "Bruce Jenner," a lithe champion with great endurance. Finally, the team agreed on "Schwarzenegger," a rugged *and* cultured image. It is not difficult to imagine what could have happened if the individual units of the design team—those building the grill, hub caps, upholstery—were designing their components with conflicting guiding visions in mind: perhaps a Bruce Jenner exterior and Rambo interior.[77]

A guiding vision serves more than the purpose of keeping knowledge workers cognizant of the customer's needs. The vision serves as a constant reminder throughout the knowledge generation process of what knowledge to feed back into the organization.

Project teams work at a frantic pace. Individuals with well-defined skills are pulled together for a specific purpose. They work like mad on the project until it is completed without ever knowing how the organization is supposed to benefit from the experience. As Leonard-Barton observed, such individuals tend to feel like "Sisyphus in the Greek fable."

> For all eternity, Sisyphus was sentenced to haul an immense boulder painfully to the top of a hill only to see it repeatedly crash back down to the bottom. Too often, the researchers and engineers on development projects harness their mental and physical creative powers to achieve the almost impossible—often at considerable personal cost—only to wonder, at project's end, whether and why the corporation needed that particular boulder moved, or to speculate that they were climbing the wrong hill and the work was in vain.[78]

There is a notorious example of what can happen when knowledge is developed without a guiding vision. As mentioned earlier, scientists at Xerox's Palo Alto Research Center had spent years developing the elements of a graphical user interface (GUI) for computers, including icons, menus, and the mouse. Unfortunately, the high level of autonomy under which the scientists worked caused them to fail to grasp the economic potential for such inventions.

The most lasting detriment of knowledge generation without a guiding vision is that after the project is done, the knowledge remains with the individuals and not the organization. When the organization articulates a clear vision for a knowledge-generative project, however, individuals understand what knowledge they are expected to invest back into the organization. They know what knowledge matters and what does not. In 1961, for example, John F. Kennedy issued a challenge to America's space program; put a man on the moon by the end of the decade. That guiding vision inspired the aerospace community to build whatever knowledge was necessary (and to disregard what didn't matter) to reach the goal.

In the mid-1960s, one of NASA's lead contractors, MIT's Draper Laboratory, discovered that the internal guidance system they were developing for Apollo was flawed. Although admitting the mistake jeopardized the reputation of the lab, the scientists insisted on starting the project all over again. The guiding vision for the project—to put man on the moon by the end of the decade—was strong enough for the researchers to abandon knowledge that was not useful.[79]

NASA represents the essential challenge in embracing knowledge: It is extremely demanding of the organization's leadership. No matter what the ultimate goal of a knowledge initiative is, leadership is ultimately responsible for creating the set of circumstances that will foster success. And unlike the corporation that values tangible assets as primary competitive advantages in leadership, the knowledge organization requires a unique approach to leadership. We call this approach *leading with knowledge.*

LEADING
WITH KNOWLEDGE

*There is nothing more difficult to take in hand, more
perilous to conduct, or more uncertain in its success than
to take the lead in the introduction of a new order of
things.*

—Niccolò Machiavelli

We believe that information arises from the processing of data,
knowledge arises from the processing of information, and
wisdom arises from the processing of knowledge. As senior-
level executives come to understand the economic power of knowledge,
the question becomes not whether one should move to becoming a
knowledge organization but, rather, how one navigates that direction
most quickly.

LEADERSHIP IN KNOWLEDGE ORGANIZATIONS

Throughout this book, we have emphasized that knowledge resides at all
levels of the organization. The knowledge organization requires an

acceptance that the people at the top, or even a group at the top, do not constitute the repository of all knowledge. Indeed, sometimes the most valuable knowledge can be found at the levels where organizational members are closest to customers and suppliers. But the leaders at the top of the organization determine how quickly and how effectively an organization can become a true knowledge organization. Successful knowledge organizations are successful because they have leaders who come to understand the relationship between leadership and knowledge. Such leaders stand apart because they have an ability to view the world differently, to change people's frame of reference.

There is an old saw that goes, "If you always do what you have always done, you will always get what you have always got—probably a little less."

It is interesting today to see how frequently companies pattern their activities after other companies, doing so with some sort of internal mind-set that they are going to get better results than the companies they patterned themselves after. The idea of trying to do what everyone else does and somehow achieving an advantage is interesting. The point is that in a knowledge organization you really must do things differently. The key notion is that to *do* things differently, you must *view* things differently.

This takes us to the very core of our model—the role and importance of vision in the knowledge organization (see Figure 10.1).

THE ROLE OF VISION

When physical assets are the primary measure of corporate value, it stands to reason that physical trappings—huge offices, priceless art, and views from tower suites—become corollary measures of executive success. The style and amount of executive amenities, which might be called "executive aristocracy," have notable implications. Perks of the executive nobility—such as style of travel; the grandeur and comfort of work areas; the crowds of minions who follow, carry, and inform; and the gilded accoutrements of something as simple as lunch—lead to success's creating a barrier between the executives and the customer. In a way, the higher you go the further away you get—from markets, from customers, from objective reality.

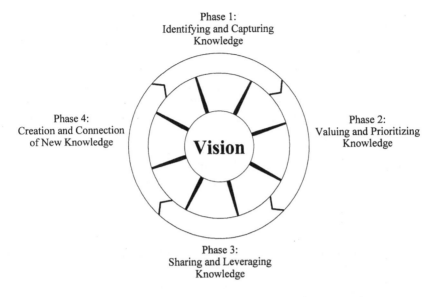

Figure 10.1. A Strategic Model for Conceptualizing and Leveraging Knowledge
SOURCE: Copyright © 1999 by Richard C. Huseman, Ph.D., and Jon P. Goodman, Ph.D.

We have heard, far too many times, apologias from executive suites for missed numbers, lost markets, and shoddy performance—and the resulting recommendations to downsize, reengineer, and let them all eat cake. The old joke about a recession being when you lose your job and a depression being when the economist loses his has something in common with this. The real pain always seems to be blamed on outside forces: shifting markets, overregulated industries, and monetary policy. This ignores the uncomfortable truth that companies don't fail, people do.

In the emerging world of knowledge organizations what you know is far more important than where you sit. Status is out—smarts are in. If, for example, you were to visit Intel's offices, you would be hard put to determine status and power by looking at personal workspaces, which are nearly all the same size, regardless of position.

The executive who understands the growing importance of knowledge in the organization fully realizes that the most important part of his or her job is to impart vision—not only strategic vision but the vision that has to do with organizational culture and values. And those values are embodied in the organization's people. What and who does the knowledge organization reward and value? Does it embody its talk?

We must continue to examine how members of the knowledge organization are recruited, retained, and rewarded. If you agree that the organization's most important assets walk out the door every night and whether they'll show up the next day is very much tied to the culture and values of the organization, you must examine the vision and values of the organization.

Indeed, the centerpiece of our model, vision, is what determines how effectively the model can be employed in any given organization. With that understanding firmly in mind, a final review of the four phases is perhaps an appropriate summary.

PHASE 1: IDENTIFYING AND CAPTURING KNOWLEDGE

As we discussed in previous chapters, companies must audit and describe the nature of their knowledge assets, determine where knowledge resides, and develop systems that allow for the codification and archiving of that knowledge.

The first part, the identification and description of the knowledge assets, involves (at the very least) a complete inventory of the following:

- Patents
- Copyrights
- Trademarks
- Trade secrets
- Manufacturing of processing know-how (and the underlying "know-who")
- Operational manuals
- Market information
- Competitor information
- Employee competence/capability inventory

When this information is compiled, relational databases and shared information retrieval systems can be established so that all who need to know can know and information becomes part of a dynamic process of ingesting, archiving, updating, and timely retrieval methods. Without robust retrieval systems, all the best efforts of codifying and collecting are worthless. Time, thought, and effort have to be invested in developing and *testing* the key words, associative systems, or content tables that let the user know what's archived or put into a database.

PHASE 2: VALUING AND PRIORITIZING KNOWLEDGE

In many cases, we have been doing all the right things for the wrong reasons. When we implement elaborate physical inventory systems but neglect intellectual assets, we fail to communicate our belief in the value of knowledge. Our accountants have done a good job of accurately telling us where we have been. We can install rich, robust inventory systems that tell us everything we need to know about how fast our most expensive products are turning, how soon we need to order components, how empty the bins may be. But there are precious few systems that would prompt executives to capture Harry's knowledge before he retires, value patents that were shelved because of lack of strategic fit, or allow for the sharing of market tidings as they pop up in the field.

In the knowledge organization, the future value of knowledge and its value to the company are now the first order of business. In previous chapters, we have shared some of the practices emerging in different companies to value and prioritize knowledge. There is no prescription, which is why so much of this information is something less than the ideal formulary for success. The fundamental action required is to view "knowing" as having value and, from there, derive comprehensive lists of what is known, who knows, where knowledge is generated, where it is housed, and who needs it. In essence, the knowledge organization rests on the belief that we must view that which is known and knowable as being describable and tangible and as having boundaries. We must compel ourselves to convert the tacit to the explicit.

PHASE 3: SHARING AND LEVERAGING KNOWLEDGE

But when we codify and archive, have we achieved anything meaningful?

Knowledge and the conditions for its transfer must become omnipresent in the corporation. We must develop systems that share core knowledge throughout the organization and allow us to piggyback—

through information—one person's knowledge onto another's. Knowledge can be leveraged. This is at the heart of state-of-the-art practices.

When we speak of state of the art, we are describing products, processes, or technologies that have advanced from other less-developed ones. The knowledge gained in producing X leads to X^2. One technology informs another, and the output of one system is the input of another. Because *people,* not technologies or machines, are the generators of this knowledge, knowledge organizations create a new internal democracy. Systems that allow for sharing of salient information about success and failure, cross-pollination of ideas, and lifelong learning are systems that will support the diffusion of valuable knowledge throughout the organization.

The imperative for knowledge organizations is to accept that knowing is everywhere, that a title does not imply intellectual transcendence, and that the care and feeding of all good minds means providing an environment that demonstrates commitment to ideas and the people who generate them.

The 21st-century corporation will be competing for the best and brightest people even more intensely than it will compete for customers.

PHASE 4: CREATION AND CONNECTION OF NEW KNOWLEDGE

When an organization knows what it knows, values and prioritizes that knowledge, and develops systems for leveraging and sharing, it leads directly to the creation of new knowledge. When that new knowledge is then connected to the main body of knowledge (Phase 1), the result is a system that transforms the organization. This leads to a more dynamic culture and, most important, provides an environment in which the generation and use of critical knowledge becomes organic, goal seeking, and sustainable.

The model is designed to illustrate the self-generating nature of knowledge systems and knowledge organizations. A company's success in the coming years will be directly related to the degree that it can design systems that continuously lead to the development of more and newer knowledge. Every knowledge system can be viewed as a sample of one, but what we've covered in the previous chapters can be a way to generate critical thinking, creative strategies, guideposts, and checklists in the development of these systems.

RISK TAKING AND THE KNOWLEDGE ORGANIZATION

The path to becoming a knowledge organization is not easy. Although our understanding of knowledge and its role in organizations is growing rapidly, in many ways we are in new and sometimes uncharted territory. We are required to make new types of investments, design new systems, and view employees and customers differently than many of us have in the past. Many of the decisions we make as we implement knowledge concepts involve various degrees of risk taking. As always, the risks are proportionate to the rewards. In this case, however, the most serious risk for corporate leaders is *not* to make decisions that will move them to becoming a knowledge organization. Perhaps the notion of risk taking in a knowledge organization is placed in an appropriate perspective in the following:

> *"Come to the edge"*
> *"We can't. We are afraid."*

> *"Come to the edge."*
> *"We can't. We will fall!"*

> *"Come to the edge"*

> *And they came.*
> *And he pushed them.*

> *And they flew.*

> *Come let us fly together.*
>
> —Guillaume Apollinaire

NOTES

uotations at the beginning of each chapter come from *The Forbes Book of Quotations: Thoughts on the Business of Life,* edited by Ted Goodman, Black Dog & Leventhal Publishers, New York, 1997.

Articles from many of the periodicals quoted in the text were found through Lexus Nexus, a periodical research service used by a variety of academic and organizational research institutions. The referenced articles were originally printed in the following periodicals: *Boston Globe, Boston Herald, Business Week, Forbes, Forbes ASAP, Fortune, Harvard Business Review, Inc., Investor's Business Daily, San Jose Business Journal,* and *Training: The Magazine of Human Resources Development.* For more information regarding Lexus Nexus articles, please contact your local library or reference the individual periodical directly.

Introduction

1. Derived from data provided by the Bureau of Labor Statistics.

2. Steve Perlstein, "Moving Beyond the Cult of the Entrepreneur," *Washington Post,* July 2, 1989.

3. John Micklethwait and Adrian Woolridge, *The Witch Doctors: Making Sense of the Management Gurus* (New York: Random House, 1996).

4. Chester I. Barnard, *The Functions of the Executive* (Cambridge, MA: Harvard University Press, 1938).

5. Ibid., 217.

6. Douglas McGregor, *The Human Side of Enterprise* (25th anniversary printing) (New York: McGraw-Hill, 1985).

7. Ibid., 24.

8. Ibid., 49.

9. Ibid., vii.

10. Ibid., 125-126.

11. Karl Weick, *The Social Psychology of Organizing* (Reading, MA: Addison-Wesley, 1969).

12. Ibid., 39.

13. Ibid.

14. Lewis Carroll, *Through the Looking-Glass* (London: Macmillan, 1872).

15. Ibid., Quotation from the Lewis Carroll Web site at http://www.cstone.net/library/glass/alice-lg.html.

16. The results of this survey were presented in two reports released in January 1998 by the Annenberg Center for Communication at the University of Southern California. Richard C. Huseman and Jon P. Goodman were the project directors on both these reports.

1. *Knowledge Organizations, Their Emergence and Impact on Corporate Education and Training.*

2. *Workforce Education: Corporate Training and Learning at America's Leading Companies.*

Chapter 1

1. Without a national transportation system or communications network, businesses were primarily focused on their immediate geographic markets. This barred them from achieving any economies of scale or any leverage on their market. Alfred D. Chandler with Herman Daems, eds., presents this history in *Managerial Hierarchies* (Cambridge, MA: Harvard University Press, 1980), 11.

2. McCallum was not the sole architect of this form of hierarchy. The principals at other railroad companies contributed their practices to this emerging model. Alfred D. Chandler's *The Railroads, The Nation's First Big Business* (New York: Harcourt, Brace & World, 1965) gives an in-depth review of the people and events that shaped the first classic corporate structures in U.S. business history. Quotation from Chandler, *The Railroads.*

3. Richard Tedlow in his book *New and Improved* (New York: Basic Books, 1996), 6-8, describes three phases of marketing in the United States. The first is fragmentation, marked by high-margin, low-volume businesses restricted by transportation costs. The second phase, unification, was realized by men such as Henry Ford. This included high-volume, low-margin businesses that incorporated the whole nation into a mass market. The third phase, segmentation, is characterized by high-volume, value pricing, and market divisions along the lines of demographics and psychographics. In the case of the automobile industry, this trend was from the uniformity of Fordism to the variety of Sloanism.

4. Ford Motor is often cited as a force driving the growth of corporate America. Mark Rupert, in *Producing Hegemony* (Cambridge, UK: Cambridge University Press, 1995), 63-66, describes many of the factors—economic, political, social—that led the United States to its stature in the world economy.

5. Frederick Winslow Taylor was an evangelist for his theories. Months before his death in 1915, he praised the automobile industry for adopting his theories, although Henry Ford had publicly renounced any connection between his practices and scientific management. One of the primary vehicles for disseminating his views was *The Principles of Scientific Management* (New York: Harper & Brothers Publishers, 1934), 39-43. Quotation from p. 39.

6. Ford expected the most disciplined work in exchange for the highest daily wage. Although he was amenable to experimentation, Ford's work expectations were as unforgiving as they were successful. Quoted in Mark Rupert, *Producing Hegemony*, 65-66.

7. The design of the American labor system was influenced by a workforce of immigrants who could not read English and, frequently, could not understand oral English. Directions thus had to be simple and direct, minimizing any misunderstandings among the workers. From Ray Marshall and Marc Tucker, *Thinking for a Living* (New York: Basic Books, 1992), 5.

8. Rupert, *Producing Hegemony*, 112.

9. Kanigel, Robert, *The One Best Way* (New York: Viking, 1997), 169-171.

10. Ibid., 169.

11. Ibid., 171.

12. Ibid., 535.

13. Strom, Sharon Hartman, *Beyond the Typewriter: Gender, Class, and the Origins of Modern American Office Work, 1900-1930* (Urbana: University of Illinois Press, 1992), 35-42.

14. The United States overtook Great Britain as the world's most productive economy in the early 1890s. Over subsequent decades, this margin widened as the United States—whose manufacturing base was never threatened in World War I or World War II—adopted the most successful production and management techniques. Rupert, *Producing Hegemony*, 68-73.

15. Tedlow, *New and Improved*, 190-199. The dominant trend in the grocery retailing industry was to reduce certain services to increase efficiency. This trend—marked by cutting out store credit, deliveries, and telephone orders—spelled the demise of the independent retailer. In 1930, Michael J. Cullen, an employee of the Kroger Company, wrote to his president. Cullen laid out the rudiments of a new kind of grocery store. The essential elements of his design included the following.

> (1) The store would be "monstrous," between 5,200 and 6,400 square feet; (2) all sales would be made in cash; (3) there would be no delivery service; (4) the store would be located in a low-rent area or warehouse district and would have ample parking; and (5) a wide variety of goods would be available—100 percent branded and nationally advertised merchandise.

Cullen's plan—although not adopted by Kroger initially—represented the coming of the national supermarket chains. Consider what a departure this was from the model of retailing dominant in the independent retailers. In a traditional grocery store, a customer would have intimate interactions with the store clerk, who did not represent the final stage of the purchase. Rather, he or she suggested what products the consumer should buy. Prices were kept under the counter, giving the clerk the flexibility to engineer the sale. With the supermarket, this dynamic shifted. The consumer was left alone to choose his or her goods. The store employee's tasks became more logistical in nature, including stocking goods and the shelves and managing customer flow through the store.

Supermarkets such as A&P integrated themselves to a point where they tried to sell every product in the store under its own private label. This led to the fall of A&P and similar national chains, but what remained was a store dynamic built on size, volume, and speed. Tedlow, *New and Improved*, p. 228.

16. Tedlow, *New and Improved*, 36.

17. Coca-Cola's promotion goal was to make the brand so ubiquitous that consumers would not be able "to escape it." The company installed hundreds of its signature red soda

fountains in pharmacies and fountains across the country. Thousands of jobbers were trained in the operation of the units. And according to company history, by 1908, 2.5 million square feet of America's walls were covered in reminders to "drink Coca-Cola." Richard Tedlow, *New and Improved,* 22-68.

18. Kanigel, *The One Best Way,* 489-500, p. 490.

19. John Kenneth Galbraith, *The Affluent Society* (Boston: Houghton Mifflin, 1958). According to Galbraith, the dynamic sector of the economy was made up of large manufacturing corporations. It was his view that the large corporation exerted an influence on its suppliers, marketing avenues, production units, and even its customers.

20. Strom, *Behind the Typewriter,* 43.

21. Kanigel, *The One Best Way,* 14.

22. Rupert, *Producing Hegemony,* 71, 76.

23. IBM for many years had a policy of not laying people off. There was a prevailing mentality of family at this and other corporations. Watson was quoted by James Traub, "Loyalty: A Spasm of Layoffs and Downsizing in the 1980s Obliterated What Was Left of Corporate Loyalty," *Business Month,* October 1990, 85.

24. William Whyte, *The Organization Man* (New York: Simon & Schuster, 1956), 269.

25. Whyte was aghast by Monsanto's approach. "As Bell Labs and General Electric prove," the sociologist said, "there are many brilliant men who will, given the right circumstances, find industrial research highly absorbing. For company self-interest, let alone society's, a management policy that repels the few is a highly questionable one." From Whyte, *The Organization Man,* 235-236.

26. Whyte held that young men at that time were deluded. They thought that personnel work was about directing people. They did not realize there would be so much work with stopwatches and clipboards. Whyte, *The Organization Man,* 81.

27. Bardwick, *Danger in the Comfort Zone* (New York: AMACOM, 1995), 25.

28. Ray Marshall and Marc Tucker, *Thinking for a Living,* 31.

29. Tedlow, *New and Improved,* 347.

30. John Case, *From the Ground Up* (New York: Simon & Schuster, 1992), 17, 44.

CHAPTER 2

1. Igor Ansoff, *The New Corporate Strategy* (New York: Wiley, 1988), 92.

2. Much of this section draws on the writings of business historian Robert Sobel. Sobel's work *Car Wars* (New York: Truman Talley Books, 1984) provides a rich and detailed history of the rise and fall of the American automobile industry. The narrative he follows is one in which a group of Detroit's leading industrialists became so sure of their position and so set in their ways that change became impossible in the face of foreign competition.

1955 marked the end of an era in American automobile design. Boxy economical cars were quickly displaced by long, low, heavy, and fast ones. General Motors led the way, and soon Chrysler and Ford followed, each seeking to one-up the other with a lower chassis, heavier frame, or more powerful engine. From Sobel, *Car Wars,* 10-12.

3. America became known after World War II by the credo, "bigger is better." For many years, this attitude prevailed among consumers as well. But it was a taste borne of circumstance. Americans had more disposable income and generally drove greater distances and paid less for gasoline after World War II than did Europeans. In Europe, a small car mentality was in great part derived from scarce and expensive fuel. The Rolls Royce, a car

four times as expensive as the Cadillac is actually much shorter than the largest American cars. From Sobel, *Car Wars*, 23-24.

4. The Beetle achieved in the United States what no other import had done previously. It built a good reputation for itself. The timing of its introduction could not have been better. By 1959, the car had become the symbol among youth that felt materialism had corrupted the American dream. From Sobel, *Car Wars*, 45-49.

5. In the estimation of Detroit's car executives, the popularity of the Beetle was attributed to the "fringe" of the consumer pool. It remained to be seen, however, whether the Big Three could capture that sector of the market with their compact models. In the case of competing with Volkswagen, the answer was no. From Sobel, *Car Wars*, 75.

6. Sobel, *Car Wars*, 84, 92, 111.

7. Ibid., 161.

8. Ibid., 150.

9. Ibid., 146.

10. Henry Ford II's admission that he was a "small-car man" stood in stark comparison to his father's infamous line "you can have any color car you like, so long as it's black." This marked a turning point in the history of automotive marketing, as the market passed into the "segmentation" phase. From Sobel, *Car Wars*, 147, 150, 203-205, 219.

11. Ibid., 203, 263.

12. Ibid., 77-80.

13. Ralph Nader, *Unsafe at Any Speed: The Designed-in Dangers of the American Automobile* (New York: Grossman, 1965).

14. Sobel, *Car Wars*, 193-195.

15. Sobel, *The Age of Giant Corporations: A Microeconomic History of American Business, 1914-1992* (Westport, CT: Greenwood, 1993), 240.

16. Sobel, *Car Wars*, 142-143.

17. Ibid., 142.

18. Ibid., 143.

19. *Fortune* magazine has published, the list of the largest companies in the United States and in the world since 1972. This list has recently become available on the Internet (http://www.fortune.com) and is searchable by industry, country, SIC code, and numerous other variables.

20. John Case, *From the Ground Up* (New York: Simon & Schuster, 1992), 54-60.

21. Ibid.

22. Lester Thurow, *Head-to-Head* (New York: William Morrow, 1992), 164-176.

23. The German apprenticeship program is one part of a national effort to train workers for specific industries. Companies develop programs customized to their individual needs and experience a fraction of the employee defections that American corporations do. From Ray Marshall and Marc Tucker, *Thinking for a Living* (New York: Basic Books, 1992), 45-46.

24. Japan's "dual economy" is an interesting foil to the era of the classic corporation in the United States, when large corporations were adored by economists and idealized by young businesspeople. From Sobel, *Car Wars*, 145.

25. In Tedlow's third phase of marketing—segmentation—consumers are classified and targeted according to various demographic and psychographic traits. Large corporations now target segments that they would never have considered twenty years ago. From Steve Perlstein, "Moving Beyond the Cult of the Entrepreneur," *Washington Post*, July 2, 1989.

26. John Kenneth Galbraith, *The Affluent Society* (Boston: Houghton Mifflin, 1958).

27. S. S. Moses, "Mr. Justice Brandeis, Competition and Small Business: A Dilemma Reexamined," *Yale Law Journal,* 69 (1956):65-75.

28. These data come from *The State of Small Business: A Report of the President,* 1994 edition (Washington, DC: Government Printing Office, 1994).

29. These data come from various indices in the U.S. Department of Labor Statistics on-line databases (http://www.bls.gov).

30. Case, *From the Ground Up,* 75.

31. If the reader questions the potential of a company that does less than $100 million of business per year, consider the fact that Wal-Mart existed for 30 years with $3 million in revenues per year. As of 1997, it did over $2 billion and ranks as the largest employer in the United States. From Anna Brady, "Small Is as Small Does," *Journal of Business Strategy* (March-April 1995). SOES story from Edward O. Welles, "Bad Boys of Capitalism," *Inc.,* January 1997.

32. Gary McWilliams, "Whirlwind on the Web," *Business Week,* April 7, 1997.

33. Otis Port, "Gordon Moore's Crystal Ball," *Business Week,* June 23, 1997.

34. Jon Bigness, "Hot Metal in Chips," *Chicago Tribune,* September 23, 1997.

35. Tom Quinlan, "Experts Skeptical about Chip Breakthrough Claims: Developers Say Design Could Advance Industry by 10 Years," *Chicago Tribune,* December 29, 1997.

36. "Paradox Lost," *The Economist,* September 28, 1996.

37. Paul David, professor of economic history at Stanford University, has done considerable research into the impact of electricity on the structure and functioning of the manufacturing plant. From Michael Rothchild, "The Coming Productivity Surge," *Forbes,* March 29, 1993.

38. The Public Broadcasting Service has put an informative history of the Internet on-line at http://www.pbs.org/internet/timeline/.

39. In August 1996, the U.S. Bureau of Labor Statistics released a special issue on computers and employment. The report focuses on the impact of the computer on business and society and is on-line at http://stats.bls.gov/ces8mlr.htm. From Jacqueline Warnke, "Computer Manufacturing: Change and Competition," *Monthly Labor Review* (August 1996):18-29.

40. Warnke, "Computer Manufacturing: Change and Competition."

41. These statistics were brought up-to-date by cross-referencing the MIPS (million instructions per second) count for the Pentium II, reported to be 500 by Michele Hostetler and Nick Turner in "Advances in Technology Aided Battle of Bull Run," *Investor's Business Daily,* January 20, 1998, with current prices for computers outfitted with the Pentium II chip. Ziff-Davis's NetBuyer site on the Internet indicated that such systems could be purchased, on average, for $1,000.

42. Warnke, "Computer Manufacturing: Change and Competition."

43. Ibid.

44. Ibid.

45. Ibid.

46. Howard Gleckman et al., "The Technology Payoff," *Business Week,* June 14, 1993.

47. Ibid.

48. Ibid.

49. Ibid., 57.

50. Ibid.

51. Ibid.

52. William H. Davidow and Michael S. Malone, *The Virtual Corporation* (New York: HarperBusiness, 1992), 79.

53. Judith Bardwick, *Danger in the Comfort Zone* (New York: AMACOM, 1995).

54. Optimal performance levels occur at a point where the worker does not feel overly secure (as is the case with entitlement) and does not feel an undue amount of fear (as is the case in the face of downsizing). From Bardwick, *Danger in the Comfort Zone*, 10-33, p. 3.

55. On the surface, rapid and unchecked growth would seem to be an ideal situation. Bardwick argues that the U.S. position of global leader, combined with massive growth in corporations, stole any sort of incentive for managers to perform. This is the entitlement mentality. Bardwick, *Danger in the Comfort Zone*, 10-12.

56. Ibid., 25.

57. Ibid., 27-31.

58. Service industries are mostly responsible for the slowdown in productivity, but starting in 1990, manufacturing also began to slump. From James C. Cooper and Kathleen Madigan, "Desperately Seeking a Dose of Productivity," *Business Week*, February 19, 1990.

CHAPTER 3

1. Alfred Chandler wrote a chapter in Lance Berger's *The Change Management Handbook* (New York: Irwin, 1994), 25-26, titled "The History of Business Change." In it, he assesses the competitive, technological, and financial background of several industries as they underwent dramatic change, beginning for many in the mid-1970s.

Mergers and acquisitions remain a technique to gain competitive advantage. When network computing giant Cisco Systems began to show signs of losing its grip on market share in the first quarter of 1997, *Business Week* announced the arrival of new gorillas on the industry scene. Cisco CEO John T. Chambers has been busy fending off competition with an aggressive acquisition spree. In the three years before 1997, the company spent over $5.5 billion picking up companies that would complement its strengths or cover up its weaknesses. From Andy Reinhardt, "Cisco: Crunch Time for a High-Tech Wiz," *Business Week*, April 28, 1997.

2. This era of mergers, acquisitions, and downsizing has been dubbed "corporate Darwinism." It represented an end of the assumed social contract between the corporation and the Organization Man. As the corporation became threatened as never before, lifetime employability ceased to be an option. From Sami Abbasi, Kenneth Hollman, and Joe Murrey, "Merger Mania: Human and Economic Effects," *Review of Business*, June 22, 1991.

3. Specialty investment banking firm, Houlihan Lokey Howard and Zukin prepare a newsletter on the most current state of M&A activity, called *MergerStat Review*.

4. This example was used in Clemens Work and Jack Semonds, "What Are Mergers Doing to America?" *U.S. News & World Report*, July 22, 1985.

5. Michael Hammer and James Champy, *Reengineering the Corporation: A Manifesto for Business Revolution* (New York: HarperBusiness, 1993).

6. Ibid., 32-35.

7. *Chief Executive* magazine said in May 1996 that Hammer and Champy's book had sparked the creation of a new industry, "led by consultants, academics, and business gurus marketing the techniques of business process redesign (BPR). What began as the latest incarnation of continuous improvement quickly was seized on by many companies as a way to improve bottom line results through expense reduction, better known as downsizing." This informative article includes the transcript of a panel discussion with CEOs from Andersen Consulting, Congress Financial Corp., Astra Merck, American Standard, and

others. From J. P. Donlon, Meryl Davids, and Joe Queenan, "Is Re-Engineering a Fad?" *Chief Executive,* May 1996, 52.

8. According to the Renaissance thinker Erasmus, "Only the hand that erases can write a true thing." William Bridges writes about Cray in *Job Shift* (Reading, MA: Addison-Wesley, 1994), 207.

9. Dunlap's commentary appeared in Alan Downs, *Corporate Executions* (New York: AMACOM, 1995), 22.

10. Transcript of a speech, "Reflections on the Downsizing Debate," made by Frank Calamita. In *HR Focus* (July 1996), p. 9.

11. Michael Schrage, "IBM Rethinking Cherished Policy of No Layoffs," *Washington Post,* June 27, 1986.

12. Jane Applegate, "From Executive to Entrepreneur," *Working Woman,* July 1992.

13. Mike Meyers, "Fear and Unease Replace Confidence, Job Security at IBM, Kodak," *Chicago Tribune,* October 3, 1993.

14. The "Great Yellow Father" reference was noted in Claudia Deutsch, "Kodak to Lay Off 10,000 Employees in a 10% Cutback," *New York Times,* November 12, 1997.

Data on Kodak's 1997 downsizing announcement was made in Tim Smart, "Ax and Ye Shall Receive?" *Washington Post,* November 13, 1997.

15. Applegate, "From Executive to Entrepreneur."

16. Smart, "Ax and Ye Shall Receive?"

17. "The Year Downsizing Grew Up," *The Economist,* December 21, 1996.

18. *Corporate Downsizing, Job Elimination, and Job Creation* (New York: American Management Association, 1996). The American Management Association conducts the most comprehensive regular study of corporate downsizing in this country. This study is a valuable resource for the executive who wants to be current on the state of corporate America. Updated every year, the study reports downsizing statistics, trends, and rationales among the organization's 9,500 members, which, in total, employ one fourth of the U.S. workforce. Over 85% of surveyed firms gross more than $10 million annually, putting them in the top 5% of all U.S. corporations. For the 1996 study, the survey sample included 1,441 human resource managers.

19. Louis Uchitelle and N. R. Kleinfeld, "On the Battlefields of Business, Millions of Casualties," *New York Times,* March 3, 1996. This is the first article in a series called "The Downsizing of America" that the *Times* ran in March and April 1996. It represented, in the minds of many social historians, a culmination of a growing sense of insecurity in the American workplace. Each of the articles examines a different aspect of downsizing and its impact.

20. Ibid.

21. Mary Kane, "Dunlap Has History of Success," *The Plain Dealer,* December 31, 1995.

22. Jim Mitchell, "Dunlap's Math: 1 + 1 = 3," *Dallas Morning News,* July 18, 1995.

23. Barbara Sullivan, "Hatchet Man or Savior?" *Chicago Tribune,* January 17, 1997.

24. Downs, *Corporate Executions.*

25. Allen Sloan, "The Hit Men," *Newsweek,* February 26, 1996. This article—introduced with the cover title "Corporate Killers"—drew sharp criticism and public interest when it ran. Some members of the media had underestimated the level of anxiety that existed in the general public. When Ann Landers told a disgruntled downsized worker in 1995 that his problem was a "bad attitude," the columnist was bombarded with 6,000 angry letters. It was the largest response the writer had received from an article.

26. Downs, *Corporate Executions,* 14.

27. *Harper's Magazine* brought together a group of individuals to discuss the rules of "new capitalism." The discussion, which took place at the Occidental Grill, a restaurant in Washington, D.C., was captured in a May 1996 article, "Does America Still Work?" The round table consisted of the following men:

▶ Albert Dunlap, former CEO of Scott Paper, current CEO of Sunbeam Corporation
▶ Robert Reich, former U.S. secretary of labor
▶ George Gilder, author of *Wealth and Poverty*
▶ Edward Luttwak, fellow, the Center for Strategic and International Studies, Washington, D.C.
▶ Ronald Blackwell, chief economist, UNITE, a trade union formed by the merger of the Amalgamated Clothing and Textile Workers Union and the International Ladies' Garment Workers' Union

28. Clara Jeffery, "The Wall Street Effect," *Harpers Magazine,* May 1996.

29. "Does America Still Work?" 35.

30. Ibid.

31. Ibid.

32. Ibid.

33. "The Year Downsizing Grew Up," p. 35.

34. American Management Association, *Corporate Downsizing,* 1996.

35. Robert Tomasko presented the results of a survey of 1,000 companies by a leading actuarial firm in *Rethinking the Corporation* (New York: AMACOM, 1993), 23.

36. In 1993, Watson Wyatt International released its downsizing report, "Best Practices in Corporate Restructuring." For more information on this report, please visit the Watson Wyatt International website www.watsonwyatt.com or contact their Atlanta office at Watson Wyatt International, Suite 432, 4170 Ashford-Dunwoody Road, N.E., Atlanta, GA 30319; phone (800) 388-9868.

37. Bruce Nusbaum, "The End of Corporate Loyalty?" *Business Week,* August 4, 1986.

38. N. R. Kleinfield, "The Company as Family, No More," *New York Times,* March 4, 1996. In the second of its seven-part series, the *New York Times* takes a close look inside a three-year restructuring of newly merged Chase Manhattan and Chemical Banks. The article deals with the dual pressures of being downsized or being spared for an uncertain amount of time.

39. Ibid., A1.

40. Ibid., A1.

41. Bardwick, *Danger in the Comfort Zone* (New York: AMACOM, 1995), 41-45.

42. Kleinfield, "In the Workplace Musical Chairs."

43. American Management Association, *Corporate Job Creation, Job Elimination, and Downsizing,* 1997.

44. Bardwick, *Danger in the Comfort Zone,* 66.

45. American Management Association, *Corporate Downsizing,* 1996.

46. John Case, *From the Ground Up* (New York: Simon & Schuster, 1992), 51.

CHAPTER 4

1. Robert Ford, "Human Relations in Industry: Summer Conferences of the YMCA" (paper presented to the Management History Division of the Academy of Management, 1991).

2. Ibid.

3. Richard C. Huseman, "Executive Education 2000: Emerging Paradigms in Management/Executive Education" (unpublished report, University of Central Florida, Orlando, Florida, August 1996).

4. Ibid.

5. Ibid.

6. John A. Byrne, "Where the Schools Aren't Doing Their Homework: Critics Say They Churn out MBAs Lacking Leadership Skills and Operations Know-How," *Business Week,* November 28, 1988.

7. Julie Cohen Mason, "Business Schools: Striving to Meet Customer Demand," *Management Review* (September 1992).

8. Alan Deutschman, "The Trouble with MBAs," *Fortune,* July 29, 1991.

9. Leslie Wines, "Pragmatic Courses for Trying Times," *Journal of Business Strategy* (March-April 1996).

10. Stan Davis and Jim Botkin, *The Monster under the Bed* (New York: Simon & Schuster, 1994).

11. Ibid., 90-91.

12. Jennifer Reingold, "When the Best B-School Is No B-School," *Business Week,* October 20, 1997.

13. Ray Marshall and Marc Tucker, *Thinking for a Living* (New York: Basic Books, 1992), 98.

14. Thomas Stewart, *Intellectual Capital: The New Wealth of Organizations* (New York: Doubleday/Currency, 1997), 94.

15. Robert Schank, *Virtual Learning* (New York: McGraw-Hill, 1997), 7.

16. Stewart, *Intellectual Capital,* 94.

17. Ibid., 94.

18. Ibid., 94.

19. Peter M. Senge, *The Fifth Discipline: The Art and Practice of the Learning Organization* (New York: Doubleday, 1990).

20. Ibid., 14.

21. Ibid., 68-73.

22. Ibid., 73-7.

23. Ibid., 70-71.

24. Senge, *The Fifth Discipline,* 176.

25. Arie de Geus, "The Living Company," *Harvard Business Review* (March-April 1997).

26. Senge, *The Fifth Discipline,* 178.

27. Case, *From the Ground Up* (New York: Simon & Schuster, 1992), 48.

28. Senge, *The Fifth Discipline,* 178-181.

29. Ibid., 180.

30. Ibid., 181.

31. David Stamps, "Communities of Practice: Learning and Work as Social Activities," *Training,* February 1997.

32. Ibid.

33. Stewart, *Intellectual Capital,* 96.

34. Ibid., 97.

35. de Geus, "The Living Company."

36. Ibid.

37. The American Management Association has polled its membership every year since 1991 on its downsizing practices. Its 1997 report was titled *Corporate Job Creation, Job Elimination, and Downsizing.*

38. Ibid.

CHAPTER 5

1. Richard C. Huseman and Jon P. Goodman, *Workforce Education: Corporate Training and Learning at America's Leading Companies,* Annenberg Center for Communication at the University of Southern California, January 1998. Full-length versions of these reports are available by calling the Annenberg Center at 213-743-2344, and asking for the Corporate Knowledge Center.

2. Thomas Bartlett, "The Hottest Campus on the Internet," *Business Week,* October 20, 1997.

3. Thomas Bartlett, Alan Gallo, and John Johnsrud, "20 Leading Executive M.B.A. Programs," *Business Week,* October 20, 1997, 80.

4. Steve Blickstein, "Does Training Pay Off?" *Across the Board,* June 1996.

5. Ibid.

6. Robert M. Fulmer, "The Evolving Paradigm of Leadership Development," *Organizational Dynamics* (March 1997).

7. Ibid.

CHAPTER 6

1. Thomas H. Davenport and Laurence Prusak, *Working Knowledge* (Boston: Harvard Business School Press, 1998), 9.

2. Leif Edvinsson and Michael S. Malone, *Intellectual Capital* (New York: HarperBusiness, 1997), 11.

3. Quoted in *Customer Capital: Supplement to Skandia's 1996 Annual Report.*

4. John Rutledge, "You're a Fool if You Buy into This," *Forbes ASAP,* April 7, 1997.

5. Stan Davis and Jim Botkin, *The Monster under the Bed* (New York: Simon & Schuster, 1994), 42-43.

6. Peter Drucker, "The Coming of the New Organization," *Harvard Business Review* 66 (January-February 1988):45-53.

7. Davenport and Prusak, *Working Knowledge,* 229.

8. Ibid., 4.

9. Our working definition of knowledge is an amalgam of several authors' attempts, but it most closely resembles that of Thomas Davenport and Laurence Prusak in *Working Knowledge.*

10. Edward O. Welles, "Why Every Company Needs a Story," *Inc.,* May 1996.

11. Ibid.

12. Davenport and Prusak, *Working Knowledge,* 6.

13. Ikujiro Nonaka and Hirotaka Takeuchi, *The Knowledge Creating Company* (Oxford: Oxford University Press, 1995), 69.

14. Ibid., 153.

15. Dorothy Leonard and Jefferey F. Rayport, "Spark Innovation through Empathic Design," *Harvard Business Review* (November-December 1997).

16. Karl Weick, "Prepare Your Organization to Fight Fires," *Harvard Business Review* (May-June 1996).

17. Ibid.

18. Ibid.

19. Francine Proctor, "Instinct: That Little Voice Is a Practical Tool in Decision Making," *San Jose Business Journal,* June 3, 1996.

20. James C. Collins and Jerry I. Porras, Built To Last (New York: HarperBusiness, 1994), 50.

21. Ibid., 51.

22. Ibid.,

23. Ibid., 70-71.

24. Thomas Stewart, *Intellectual Capital: The New Wealth of Organizations* (New York: Doubleday/Currency), 12.

25. Davenport and Prusak, *Working Knowledge,* 14.

26. "The Spawning of a Third Sector: Information," *Business Week,* November 7, 1994.

27. Davenport and Prusak, *Working Knowledge,* 54.

28. David Kirkpatrick, "Why Microsoft Can't Stop Lotus Notes," *Fortune,* December 12, 1994.

29. Ibid.

30. Amy Cortese and Ira Sager, "Gerstner at the Gates," *Business Week,* June 19, 1995.

31. Paul Judge, "Will Manzi's Minions Walk, Too?" *Business Week,* December 25, 1995.

32. John W. Verity and Amy Cortese, "Cyber-Networks Need a Lot of Spackle," *Business Week,* June 26, 1995.

33. David Kirkpatrick, "IBM Moves to Fix Its Microsoft Problem," *Fortune,* July 10, 1995.

34. Kirkpatrick, "Why Microsoft Can't Stop Lotus Notes."

35. "The Lotus Eater," *The Economist,* June 10, 1995.

36. Cortese and Sager, "Gerstner at the Gates."

37. Ira Sager, "Serious Fun for IBM," *Business Week,* June 17, 1996.

38. Jeffrey Krasner, "Rolm Purchase Proved Disastrous Move," *Boston Herald,* June 8, 1995.

39. Joann Muller, "A Not-So-Odd Couple: Lotus Is Thriving in the World of IBM," *Boston Globe,* July 13, 1997.

40. Kirkpatrick, "Why Microsoft Can't Stop Lotus Notes."

41. Krasner, "Rolm Purchase Proved Disastrous Move."

42. Muller, "A Not-so-odd Couple."

43. Ibid.

44. Ibid.

45. Alan Farnham, "How Safe Are Your Secrets?" *Fortune,* September 8, 1997.

46. Robert Renzer and Carrie Shook, "Whose Rolodex Is It, Anyway?" *Forbes,* February 23, 1998.

47. Farnham, "How Safe Are Your Secrets?"

48. "Economy of the Mind," *The Economist,* December 23, 1989.

49. Jeffrey Young, "Spies Like Us," *Forbes,* June 3, 1996.

50. Farnham, "How Safe Are Your Secrets?"

51. Robert Sobel, *Car Wars* (New York: Truman Talley Books, 1984), 142.

52. Ibid., 126.

53. William H. Davidow and Michael S. Malone, *The Virtual Corporation* (New York: HarperBusiness, 1992), 119-120.

54. Ibid., 117-118.

55. Ibid., 118.

56. Kathy Rebello, "Inside Microsoft," *Business Week,* July 15, 1996.

57. Ibid.

58. "Microsoft's Contradiction," *The Economist,* January 31, 1998.

59. Rebello, "Inside Microsoft."

60. Randall E. Stross, "Microsoft's Big Advantage: Hiring Only the Supersmart," *Fortune,* November 25, 1996.

61. Ibid.

62. Ibid.

CHAPTER 7

1. Dorothy Leonard-Barton, *Wellsprings of Knowledge* (Boston: Harvard Business School Press, 1995), 261-262.

2. Ibid., 11-12.

3. Richard D. Huseman and Jon P. Goodman, *Knowledge Organizations: Their Emergence and Impact on Corporate Education and Training.* Report for the Corporate Knowledge Center, the Annenberg Center for Communication at the University of Southern California, November 1997.

4. Leonard-Barton, *Wellsprings of Knowledge,* 156.

5. Michael Polanyi, "The Tacit Dimension," in *Knowledge in Organizations,* ed. Laurence Prusak (Boston: Butterworth-Heinemann, 1997), 136.

6. Thomas A. Stewart, "GE Keeps Those Ideas Coming," *Fortune,* August 12, 1991.

7. Ibid.

8. Topics evaluated include general management skills; managing human performance; managing organizational change; managing the virtual workplace; leadership training; relationship management; general communication skills; presentation skills; critical thinking skills; creativity training; diversity/ethics/values training; teamwork/team building skills; PR/external communication skills; information technology training; financial training; sales/customer service training; product/industry training; technology applications training; total quality management; business/market strategy training; and legislation and regulatory issues training.

9. Leonard-Barton, *Wellsprings of Knowledge,* 264-265.

CHAPTER 8

1. William H. Starbuck, "Learning by Knowledge Intensive Firms," in *Knowledge in Organizations,* ed. Laurence Prusak (Boston: Butterworth-Heinemann, 1997), 150.

2. Thomas A. Stewart, "Brainpower," *Fortune,* June 3, 1991.

3. Ibid.

4. Tim Carvel, "It's a Seller's Market for Nerds: Silicon Valley's Hiring Frenzy," *Fortune,* December 9, 1996.

5. Matt Krantz, "A Tech Banker Assigns Value to Intangibles," *Investor's Business Daily,* January 14, 1998.

6. Zaher Z. Zantout and George P. Tsetsekos, "The Wealth Effects of Announcements of R&D Expenditure Increases," *Journal of Financial Research* (June 22, 1994).

7. Leif Edvinsson and Thomas Malone, *Intellectual Capital* (New York: HarperBusiness, 1997), 16.

8. Annie Brooking, *Intellectual Capital* (London: International Thomson Business Press, 1996), 83.

9. Robert S. Kaplan and David P. Norton, "Putting the Scorecard to Work," *Harvard Business Review* (September-October 1993).

10. Robert S. Kaplan and David P. Norton, "The Balanced Scorecard: Measures That Drive Performance," *Harvard Business Review* (January-February 1992).

11. Ibid.

12. Stewart, "Brainpower."

13. Thomas Stewart, *Intellectual Capital: The New Wealth of Organizations* (New York: Doubleday/Currency, 1997), 224.

14. Ibid., xvii.

15. Thomas Stewart, "Grab Your Pencil—It's a Knowledge Quiz," *Fortune,* December 8, 1997.

16. Edvinsson and Malone, *Intellectual Capital,* 20.

17. Ibid., 133.

18. Ibid., 98.

19. Ibid., 118.

20. Stewart, *Intellectual Capital,* 144.

21. Ibid., 143.

22. Edvinsson and Malone, *Intellectual Capital,* 90-91.

23. Don Peppers and Martha Rogers, *The One-to-One Future* (New York: Doubleday, 1993).

24. Ibid., 17.

25. Edvinsson and Malone, *Intellectual Capital,* 93.

26. Dorothy Leonard-Barton, *Wellsprings of Knowledge* (Boston: Harvard Business School Press, 1995), 200.

27. Edvinsson and Malone, *Intellectual Capital,* 94-95.

28. Ibid., 96-98.

29. Skandia's 1995 report on intellectual capital, *Value-Creating Processes,* 96-98.

30. Edvinsson and Malone, *Intellectual Capital,* 97.

31. Ibid., 55.

32. Edvinsson and Malone, *Intellectual Capital,* 11.

33. Stewart, *Intellectual Capital,* 89-90.

34. Skandia's 1996 report on Intellectual Capital, *Customer Value,* 16.

35. Edvinsson and Malone, *Intellectual Capital,* 108-109.

36. Ibid., 108.

37. Stewart, *Intellectual Capital,* 85.

38. Edvinsson and Malone, *Intellectual Capital,* 34-35.

39. Joseph Oberle, "Human Resource Accounting," *Training,* July 1989.

40. Skandia's 1996 report on intellectual capital, *Customer Value.*

41. Ibid., 12.

42. Riel Miller, *Measuring What People Know* (Paris: Organisation for Economic Co-Operation and Development, 1996), 20.

43. Oberle, "Human Resource Accounting."

44. Stewart, *Intellectual Capital*, 85.

45. Edvinsson and Malone, *Intellectual Capital*, 126-129.

46. Yash P. Gupta and Jahangir Karimi, "Telecommuting: Trend of Future Firms Must Consider Safety, Liability," *Denver Post*, August 17, 1997.

47. Edvinsson and Malone, *Intellectual Capital*, 129.

48. Skandia's 1994 report, *Visualizing Intellectual Capital in Skandia*, 11.

49. Ibid., 15.

50. Edvinsson and Malone, *Intellectual Capital*, 133.

51. Karl Sveiby, *The New Organizational Wealth* (San Francisco: Berrett Koehler, 1997), 186.

52. Edvinsson and Malone, *Intellectual Capital*, 139.

53. "A Business Researcher's Interest," www.brint.com.

54. Skandia's report *Value-Creating Processes*, 7.

55. Edvinsson and Malone, *Intellectual Capital*, 42.

56. Skandia's 1994 report, *Visualizing Intellectual Capital in Skandia*, 3.

57. Edvinsson and Malone, *Intellectual Capital*, 49.

58. Ibid., 55-56.

CHAPTER 9

1. Michael Polanyi, "The Tacit Dimension," in *Knowledge in Organizations*, ed. Laurence Prusak (Boston: Butterworth-Heinemann, 1997), 136.

2. Thomas Stewart, *Intellectual Capital: The New Wealth of Organizations* (New York: Doubleday/Currency, 1997), 114.

3. Thomas H. Davenport and Laurence Prusak, *Working Knowledge* (Boston: Harvard Business School Press, 1998), 72-73.

4. Stewart, *Intellectual Capital*, 99.

5. Anne H. Souhanov, ed., *The American Heritage Dictionary of the English Language* (Boston: Houghton Mifflin, 1992), 1091.

6. Prusak was a panelist at a conference presented by the University of California at Berkeley. The research associate for this study, Dan Rabinovitch, attended the conference.

7. Steven Wallman, "SEC Love IC," interview by Rich Karlgaard, *Forbes ASAP*, April 7, 1997.

8. Ibid.

9. John Rutledge, "You're a Fool if You Buy into This," *Forbes ASAP*, April 7, 1997.

10. Ibid.

11. Stewart, *Intellectual Capital*, 118.

12. Ibid., 117.

13. Davenport and Prusak, *Working Knowledge*, 90-92.

14. Ibid.

15. Ikujiro Nonaka and Hirotaka Takeuchi, *The Knowledge Creating Company* (Oxford: Oxford University Press, 1995), 62-70.

16. Scott D. Cook and Dvora Yanow, "Culture and Organizational Learning," *Journal of Management Inquiry* (December 1993):373-390.

17. Ibid., 380.

18. Dorothy Leonard-Barton, *Wellsprings of Knowledge* (Boston: Harvard Business School Press, 1995), 14-15.

19. Tim Wilson, "Intranets Reach Critical Mass," *Communications Week,* February 17, 1997.

20. David Strom, "Art, Geeks and Power Ploys: How to Build Your Intranet," *Forbes,* August 26, 1996.

21. Ibid.

22. Ibid.

23. Ian Campbell, "The Intranet: Slashing the Cost of Business," *International Data Corporation,* 1997.

24. Ibid.

25. Ibid.

26. Terry Curtis et al., "Nortel's Intranet," *Telesis,* December 1996.

27. Campbell, "The Intranet: Slashing the Cost of Business."

28. Stewart, *Intellectual Capital,* 118.

29. Wanda J. Orlikowski, "Learning from Notes: Organizational Issues in Groupware Implementation," in *Knowledge Management Tools,* ed. Rudy L. Ruggles III (Boston: Butterworth-Heinemann, 1997), 231-246.

30. Ibid., 235.

31. Byron Reimus, *Knowledge Sharing within Management Consulting Firms* (sponsored by *Consultants News*) (Fitzwilliam, NH: Kennedy).

32. Orlikowski, "Learning from Notes," 242.

33. Ibid., 240.

34. Reimus, "Knowledge Sharing," 11-13.

35. Ibid.

36. Author's conversations with Michael Stelzer, Ernst & Young.

37. Nonaka and Takeuchi, *The Knowledge Creating Company,* 74.

38. Leonard-Barton, *Wellsprings of Knowledge,* 29.

39. Ibid., 29-56.

40. Ibid., 31.

41. Ibid., 33.

42. Ibid., 64.

43. Ibid., 64-65.

44. Ibid., 59.

45. Ibid., 72.

46. Ibid., 79.

47. Ibid.

48. Andrew S. Grove, "How to Make Confrontation Work for You," *Fortune,* July 23, 1994.

49. Ibid.

50. Nonaka and Takeuchi, *The Knowledge Creating Company,* 100.

51. Ibid., 95-100.

52. Jeremy Bernstein, *Three Degrees Above Zero: Bell Labs in the Information Age* (New York: Scribner, 1984).

53. Elizabeth Corcoran, "The Changing Role of U.S. Research Labs," *Research-Technology Management* (July-August 1994).

54. John Carey, "What Price Science," *Business Week,* March 26, 1997.

55. Randall E. Stross, "Mr. Gates Builds His Brain Trust," *Fortune,* December 8, 1997.

56. Ibid.

57. The *Chicago Tribune,* for example, told the story of Art Fry's accidental invention of Post-it Notes. Art Fry, a researcher at 3M, was trying to find a way to hold his place in

his church songbook, without tearing the pages. He remembered fellow researcher Spencer Silver's efforts to make a strong new adhesive. Silver, however, came up with a weaker adhesive that allowed for easy separation of the joined surfaces. Fry thought this might be the answer to his problem. It was. And to ours, too. For what would life be without Post-it Notes? From Wilma Randle, "Got a Minute? Here's Some Trivial News You Can't Use," *Chicago Tribune,* August 5, 1996.

58. Leonard-Barton, *Wellsprings of Knowledge,* 117.

59. Ibid., 118.

60. Malone was quoted by Tom Peters in "Let Us Celebrate Bold Botches," *Forbes ASAP,* October 25, 1993.

61. Ibid.

62. Leonard-Barton, *Wellsprings of Knowledge,* 11.

63. This section is based on Leonard-Barton's discussion of the characteristics of employees that managers should consider when implementing new technologies and systems. From *Wellsprings of Knowledge,* 94-97.

64. Thomas A. Hemphill, "U.S. Technology Policy, Intraindustry Joint Ventures, and the National Cooperative Research and Production Act of 1993: Goals and Achievements of the NCRPA," *Business Economics,* October 1997.

65. Leonard-Barton, *Wellsprings of Knowledge,* 152.

66. Association of University of Technology Managers, "Licensing Survey FY 1991-1995." For more information on this report, please contact the Association of University Technology Managers, Inc., 49 East Avenue, Norwalk, CT 06851. Phone: (203) 845-9015. E-mail: autm@ix.netcom.com.

67. Joan C. Hamilton, "A Wellspring Called Stanford," *Business Week,* August 25, 1997.

68. James Aley, "The Heart of Silicon Valley," *Fortune,* July 7, 1997.

69. Hamilton, "A Wellspring Called Stanford."

70. Aley, "The Heart of Silicon Valley."

71. Leonard-Barton, *Wellsprings of Knowledge,* 153.

72. Davenport and Prusak, *Working Knowledge,* 53.

73. Leonard-Barton, *Wellsprings of Knowledge,* 157-158.

74. Nonaka and Takeuchi, *The Knowledge Creating Company,* 79.

75. Peter M. Senge, *The Fifth Discipline: The Art and Practice of the Learning Organization* (New York: Doubleday, 1990), 150.

76. Ibid., 206.

77. Leonard-Barton, *Wellsprings of Knowledge,* 87-88.

78. Ibid., 87.

79. Ibid., 208-209.

Index

A&P, 11, 221 (n15)
Abernathy, William, 25
Academia:
    scientific management in, 12
    See also Universities
Accounting systems measuring intellectual
    capital:
    measuring customer capital, 165-168,
        169, 171
    measuring human capital, 170-173,
        180-182
    measuring structural capital, 168-170
    need for, 157-160
    organization-specific nature of, 160-164
    Skandia report on, 104, 163-164, 164
        (table), 167-168, 169-170, 171,
        172-176
    use of, in "Knowledge Organizations"
        survey, 148, 150, 152, 153
Acquisitions. *See* Mergers and acquisitions
    (M&A)
Administrative support:
    classic corporation style of, 4, 10, 12
    impacts of downsizing on, 47, 53
Advertising. *See* Mass marketing
Aetna Life & Casualty, information
    technology reducing workforce, 36-37
Affluent Society, The (Galbraith), 12, 29, 221
    (n19)
Akers, John, 184
Alcoa, research at, 200
Aley, James, 205, 234 (n68)
Allard, J., 128
Allchin, Jim, 119

Allen, Robert, 49
American Airlines, 159
American Management Association (AMA),
    downsizing polls, 46, 53, 56, 78, 226
    (n18)
Andersen Center, corporate training facility,
    101
Anderson Consulting, management of
    knowledge database, 194
Annenberg Center for Communication (USC):
    corporate education and training survey,
        xv-xvi.
    workforce education survey, 83-91.
Ansoff, Igor, 19
Answer Center (General Electric), 108-109,
    186
Anxiety. *See* Fear
Apple Computer, 200, 204
Apprenticeship programs, 28, 184-185, 223
    (n23)
Arthur Anderson, training by, 101
Aspen Institute for Humanistic Studies, 64-65
Assembly line production:
    Ford's development of, 5-8
    success of, 6-7, 12, 13, 16
Assets:
    intellectual capital as, xv, 116-125, 146,
        157-158, 159-160, 164-173, 177-178
    See also Accounting systems measuring
        intellectual capital
AT&T, 64
    downsizing, 49, 51-52, 53
    postwar growth, 38-39
    rigidity of regulations, 15

Audits. *See* Accounting systems measuring
    intellectual capital
Authority, hierarchical, xi-xii, 4, 7-8, 10,
    15-16, 38-40, 72, 183
Automated teller machines (ATM), 35, 36
Automobile industry:
    development of assembly line production,
       5-8
    downsizing in, 46
    international competition impacting,
       20-28, 24 (table), 26 (tables), 28, 72,
       125-127, 196, 222 (nn2,4,5)
    market segmentation in, 109, 220
       (nn3,10)
    United States dominance in, 13, 15, 26
    See also specific companies
Autonomy, of individuals in workforce,
    xi-xii, 57, 142, 194-195

Balanced Scorecard, The (Kaplan & Norton),
    161-162, 231 (n9)
Banking industry:
    data intensive nature of, 106
    information technology impacting,
       35-36, 37
    mergers in, 50-51, 54-55, 227 (n39)
    scientific management in, 12
    telecommuting in, 172
    See also Skandia
Bardwick, Judith, 38, 39, 55, 56, 224
    (nn54,55,56)
Barnard, Chester, xi
Bateson, Gregory, 106
Bateson, John, 193
Bayh-Dole Act (1980), 205
Bell, Gordon, 201
Bell Laboratories, 200, 222 (n25)
Benchmarking, 147, 174
Bennis, Warren, xii
Bernstein, Jeremy, 200
Best Practices in Corporate Restructuring
    (Watson Wyatt), 44
Bethlehem Steel Company, 7
Billing, information technology impacting, 36
Blackwell, Ronald, 226 (n27)
Block, Chris, 30
Block Trading (company), 30
Boeing Company, downsizing by, 49 (table)
Borgs, Christian, 201
Botkin, Jim, 67, 227 (nn10,11)
Brand names. *See* National brands

Bridges, William, 44, 225 (n8)
Brooking, Annie, 160-161, 231 (n8)
Brown, John Sealy, 70
Brummet, R. Lee, 170
Budgets, for training, 99-102, 101 (figure),
    154 (table), 170-171
Built to Last (Collins & Porras), 114 (n20)
Burke, Jeff, 30
Burke, Jim, 114
Business process redesign (BPR). *See*
    Restructuring
Business schools:
    course content, 65-66
    criticisms of, 66-68, 69-70
    future expectations of using, in *Workforce
       Education* survey, 91 (figure), 92
    historical development of, 62-63, 64-65
    management fads in, x
    partnering with, for MBT training,
       98-99, 99 (figure)
    See also MBA programs

Cadence Design Systems, Inc, 189-190
Campbell, Ian, 188, 233 (n24)
Campbell's Soup, 124-125
Canadian Imperial Bank of Commerce
    (CIBC), 69
Candler, Asa G., 5, 11
Candler, Charles Howard, 11
Car Wars (Sobel), 20, 21-23, 222
    (nn2,3,4,5,10)
Carendi, Jan, 174, 175
Carnegie Foundation for the Advancement of
    Teaching, 12
Carroll, Lewis, xv
Case, John, 30, 57, 223 (n30), 227 (n47)
Centesimus Annus (John Paul II), 115
CEOs:
    education of. *See* Business schools; MBA
       programs
    responsibilities for downsizing from,
       47-49, 51-52, 226 (n27)
Chambers, John, T., 224-225 (n1)
Champy, James, 43, 44, 53, 225 (nn6,7)
Chandler, Seth, 63
Change:
    corporate universities as response to,
       67-69
    discontinuous, 19-20, 41
    domestic competition impacting, 29-32

downsizing as strategy against. *See*
Downsizing
future constancy of, xiv-xv
information technology impacting, xv,
32-38
international competition impacting, xv,
20-28, 23 (table), 26 (tables), 28, 222
(nn2,4,5)
knowledge as manager of, 128-131
magnitudes of, 38
realignment as strategy against, 42,
224-225 (nn1,2,3)
restructuring as strategy against, 43-44,
225 (nn7,8)
Chaos, creative, 195, 198-200
Chaparral Steel, 140, 185, 203
Chase Manhattan Bank, merger, 54-55, 227
(n39)
Chayes, Jennifer Tour, 201
Cheerios, market research by, 109
Chemical Bank, merger, 54-55, 227 (n39)
Cheng, C. S., 63
Chevrolet. *See* General Motors (GM)
Chief Executive Officers. *See* CEOs
Chrysler Corporation, 20, 24
Churches. *See* Religious organizations
Cisco Systems, 224-225 (n1)
Clark, Kim, 25
Classroom training:
proportion of, in *Workforce Education*
survey, 83, 84-85, 84 (figure)
See also Business schools; Corporate
universities; MBA programs;
Universities
Cleese, John, 202
Coca-Cola, mass marketing strategies by, 11,
221 (n17)
Collins, James C., 114, 115, 229
(nn20,21,23)
Combination, as knowledge transfer method,
185-186
Communication:
enhancing group learning process, 76-77
redundancy as positive attribute in, 195,
199
rigid channels of, 4
with customers, 164 (table), 168
Communication technology. *See* Information
technology
Communities of practice, 75-78
Company knowledge, defined, 158
Compaq Computer, 31

Competition. *See* Domestic competition;
International competition
Competitiveness:
diminishing Japanese, 196
information technology enhancing, 37
inhibiting sharing knowledge, 191-192
Japanese economic system facilitating,
28, 223 (n24)
knowledge as primary tool of, 125-127,
139-141, 183
rankings of industrial countries by, 27-28
through mergers and acquisitions, 42,
224-225 (nn1,2,3)
Computer-based training (CBT):
in "Knowledge Organizations" survey,
154, 154 (table)
in *Workforce Education* survey, 83-84, 84
(figure), 85, 94, 95-96, 99
See also Multimedia-based training (MBT)
Computers:
direct sales of, 31-32
graphical user interface (GUI)
development, 200, 208
impacting productivity rates, 34, 187,
224 (n39)
impacting rates of change, 32-33, 37-38
price and speed of, 34, 35 (table), 37-38,
224 (n41)
software for, 116-119, 120-121,
122-123, 129, 147, 165, 190-193
theft of information from, 123, 125
training via. *See* Computer-based training
(CBT)
See also Information technology (IT);
Internet; *specific companies*
Conceptualization and leveraging knowledge
model. *See* Knowledge
conceptualization and leveraging
model
Conflict, creation of knowledge through,
195-199
Confrontation:
constructive, 198
See also Conflict
Consultants:
as corporate gypsies, 172
corporations partnering with, for
training, 88, 89 (figure), 90, 91
(figure), 98, 99 (figure), 154
culture of, inhibiting sharing of
knowledge, 191-192
management fads and, x

Consumer electronics industry:
    Japanese dominance in, 27
    See also Computers
Consumers. *See* Customers
Cook, Scott D., 184, 185, 233 (nn16,17)
Core rigidities, failure from, 195-196
Corporate education. *See* Business schools;
    Corporate universities; Learning
    organizations
Corporate Executions (Downs), 48
Corporate universities:
    as response to changing conditions, 67-69
    in "Knowledge Organizations" survey,
        140-141, 143, 154
    in *Workforce Education* survey, 82,
        85-86, 87 (figure), 100-102
Corporate yellow pages, knowledge mapping
    tool, 179-180
Corporations, classic:
    domestic competition impacting, 29-32
    favoring average vs. brilliant managers,
        14, 131, 222 (n25)
    hierarchical structure, xi-xii, 4, 7-8, 10,
        15-16, 38-40, 72, 183
    historical evolution, 3-4
    impacts of scientific management on. *See*
        Scientific management
    international competition impacting,
        20-28, 23 (table), 26 (tables), 28, 72,
        125-127, 222 (nn2,4,5)
    loyalty of employees to, 13-16, 53, 221
        (n23)
    mental models blocking vision of, 72-75
    realignment as strategy against change,
        42, 224-225 (n1)
    restructuring as strategy against change,
        43-44, 225 (nn7,8)
    size of, impacting success, ix-x, 12, 28,
        38-39, 52, 57-58, 221 (n19), 223
        (n24), 224 (n55)
    success of, 13, 16-17, 220-221 (nn4,14)
    See also Managers; Workforce
Corvair automobiles, 24-25
Cost analysis, decisions based on, 4
Craftsman-apprentice programs, 28,
    184-185, 223 (n23)
Cray, Seymour, 44
Creative chaos, 195, 198-200
Creative tension, 207
Cullen, Michael J., 221 (n15)
Culture:
    at IBM, 119-120

    at Lotus, 121-122
    at Microsoft, 130-131, 201
    inhibiting knowledge sharing, 191-192
    within knowledge organizations, 136,
        144, 146-147, 150, 151 (table), 153,
        183, 186
    See also Leadership
Customer satisfaction, 165-166, 167, 181
Customer service:
    by Skandia, 167, 169
    information technology enhancing, 37
    rising expectations by consumers of,
        165-166
    Xerox training for, 75-76
Customers:
    direct communications to, 164 (table),
        168
    impacts of scientific management on, 221
        (n15)
    information technology (IT) literacy, 164
        (table), 168
    lack of responsiveness to, xii, 21-23, 26
    loss of confidence in American
        automobiles, 25
    measuring customer capital, 165-168,
        169, 171
    research on preferences of, 11, 109, 147,
        166
    size symbolic of success for, 21, 222 (n3)
Czechoslovakia, assembly line production in,
    13

Danger in the Comfort Zone (Bardwick), 38,
    224 (n54)
Dartmouth, business seminars, 62-63
Data:
    defined, 105-106
    knowledge vs., 108
Datsun. *See* Nissan
Davenport, Thomas H., 103-104, 106, 108,
    179, 184, 229 (nn1,8,9,12)
David, Paul, 224 (n37)
Davidow, William H., 37-38, 126, 127, 224
    (n52), 230 (nn54,55)
Davis, Stan, 67, 227 (nn10,11)
De Geus, Arie, 72-73, 228 (n25)
De-skilling, term definition, 9
Decision making:
    based on cost analysis, 4
    based on more vs. less knowledge, 104
    intuition as, 112-113

judgment essential to, 110
Dell, Michael, 31-32
Dell Computer, 31-32
Delorean, John, 20
Demming, W. Edwards, 125
Demographics, market segmentation and, 220 (n3), 222 (n10), 223 (n25)
Department of Defense (DOD), rigid regulations in, 15
Deutschman, Alan, 67, 227 (n8)
Dietz, Don, 112-113
Direct sales, of personal computers, 31-32
Distance learning. *See* Multimedia-based training (MBT)
Dodge, Mark, 187
Domestic competition:
    era of predictable, 16, 57
    impacts of, 29-32
Douglas Aircraft Company, 188-189
Dow Chemical, 124, 173
Downs, Alan, 48
Downsizing:
    as "corporate Darwinism," 225 (n2)
    efficacy of, 52-53
    impacts on workforce, 35-37, 45-46, 51-57, 172, 224 (n54), 226 (nn19,25), 227 (n39)
    rates of, 30
    responsibilities for, 46-52, 49 (table), 54, 226 (nn18,27)
    restructuring and, 44, 45, 47, 53, 225 (n7)
    training helping recovery from, 78
Drucker, Peter, 106
Dubiel, John, 187
Duke University, GEMBA (Global Executive MBA program), 97-98
Dunlap, Albert, 47-48, 51, 226 (n27)
DuPont, 36

Eastman Kodak, downsizing by, 45
Economic Espionage Act (EEA) (1996), 123
Education and training survey. *See* "Knowledge Organizations: Their Emergence and Impact on Corporate Education and Training" survey
Education. *See* Business schools; MBA programs; Training
Edvinsson, Leif, 104, 160, 163, 165, 166, 167-168, 171, 173, 174-175, 176, 231 (nn7,22), 232 (nn27,50,55,57,58)

Electricity, discovery of, 33-34, 224 (n37)
Electronic fund transfer (EFT) technologies, 35
Emmons, G. E., 63
Employees. *See* Managers; Workforce
Employment offices. *See* Personnel offices
England. *See* Great Britain
Entitlement, mentality of, 38-40, 54-55, 224 (nn54,55)
Entrepreneurs:
    and failure, 202
    at Lotus, 121-122
    small business innovations and, 29-32
Environment:
    adaptation to, in learning organizations, 70-75
    knowledge conveying truth about, 109-110
    pace of evolution in threatening, xiv-xv
    responsiveness to, xii
Ernst & Young, management of knowledge database, 194
Euchner, James, 76
Europe:
    industrial corporations in, 27 (table)
    See also specific countries
Executives. *See* CEOs; Managers
Experience:
    apprenticeship programs, 28, 184-185, 223 (n23)
    as element of knowledge, 108-109, 130
Experimentation:
    creation of knowledge through, 199-202
    See also Research
Exports. *See* Automobile industry, international competition impacting
Externalization, knowledge transfer method, 186

Factories:
    power sources in, 33-34, 224 (n37)
    See also Scientific management
Failure:
    experimentation and, 202
    from rigidity of success, 195-196
Family income, growth rate, 16
Farnham, Alan, 123, 125, 230 (nn45,50)
Fear, of downsizing, 54-55, 56, 224 (n54)
Federal Express, MBT training by, 102

Fifth Discipline, The: The Art and Practice of the Learning Organization (Senge), 70, 139, 228 (n19)
First Bank System, Inc., 50
First Interstate Bank Corporation, merger, 50-51
Flamholtz, Eric, 170
Flexibility, balance between stability and, xii-xiii
Focus groups, 147
Ford, Henry, development of mass production system, 5-8, 10, 61, 220 (nn3,5,6)
Ford, Henry, II, on small cars, 23, 222 (n10)
Ford Motor Company:
    assembly line system, 5-8, 10, 220 (n3)
    compact cars by, 24
    customer capital measures, 165
    growth of United States economy and, 220 (n4)
    sales in United States, 21
    shared vision in, 207
Foreign competition. *See* International competition
Fortune magazine, 223 (n20)
Forward, Gordon, 185
France:
    assembly line production in, 13
    automobile sales in United States, 21
    United States corporate profits vs., 16
    workforce productivity rates in, 27
From the Ground Up (Case), 30, 57, 227 (n47)
Fry, Art, 234 (n57)
Functions of the Executive, The (Barnard), xi
Future projections:
    desirability of MBAs, 93-94, 154-155
    establishing corporate universities, 86, 87 (figure)
    intellectual capital accounting systems, 148
    scenario planning at Shell, 74-75
    time allocation for training, 81, 154, 155, 231 (n8)
    training budgets, 99-102, 101 (figure)
    training methods, 84-85, 84 (figure), 86, 87 (figure), 90-92, 91 (figure)
    H. G. Wells on, xiii

Galbraith, John Kenneth, 12, 29, 221 (n19)
Galvin, Bob, 68

Gardner, Howard, 107
Gasoline prices, 73
Gates, Bill:
    demand for brilliance in workforce, 131
    importance of research to, 200-201
    Internet strategy by, 128, 129, 131
    on Lotus Notes, 119
    See also Microsoft
GEMBA (Global Executive MBA program), 97-98
Gemini Consulting, management of knowledge database, 193
General Electric:
    Answer Center, 108-109, 186
    quality of research personnel, 222 (n25)
    suit for theft of trade secrets, 124
    Work-Out program, 148-149
General Magic, 115
General Motors (GM):
    compact cars by, 24-25, 26 (tables)
    design and marketing strategies, 20, 222 (n2)
    earnings, 16-17
    lack of workforce incentives for quality, 127
    participatory management in, xii
    production costs vs. Japanese manufacturers, 25, 26 (tables)
    sales in United States, 21
    theft of knowledge from, 124
Germany:
    apprenticeship programs, 28, 223 (n23)
    assembly line production, 13
    automobile sales in United States, 21-22, 24 (table), 222 (nn4,5)
    competitiveness rankings, 27-28
    ratio of worker wages to CEO wages, 49
    United States corporate profits vs., 16-17
    workforce productivity rates, 27
    See also Volkswagen
Gerstner, Louis V., 48, 117, 122
Gilder, George, 226 (n27)
Global competition. *See* International competition
Goldman Sachs & Company, 129
Goss, Chauncey Porter, 9, 10
Graphical user interface (GUI), 200, 208
Great Britain:
    automobile sales in United States, 21
    initiates assembly line production, 13
    ratio of worker wages to CEO wages, 49
    size of Rolls Royces vs. Cadillacs, 222 (n3)

United States corporate profits vs., 16
   workforce productivity rates in, 27
Grocery retail industry:
   scientific management and, 10-11, 221
      (n15)
   supply system of, 126
Gross domestic product (GDP), 115
Gross national product (GNP), 16, 17
Group learning. *See* Communities of practice
Groupware. *See* Lotus Notes software
Grove, Andrew, 198, 205, 234 (n49)
Gula, Allan, 37

Hahn, Eric, 120
Hammer, Michael, 43, 44, 45, 53, 225
   (nn6,7)
Harris, William T., 66
Harvard University, business school, 64
Hawkins, Rick, 76
Health care industry, scientific management
   in, 11-12
Heinz Company, 124-125
Hennesey, John, 206
Hewlett-Packard:
   corporate education in, 69
   inception of, 205
   new product design, 110, 202
Hierarchy, managerial, xi-xii, 4, 7-8, 10,
   15-16, 38-40, 72, 183
Higher-order learning, 155-156
Hiring. *See* Recruitment
Hirshberg, Gerald, 197
Home Depot, 37
Hubbard, Greg, 187
Human capital. *See* Accounting systems
   measuring intellectual capital;
   Intellectual capital (IC)
Human resource accounting (HRA) theory,
   170-171
Human resource management. *See*
   Managers; Training
Human Side of Enterprise, The (McGregor),
   xi, xii

IBM:
   downsizing by, 45, 48, 49 (table)
   hostile takeover of Lotus Corporation,
      116-123
   joint venture in research, 204
   knowledge transfer in, 184

price and speed of computers, 35 (table)
   technological innovations by, 33
   workforce as family in, 221 (n23)
Ibuka, Masura, 113-114
Immigration, impacting United States
   workforce, 8, 220 (n7)
Imports:
   of steel, 26
   See also Automobile industry,
      international competition impacting
Individual learning:
   group learning vs., 76-78
   See also Training
Industrial psychology, 64
Industry knowledge, defined, 158
Informal learning. *See* Communities of
   practice
Information:
   and intuition, 113
   defined, 106-107
   generating knowledge from, 108
   knowledge vs., 107
   management of, vs. management of
      knowledge, 193-194
   theft of, 123-125
   See also Knowledge
Information technology (IT):
   downsizing and, 46
   impacts of, xv, 32-38
   literacy of customers, 164 (table), 168
   platforms for knowledge transfer,
      186-194
   Skandia measurement of, 169-170
   See also Computers
Innovation:
   by small businesses, 29-32
   conditions enhancing, 196
   discouraged in classic corporations, 14,
      39, 222 (n25)
   impact of downsizing on, 53
   through experimentation, 199-202, 234
      (n57)
Instinct. *See* Intuition
Institute for Research on Learning (IRL),
   Xerox training program by, 75-76
Institutional investors, growth of, 49-51
Insurance industry:
   data intensive nature of, 106
   telecommuting in, 172
Intel Corporation, 32-33, 35 (table), 198,
   213

Intellectual Capital: Realizing Your Company's True Value by Finding Its Hidden Brainpower (Edvinsson & Malone), 163, 167-168, 232 (n27)
Intellectual capital (IC):
accounting systems for. *See* Accounting systems measuring Intellectual capital
as corporate asset, xv, 116-125, 146, 157-158, 159-160, 164-173, 177-178
defined, 104-105
historical development of, xi, 61
management of, in "Knowledge Organizations" survey, 139, 145-150
Skandia report on, 104, 163-164, 164 (table), 167-168, 169-170, 171, 172-176
See also Knowledge
Interactive videodisks (IVDs), for training, 102
Internalization, knowledge transfer method, 186
International competition:
era of minimal, 16
impacting corporate changes, xv, 20-28, 23 (table), 26 (tables), 28, 222 (nn2,4,5)
in automobile industry, 20-28, 24 (table), 26 (tables), 28, 72, 125-127, 196, 222 (nn2,4,5)
Internet:
Dell Computer sales on, 31-32
impacting rate of change, 34
Microsoft's focus on, 128-131
training via, 84 (figure)
Interval Research, 197
Intranets, as platform for knowledge transfer, 186-190
Intuition, as element of knowledge, 112-113
Inventory systems, 36, 37
Investors. *See* Shareholders
IT (Information technology). *See* Information technology (IT)

Japan:
automobile sales in United States, 22-23, 24 (table), 25, 26 (tables), 72, 196
competitive methods of, 125-127, 196
corporate competitiveness rankings, 27-28
economic system facilitating competitiveness, 28, 223 (n24)
industrial corporations in, 27 (table)

informal knowledge transfer, 184
loss of automobile industry advantage, 196
prediction vs. performance of economy, 22, 23 (table)
ratio of worker wages to CEO wages, 49
workforce productivity rates in, 27
Java programming language, 129, 131
Jobs, Steven, 200
John Paul II, 115
Johnson & Johnson, 114
Judgment, as element of knowledge, 110-112
Juran, Joseph, 125
Just-in-time supply system, at Toyota, 126-127
Just-in-time training, 142, 143

K-Mart, 195
Kaku, Ryuzaburo, 207
Kampouris, Emmanuel A., 43
Kanban supply system, 126-127
Kanigel, Robert, 8, 9
Kaplan, Robert, 161-162, 231 (nn9,11)
Kapor, Mitch, 121
Katzenberg, Jefferey, 129
Keiritsu (industry groupings), defined, 28
Kellogg, Harry, 159
Kimberly-Clark, product development, 109-110
Kirkpatrick, David, 117, 229 (n28)
Klann, William, 6
Kleinfield, N. R., 55, 227 (nn39,40)
Knowledge:
as corporate asset, xv, 116-125, 146, 157-158, 159-160, 164-173, 177-178
as manager of change, 128-131
as primary tool of competitiveness, 125-127, 139-141, 183
as renewable resource, 61-62, 137
data as element of, 105-106
defined, 103-105, 107-108
economic value of, 115-116, 151 (table), 200, 204-205
experience as element of, 108-109, 130
information as element of, 106-107, 108
intuition as element of, 112-113
judgment as element of, 110-112
mapping, 179-180
measurement of. *See* Accounting systems measuring intellectual capital
protection under law of, 123-124, 125

tacit, 178-179, 184-185, 186
theft of, 123-125
truth as element of, 109-110, 166
values as element of, 113-115, 130
See also Intellectual capital (IC);
    Knowledge conceptualization and
    leveraging model; "Knowledge
    Organizations: Their Emergence and
    Impact on Corporate Education and
    Training" survey
Knowledge assets. *See* Intellectual capital (IC)
Knowledge conceptualization and leveraging
    model, xiv (figure), 179 (figure)
    creating new knowledge, 194-209,
        216-217
    identifying/capturing knowledge, xiv
        (figure), 178-180, 214-215
    role of vision in, 177, 212-214, 213
        (figure)
    sharing/leveraging knowledge, 182-194,
        215-216
    valuing/prioritizing knowledge, 180-182,
        215
Knowledge gatekeepers, defined, 206
Knowledge management:
    difficulty of, 103
    historical development of, xi, 61
    intranets for, 186-190
    Lotus notes for, 190-193
    term usage, 61-62
"Knowledge Organizations: Their Emergence
    and Impact on Corporate Education
    and Training" survey, xv-xvi
    continual learning and, 141-145, 146
        (figure)
    exemplars of, 153-155, 154 (table), 231
        (n8)
    knowledge as primary competitive
        advantage, 139-141
    knowledge organizations defined,
        136-139, 137 (figure), 146, 155
    managing intellectual capital, 139,
        145-150
    self-perceptions as, 141, 150-153, 151
        (table)
    See also Learning organizations
Knowledge workers. *See* Managers;
    Workforce
KPMG Peat Marwick, management of
    knowledge database, 193
Krantz, Matt, 159, 231 (n5)
Krasner, Jeffrey, 121, 230 (n41)

Kroger Company, 221 (n15)

Laborers. *See* Workforce
Lake Geneva (Wis.) YMCA conferences, 63
Landers, Ann, 226 (n25)
Lauzon, Armand, 149
Layoffs. *See* Downsizing
Leadership:
    in knowledge organizations, 209, 212
    vision and, 212-214, 213 (figure)
    See also Culture; Vision
Learning by doing, 186
Learning centers. *See* Corporate universities
Learning organizations:
    adaptation to environment by, 70-75
    as survival strategy, x, xvi
    communities of practice, 75-78
    defined, 70, 131, 158
    favoring brilliant over average employees,
        131, 159, 213, 216
    historical development of, xi-xiii, 61
    intellectual capital vs. traditional assets
        in, xv
    leadership in, 209, 212
    mental models impacting, 72, 73, 74
    replacing traditional training, 69-70, 138,
        141-143, 144-145, 146 (figure)
    systems thinking, 71
    See also "Knowledge Organizations:
        Their Emergence and Impact on
        Corporate Education and Training"
        survey
Leonard-Barton, Dorothy, 139-140, 142,
    155-156, 166, 185, 195, 196, 197,
    202, 206, 208, 230 (nn1,2,4), 232
    (n26), 233 (nn18,38), 234
    (nn43,44,45,59), 235 (nn71,78)
Leveraging and conceptualizing knowledge
    model. *See* Knowledge
    conceptualization and leveraging
    model
Liddle, David, 197
Lilly Tulip, 47
Lippincott, Phil, 47
Lockheed Martin, use of intranet by, 187-188
Lopez de Arriortua, Jose Ignacio, 124
Lotus Development Corporation, hostile
    takeover by IBM, 116-123
Lotus Notes software, 116-118, 119,
    120-121, 122-123, 147
    as knowledge management tool, 190-193

Luttwak, Edward, 52, 226 (n27)

M&A. *See* Mergers and acquisitions (M&A)
Machlup, Fritz, 115
Malone, Michael S., 37-38, 126, 127, 202,
    224 (n52), 230 (nn54,55)
Malone, Thomas, 160, 163, 165, 166,
    167-168, 171, 173, 175, 176, 231
    (nn7,22), 232 (nn27,50,55,57,58)
Management fads, x-xi, xvi
Managers:
    as Organization Men, 13-16, 39, 40, 54,
        221 (n23), 225 (n2)
    average vs. brilliant, 14, 131, 159, 213,
        216, 222 (n25)
    control of knowledge in classic
        corporations by, 8-10, 11
    defined, 180
    diminishing incentives/performance
        levels, 38-40, 224 (nn54,55)
    education of. *See* Business schools;
        Corporate universities; MBA
        programs
    hierarchical style of, xi-xii, 4, 7-8, 10,
        15-16, 38-40, 72, 183
    impacts of downsizing on, 47, 53-57
    percentage receiving training in
        Workforce Education survey, 80
        (figure), 81
    respecting workforce knowledge, 137,
        139-140, 149, 150, 151 (table), 153
    role of, in classic corporations, 4, 7-10
    women as, 173
    See also CEOs
Manuals:
    as knowledge transfer method, 9, 107,
        174, 186
    as training method in *Workforce*
        Education survey, 83, 84 (figure)
    on intranet systems, 189
Manufacturing plants. *See* Factories
Manzi, Jim, 118, 120
Mapping knowledge, 179-180
Marizt, Paul, 130
Market share, inadequacies of, as measure,
    165, 166-167
Marquart, David F., 128
Marshall, Ray, 223 (n23)
Martin Corporation, creation of intranet for,
    187-188
Mass marketing:

by Coca-Cola, 11, 221 (n17)
by Lotus, 122
historical development of, 5, 16, 220
    (nn1,3)
size symbolic of success in, 21, 222 (n3)
technology enabling, 5
word-of-mouth, 71
Mass production:
    development by Ford Motor of, 5-8, 10,
        220 (nn3,5)
    scientific management and, 7-13, 16
Massachusetts Institute of Technology (MIT),
    64
Matsushita, 198-199
MBA programs:
    costs of, 92, 94 (figure), 96-97
    criticisms of, 66-67
    desirability of, 93-94, 154-155
    distance learning format, 97-99, 99 (table)
    historical development of, 64-65
    reimbursement by employers for, 94-95,
        154-155
    selection factors, 94 (figure), 95-97, 97
        (figure)
    See also Business schools
MBNA, customer capital measures, 165
MBT. *See* Multimedia-based training (MBT)
McCallum, Daniel C., 4, 220 (n2)
McCreedy, Scott, 121
McDonald, Hugh, 162
McDonald's Hamburger University, 101
McDonnell, John F., 195
McGregor, Douglas, xi-xii
MCI Communications, 200
Measuring What People Know (Miller), 171
Mental models, 72-75
Mentors, training by, 68, 138, 145, 146
    (figure)
Mercedes Benz, sales in United States, 21
Mergers and acquisitions (M&A):
    as strategy to defend against change, 42,
        224-225 (nn1,2,3)
    in banking industry, 50-51, 54-55, 227
        (n39)
Michigan State, business school, 65
Micklethwait, John, x
Microsoft Corporation:
    as manufacturing or service company,
        115-116
    importance of research at, 200-201
    Internet strategy, 128-131
    software by, 118-119, 121, 123, 129

See also Gates, Bill
Mill Valley (Cal.), intellectual accounting
  meeting, 158-160
Miller, Dede, 76
Miller, Riel, 171
MIT (Massachusetts Institute of Technology),
  64
Mitroff, Ian, 72
Monsanto Chemical Company:
  intellectual capital accounting by, 173-174
  knowledge transfer in, 183
  recruitment by, 14, 222 (n25)
Monster under the Bed, The (Davis &
  Botkin), 67, 227 (n10)
Moore, Gordon, 32-33, 205
Moore, Jim, 118
Moore's Law, 32-33
Moreno, Dennis, 113
Morita, Akio, 114
Motivational speakers, management fads
  and, x
Motorola, joint venture in research, 204
Motorola University, 68-69, 100
Muller, Joann, 122, 230 (n42)
Multimedia-based training (MBT):
  corporate partnering with outside
    developers for, 97-99, 99 (figure)
  current use of, 102
  future use of, 86, 100
  See also Computer-based training (CBT)
Myhrvold, Nathan, 200-201

Nader, Ralph, 25
NASDAQ, fair access to, 30
National brands, development of, 5, 10-11,
  221 (n15)
National Cooperative Research Act (NCRA)
  (1984), 204
Netscape Communications, 120, 129-130
New and Improved (Tedlow), 220 (n3), 221
  (n15)
Niche strategies, x
Nissan Design International, 197-198
Nissan Motor:
  automobile sales competition from, 22-23
  production costs, 25, 26 (table)
  value of experience to, 109
Nonaka, Ikujiro, 184, 194-195, 198-199,
  235 (n74)
Northern Telecom (Nortel), use of intranet
  by, 189

Norton, David, 161-162, 231 (nn9,11)
Notes software. *See* Lotus Notes software
Nucor Steel, 30
Nusbaum, Bruce, 54, 227 (n38)
Nynex, communities of practice, 76-77

Ohno, Taichi, 126, 127
Oil embargo, 73-75
On-the-job training, proportion of, in
  Workforce Education survey, 83, 84
  (figure)
One-to-One Future, The (Peppers & Rogers),
  165-166
OPEC (Organization of Petroleum Exporting
  Countries), 73-75
Organization Men, 13-16, 39, 40, 54, 221
  (n23), 225 (n2)
Orlikowski, Wanda, 191-193, 233
  (nn30,32,33)
Outsourcing:
  as source of intellectual capital, 172
  by exemplary knowledge organizations,
    154
  in *Workforce Education* survey, 82-92, 89
    (figure), 90 (table), 91 (figure), 97-99,
    99 (figure)
  research, 200
Ozzie, Ray, 120-121

Palo Alto Research Center (PARC), 200, 208
Papows, Jefferey, 122
Participatory management, Theory Y and,
  xi-xii
Paulk, Charles, 194
Peer training, 138, 145, 146 (figure)
Peppers, Don, 165-166, 232 (n24)
Performance evaluations, 147
Perlstein, Steve, x, 219 (n2)
Personal computers. *See* Computers
Personnel offices:
  Organization Men in, 15, 222 (n26)
  scientific management in, 10
Peters, Chris, 131
Peters, Tom, 202
Petersson, Lars-Eric, 104
Petrash, Gordon, 173
Petroleum industry, 73-75
Phoenix Designs, 36
Point-of-sale (POS) transactions, 35, 36
Polanyi, Michael, 178, 232 (n1)

Polermo, Ann, 117-118
Pontiac. *See* General Motors (GM)
Porat, Marc, 115
Porras, Jerry I., 114, 115, 229 (nn20,21,23)
Post-it Notes, 202, 234 (n57)
Price, Michael F., 54
Principals of Scientific Management (Taylor),
    10
Proctor, Francine, 112-113, 229 (n19)
Product diversification, through mergers and
    acquisitions, 42, 224-225 (n1)
Product quality:
    corporate education and, 68, 69
    impacts of downsizing on, 53, 56, 78
    United States auto makers and, 24-25, 72
Production costs:
    decreasing for personal computers, 34,
        35 (table), 224 (n41)
    General Motors vs. Nissan small cars, 25,
        26 (table)
    impacts of downsizing on, 53, 78
Productivity rates:
    computers impacting, 34, 187, 224 (n39)
    decline through entitlement mentality, 40
    electricity and, 33-34
    impacts of downsizing on, 53, 56, 78
    in commercial banking, 36
    in United States workforce, 6-7, 12, 13,
        27, 34
    relationships between education and, 170
Profits:
    higher for larger cars, 24
    impact of downsizing and training on, 78
    mass marketing and, 5
    mass production and, 7, 9
    of Dell Computer, 32
    United States corporate, 16-17
Pruitt, Howard, 113
Prusak, Laurence, 103-104, 106, 108, 179,
    181, 184, 229 (nn1,8,9,12)
Psychographics, market segmentation and,
    220 (n3), 222 (n10), 223 (n25)
Public knowledge, defined, 158
Purpose statements, 113-114, 144

Quality assurance teams, 147

Radio Corporation of America (RCA), 27
Railroads:

evolution of managerial organization in,
    3, 4, 220 (n2)
growth of corporations through, 4, 5,
    220 (n1)
RCA (Radio Corporation of America), 27
Realignment:
    as strategy against change, 42, 224-225
        (nn1,2,3)
    See also Mergers and acquisitions (M&A)
Rebello, Kathy, 130, 131, 230 (n57)
Recruitment:
    favoring average over brilliant managers,
        14, 222 (n25)
    favoring brilliant over average employees,
        131, 159, 213, 216
Red Queen hypothesis, xiv-xv
Redundancy, knowledge creation through,
    195, 199
*Reengineering the Corporation: A Manifesto
    for Business Revolution* (Hammer &
    Champy), 43, 53, 225 (nn5,7)
Reich, Robert, 51-52, 226 (n27)
Reimus, Byron, 193, 233 (n34)
Religious organizations, hierarchical
    structure of, xi
Requisite variety, knowledge creation
    through, 195, 199-200
Research:
    at Microsoft, 200-201
    expenditures on, 159, 160
    joint ventures in, 204
    on customer preferences, 11, 109, 147,
        166
    reduction of corporate, 200
    success through ignoring, 114
    university, 204-206
Restructuring:
    as strategy against change, 43-44, 225
        (nn7,8)
    downsizing and, 44, 45, 47, 53, 225 (n7)
Riordon, Richard, 50
Risk taking:
    in knowledge organizations, 136, 140,
        149-150, 151 (table), 202, 217
    increase in, after restructuring, 53
Rogers, Martha, 165-166, 232 (n24)
Rolm Corporation, IBM's purchase of,
    119-120
Roukes, Michael L., 200
Royal Dutch/Shell Group:
    scenario-planning strategies, 74-75
    training in, 77

Rutledge, John, 104-105, 182, 229 (n4), 233 (nn9,10)

Sabre (airline reservation system), 159
Sager, Ira, 119, 230 (n37)
Saint-Onge, Hubert, 70
Sakekeeny, Bob, 120
Sales departments:
    information technology impacting, 36, 189-190
    Organization Men in, 15
SatCon Technology, 107-108
Scenario planning, by Royal Dutch Shell, 74-75
Schank, Roger, 69, 228 (n15)
Scientific management:
    hierarchical management style, xi-xii, 7-8, 10, 40, 220 (n6)
    mass production and, 7-13, 16, 220 (n5), 221 (n15)
Scott Paper, downsizing by, 47
Scovill Manufacturing company, 9-10, 12
Sears, Richard W., 5
Sears, Roebuck & Company, 45, 195-196
Security:
    institutional forms of, 39
    loss of. *See* Downsizing
    sharing information vs., 192
Seeman, Patricia, 179-180
Self-reliance. *See* Autonomy
Senge, Peter, 70, 71, 72, 74, 137 (figure), 138-139, 142, 207, 228 (nn20,24,28,29)
Shareholders, 181-182
    responsibilities for downsizing from, 49-51, 52, 54
Siart, William, 50
Silver, Spencer, 234 (n57)
Silver Bay (N.Y.) business conferences, 63-64
Simon & Schuster, 196
Singer, Kurt, 125
Sinofsky, Steven, 128
Skandia, intellectual capital report, 104, 163-164, 164 (table), 167-168, 169-170, 171, 172-176
Small businesses:
    entrepreneurial innovations in, 29-32
    growth in employment in, ix
    income potential of, 223 (n31)
    larger companies acquiring or merging with, 42, 224-225 (nn1,2,3)

relations with large corporations in Japan vs. United States, 28
share of United States economy, 30
Small-order execution system (SOES), 30
Smith, Alvy Ray, 201
Smith, Bruce, 123
Snyder, Richard, 196
Sobel, Robert, 20, 21-23, 125, 126, 222 (nn2,3,4,5,10), 230 (nn52,53)
Social influences:
    of corporations, 221 (n19)
    of downsizing, 46, 50-52, 226 (n19)
    of information technology, 37-38
Social Psychology of Organizing, The (Weick), xii
Socialization, knowledge transfer through, 184-185
Society National Bank, 37
Software, for computers, 116-119, 120-121, 122-123, 129, 147, 165, 190-193
Sony, values guiding, 113-114
Southwest Airlines, 30
Sperry, M. L., 9
Stability:
    absence of, 177-178
    balance between flexibility and, xii-xiii
Stakeholders. *See* Shareholders
Stamps, David, 76, 228 (n32)
Stanford University:
    business school, 64
    research at, 205-206
Starbuck, William, 157
Starkweather, Gary, 201
Steel industry:
    falling domestic demand, 26
    scientific management in, 7, 8-9
    See also Chaparral Steel
Stewart, Thomas, 70, 103, 162, 168, 178, 180, 182, 190, 228 (n18), 232 (nn2,35), 233 (nn4,11,28)
Stock options, 122
Stock values, research and development linked to, 160
Stockholders. *See* Shareholders
Stora (paper and chemical company), 72-73
Stories/storytelling, as medium for knowledge transfer, 107-108, 180, 186
Stross, Randall E., 131, 201, 230 (n60)
Structural capital, measuring, 168-170
Sullivan, Thomas, 63

Sun Microsystems, Java programming language, 129, 131
Sunbeam Corporation, downsizing, 47, 51
Supermarkets. *See* Grocery retail industry
Surveys:
    capturing knowledge through, 147
    See also "Knowledge Organizations:
      Their Emergence and Impact on
      Corporate Education and Training"
      survey; *Workforce Education:
      Corporate Training and Learning at
      America's Leading Companies* survey
Sveiby, Karl, 173
Systems thinking, in learning organizations, 71, 137

Tacit knowledge, 178-179, 184-185, 186
Takeovers. *See* Mergers and acquisitions (M&A)
Takeuchi, Hirotaka, 184, 194-195, 198-199, 235 (n74)
Taylor, Frederick Winslow, scientific management and, 7, 8, 10, 12, 40, 62-63, 220 (n5)
Team-building, at Xerox, 75-76
Technology. *See* Computers; Information technology; Railroads; Scientific management
Tedlow, Richard, 220 (n3), 221 (n15), 223 (n25)
Telecommuters, 172
Telegraph communication, 5
Telephones, banking by, 35-36, 37
Television, training through, 37
Tension, creative, 207
Terman, Frederick Emmons, 205, 206
Thacker, Chuck, 201
Theft, of knowledge, 123-125
Theory X, xi-xii
Theory Y, xi-xii
Thermos, 166
Thompson, John, 118
3M, experimentation/innovation at, 202, 234 (n57)
Three Degrees Above Zero (Bernstein), 200
Through the Looking Glass (Carroll), xv
Time-motion studies, 7
Toyota:
    automobile sales competition from, 22-23
    production technique, 126-127
    relations with small suppliers, 28

Trade deficits, in United States, 24
Trade secrets, 123-124
Trade unions, opposition to scientific management, 9, 10
Training:
    apprenticeship programs, 28, 184-185, 223 (n23)
    budgets for, 99-102, 101 (figure), 154 (table), 170-171
    by mentors, 68, 138, 145, 146 (figure)
    communities of practice, 75-78
    information technology and. *See*
      Information technology
    learning organizations replacing
      traditional, 69-70, 138, 141-143, 144-145, 146 (figure)
    via computers. *See* Computer-based training (CBT)
    via intranets, 189
    See also Business schools; Corporate
      universities; "Knowledge
      Organizations: Their Emergence and
      Impact on Corporate Education and
      Training" survey; MBA programs;
      Universities; *Workforce Education:
      Corporate Training and Learning at
      America's Leading Companies* survey
Training manuals. *See* Manuals
Transportation systems. *See* Railroads
Truth, as element of knowledge, 109-110, 166
Tsetsekos, George P., 160
Tucker, Marc, 223 (n23)

Unemployment, falling levels of, 45-46
Unions, trade, opposition to scientific management, 9, 10
United Kingdom. *See* Great Britain
United States:
    automobile industry in. *See* Automobile industry
    corporate competitiveness rankings, 27-28
    domination of markets by, 13, 16-17, 26, 220-221 (nn4,14)
    fall from dominance by, 26-27, 27 (table)
    immigration impacting workforce, 8, 220 (n7)
    international competition impacting. *See* International competition
    ratio of worker wages to CEO wages, 49
    trade deficits in, 24

workforce productivity rates, 6-7, 12, 13, 27, 34
See also Corporations, classic; *specific corporations*
United Technologies, downsizing by, 49 (table)
Universities:
corporations partnering with, for training, 88, 89 (figure), 90, 90 (table), 91 (figure), 97-99, 99 (figure), 154
research in, 204-206
See also Business schools; Corporate universities; MBA programs
University of California, Berkeley, 205
University of Chicago, business school, 62, 65, 67
University of Southern California (USC):
corporate education and training survey. *See* "Knowledge Organizations: Their Emergence and Impact on Corporate Education and Training" survey
strategic report on workforce education. *See Workforce Education: Corporate Training and Learning at America's Leading Companies* survey
Unsafe at Any Speed (Nader), 25
Utilities industries, data intensive nature of, 106

Values:
as element of knowledge, 113-115, 130
See also Culture
Van Derlip, George, 63
Van Valen, Leigh, xiv-xv
Variety, requisite, 195, 199-200
Videodisks, interactive (IVDs), for training, 102
Videotapes:
as system for capturing knowledge, 147
as training method, in *Workforce Education* survey, 83, 84 (figure)
Japanese dominance in market for, 27
Vision:
role in knowledge conceptualization and leveraging model, 177, 212-214, 213 (figure)
shared, 207-209
Visualizing Intellectual Capital (Skandia report), 104, 163-164, 164 (table), 169-170, 171, 172-176

Volkswagen:
Beetles, 21-22, 25, 71, 222 (nn4,5)
theft of knowledge by employee, 124

W-M Data, 173
Wages, 49, 57, 220 (n6)
Wal-Mart, 30, 37, 195-196, 223 (n31)
Wall Street, responsibilities for downsizing from, 49, 49 (table), 51
Wallman, Steven, 181-182, 233 (nn7,8)
Watson, Thomas, Sr., 13
Watson Wyatt International, 44, 53, 227 (n36)
Weick, Karl, xii-xiii, 110, 111, 112, 229 (nn16,17)
Welles, Edward O., 107, 229 (nn10,11)
Wells, H. G., xiii
Wells Fargo & Company, merger, 50-51
Wellsprings of Knowledge (Leonard-Barton), 155-156, 195, 234 (n39)
Welsh, Jack, 148
West Germany. *See* Germany
Western Ontario, business school, 64
Westinghouse, H. H., 63
Whyte, William, 13, 14, 15, 40, 222 (nn25,26)
Wildon, Dave, 171
Wilson, Allan, 77
Wilson, Paul, 140
Winblad, Ann, 159
Witch Doctors, The (Micklethwait & Woolridge), x
Wolrath, Bjorn, 174, 175
Women, as managers, 173
Woodin, W. H., 63
Woolridge, Adrain, x
Workforce:
as units of production in scientific management, 7-8, 220 (n6)
assessing morale of, 150, 152, 153, 181
autonomy of individuals in, xi-xii, 57, 142, 194-195
diminishing incentives/performance levels, 38-40, 53, 127, 224 (n54)
downsizing impacting, 35-37, 45-46, 51-57, 172, 224 (n54), 226 (nn19,25), 227 (n39)
employment in small corporations, ix, 30
immigration impacting, 8, 220 (n7)
Japanese manufacturing process and, 127

knowledge transferred to management
  from, in classic corporations, 9-10,
  11, 40, 221 (n15)
machines replacing, 35-37
mergers and acquisitions impacting, 42,
  225 (n2)
participatory management by, xi-xii, 57,
  68
percentage receiving training in
  "Knowledge Organizations" survey,
  155
percentage receiving training in
  Workforce Education survey, 80
  (figure), 81
productivity rates in United States, 6-7,
  12, 13, 27, 34
replacement of skilled with unskilled, 9,
  10
respecting knowledge of, xvi, 137,
  139-140, 149, 150, 151 (table), 153
turnover rates, 122, 164 (table), 173
variety of intellectual capital within,
  171-172
wages, 49, 57, 220 (n6)
See also Intellectual capital; Training
*Workforce Education: Corporate Training and
  Learning at America's Leading
  Companies* survey:
corporate universities/learning centers,
  85-86, 87 (figure), 100-102
current and future budgets for training,
  99-102, 101 (figure)
current training methods, 83-84, 84
  (figure)

future training methods, 84-85, 84
  (figure), 86, 87 (figure), 90-92, 91
  (figure)
geographic locations of training, 82, 88
partnering with other corporations for,
  88, 89-90, 89 (figure), 91-92, 91
  (figure), 97-99, 99 (figure)
partnering with outside developers,
  82-92, 89 (figure), 90 (table), 91
  (figure), 97-99, 99 (figure)
percentage of employees receiving
  training, 80-81, 80 (figure)
sample and methodology, 79-80, 81
  (table)
types of employees receiving training, 80
  (figure), 81
use and costs of MBA programs, 92-99,
  94 (figure), 97 (figure), 99 (figure)
World Wide Web. *See* Internet; Intranets
Wriston, Walter, 159

Xerox Corporation, 45, 75-76

Yanow, Dvora, 184, 185, 233 (nn16,17)
YMCA, business seminars, 63
Youth culture, automobiles as symbol for, 21,
  222 (n4)

Zantout, Zaher Z., 160
Zisman, Michael, 122

ABOUT THE AUTHORS

Richard C. Huseman, Ph.D., is the founding editor of the Corporate Knowledge Center at the University of Southern California and currently serves as Professor of Management at the University of Central Florida. He has had a variety of experiences in business school settings, serving as professor, department head, and dean. In the corporate arena, Dr. Huseman has engaged in speaking, consulting, and knowledge sharing for numerous global corporations including 3M, AT&T, Coca Cola, IBM, and Mobil. He is a highly recruited speaker for executive development programs both nationally and internationally. His presentations focus on knowledge management, change management, and relationship management as the primary ways organizations can leverage their competitive position.

Dr. Huseman has coauthored nine books, including *Managing the Equity Factor* (1989), which has been translated into Russian, German, Chinese, Portuguese, and Greek. He has written more than 100 articles and papers for journals and national and international professional meetings.

Jon P. Goodman, Ph.D., is the architect, founder, and executive director of EC², the Annenberg Incubator Project at the University of Southern

California, and Director of Distance Learning at the Annenberg Center for Communication at USC. Under her direction, EC^2 has recruited a unique combination of technologists, creative artists, and industrial partners to create this focal point for media innovation. She previously was Director of the Entrepreneur Program at USC. She founded the University of Houston's Economic Development Project and is a cofounder of Health Trends, Inc., a large venture-backed health care company merged with National Rehabilitation Centers, Inc.

Dr. Goodman is moderator of *Something Ventured,* a 26-part series that is being repeated for the fifth season on PBS. She also is a frequent commentator on CNN, *Nightly Business Report,* and *Marketplace,* as well as the *Wall Street Journal* and other business publications. In 1997, she was named by *Wired* magazine as one of the 20 people in the nation who will help shape the future of the entertainment industry.